Researching Discourse

This book offers a 'how-to' guide to conducting research in discourse analysis. Organised around different approaches to discourse analysis and working with different types of discourse data, the book will help students answer questions such as: Which approach should I take? What kind of data should I analyse and how do I set about collecting it? What consideration should I give to ethics? How do I make my analyses systematic and rigorous? How do I report my findings?

Both qualitative and quantitative (corpus-based and experimental) methods are covered. Illustrated with far-ranging, detailed, and original case-studies, each chapter follows a consistent format that takes readers step by step through the research process, from design to implementation and presentation. Chapters can be read independently of one another.

This is the ideal companion for any student undertaking research in discourse analysis within English language, linguistics, applied linguistics, and communication studies programmes.

Christopher Hart is Professor of Linguistics at Lancaster University, UK. His research is focussed on the link between language, cognition, and social action in political contexts of communication. He is the author of *Critical Discourse Analysis and Cognitive Science* (2010) and *Discourse, Grammar and Ideology* (2014).

Researching Discourse
A Student Guide

Edited by Christopher Hart

LONDON AND NEW YORK

First published 2020
by Routledge
2 Park Square, Milton Park, Abingdon, Oxon OX14 4RN

and by Routledge
52 Vanderbilt Avenue, New York, NY 10017

Routledge is an imprint of the Taylor & Francis Group, an informa business

© 2020 selection and editorial matter, Christopher Hart; individual chapters, the contributors

The right of Christopher Hart to be identified as the author of the editorial material, and of the authors for their individual chapters, has been asserted in accordance with sections 77 and 78 of the Copyright, Designs and Patents Act 1988.

All rights reserved. No part of this book may be reprinted or reproduced or utilised in any form or by any electronic, mechanical, or other means, now known or hereafter invented, including photocopying and recording, or in any information storage or retrieval system, without permission in writing from the publishers.

Trademark notice: Product or corporate names may be trademarks or registered trademarks, and are used only for identification and explanation without intent to infringe.

British Library Cataloguing-in-Publication Data
A catalogue record for this book is available from the British Library

Library of Congress Cataloging-in-Publication Data
Names: Hart, Christopher (Linguist) editor.
Title: Researching discourse : a student guide / edited by Christopher Hart.
Description: London ; New York : Routledge, 2020. | Includes
bibliographical references and index.
Identifiers: LCCN 2019046982
Subjects: LCSH: Discourse analysis. | Discourse analysis–Methodology.
Classification: LCC P302 .R4825 2020 | DDC 401./41–dc23
LC record available at https://lccn.loc.gov/2019046982

ISBN: 978-1-138-55107-7 (hbk)
ISBN: 978-1-138-55108-4 (pbk)
ISBN: 978-0-367-81504-2 (ebk)

Typeset in Goudy
by Swales & Willis, Exeter, Devon, UK

Contents

List of contributors	vii
Acknowledgements	ix

Editor's introduction   1
CHRISTOPHER HART

1 Introduction to discourse: definitions, debates, and decisions   6
ALISON SEALEY

2 Conversation analysis   19
GREG MYERS

3 Discourse analysis and ethnography   36
KARIN TUSTING

4 Discourse analysis and systemic functional linguistics   54
VERONIKA KOLLER

5 Analysing metaphor in discourse   77
VERONIKA KOLLER

6 Cognitive linguistic critical discourse analysis   97
CHRISTOPHER HART

7 Corpus-assisted discourse analysis   124
PAUL BAKER

8 Multimodal discourse analysis   143
CHRISTOPHER HART

vi   *Contents*

9 Digitally mediated discourse analysis   180
JOHANN W. UNGER

10 Experimental methods in discourse analysis   201
CHRISTOPHER HART

Index   228

Contributors

Paul Baker is Professor of English Language in the Department of Linguistics and English Language at Lancaster University, UK. He has written 19 books which involve corpus linguistics, discourse analysis and/or research in gender, sexuality, health, and media language. He is the commissioning editor for the journal *Corpora*.

Christopher Hart is Professor of Linguistics in the Department of Linguistics and English Language at Lancaster University, UK. His research is focussed on the link between language, cognition, and social action in political contexts of communication. He is the author of *Critical Discourse Analysis and Cognitive Science: New Perspectives on Immigration Discourse* (2010) and *Discourse, Grammar and Ideology: Functional and Cognitive Perspectives* (2014). He has edited several books including *Contemporary Critical Discourse Analysis* (2014, with Piotr Cap) and *Cognitive Linguistic Approaches to Text and Discourse: From Poetics to Politics* (2019).

Veronika Koller is Reader in Discourse Studies in the Department of Linguistics and English Language at Lancaster University, UK. Her research interests are in business and political discourse, and language and sexuality. Her recent publications include *Language in Business, Language at Work* (2018, with Erika Darics) and *Discourses of Brexit* (2019, with Susanne Kopf and Marlene Miglbauer).

Greg Myers is Emeritus Professor in the Department of Linguistics and English Language at Lancaster University, UK. His most recent research has been focussed on the expression of opinions in talk, particularly in focus groups and consultation processes, taking an approach from conversation analysis. He is the author of *Matters of Opinion: Talking About Public Issues* (2004) and *Discourse of Blogs and Wikis* (2010). Until 2015, he was editor of the journal *Discourse, Context & Media*.

Alison Sealey is Professor of Applied Linguistics in the Department of Linguistics and English Language at Lancaster University, UK. She has published extensively on a wide range of subjects, with an emphasis on the role of discourse in representations of the social world. Among her recent publications are 'Translation: a biosemiotic/more-than-human perspective' (*Target. International Journal of Translation Studies*); 'Representing women, women representing: backbenchers' questions during Prime Minister's Questions, 1979–2010' (with Stephen Holden Bates, *European Journal of Politics and Gender*).

Karin Tusting is Senior Lecturer in the Department of Linguistics and English Language at Lancaster University, UK. Her research interests are in workplace literacies, particularly in relation to bureaucracy and accountability, and linguistic ethnography. Recent publications include *Academics Writing* (2019, with Sharon McCulloch, Ibrar Bhatt, Mary Hamilton, and David Barton) and the *Handbook of Linguistic Ethnography* (2019).

Johann W. Unger is Lecturer in the Department of Linguistics and English Language at Lancaster University, UK. He researches mainly in the areas of language policy and digitally mediated politics from a critical discourse studies perspective. His publications include *The Discursive Construction of the Scots Language* (2013) and the co-authored textbook *Researching Language and Social Media* (2014). He is an editor of the book series *Discourse Approaches to Politics, Society and Culture*.

Acknowledgements

This book was written at the invitation of the publishers. In the highly competitive, target-driven and performance-focussed environment that is UK higher education it isn't always easy to see the value in producing such a text, while it is all too easy to lose sight of the fact that communicating not just research findings but research know-how to new generations of students and scholars is an essential aspect of what we do or ought to be doing. In writing this book, we are reminded of this fact and are rewarded with a renewed appreciation for the merits, outside the immediate context of research targets and assessments, of producing such a book. The book is intended as a research guide for students but in producing it we as authors have also been given an opportunity to reflect on and consider explicitly aspects of the research process which are often otherwise taken for granted. This, I believe, has made us better researchers and better teachers. I'd therefore like, first and foremost, to thank Louisa Semlyen at Routledge for persuading us to undertake this project.

The book is the culmination of efforts made by colleagues in the Department of Linguistics and English Language at Lancaster University. This includes those who have directly contributed to the book by writing chapters but also a great number of other colleagues who have provided support and inspiration in all sorts of other ways. Besides the contributing authors, then, who have given their time and energy to this project both generously and enthusiastically, I'd like to thank all of my colleagues and friends in the department, academic and administrative, for making it such a wonderful – stimulating, collegial, and, above all, fun – environment in which to work.

Of course, the book is a product of the experiences we have had, accumulated collectively over many years, in teaching discourse analysis and working with students on dissertations and other research projects in various different approaches to discourse analysis. Those experiences are, for us, a motivation and a learning curve. I'd therefore like to thank the many students who over the years, at undergraduate and postgraduate level, have studied with us and have, as a result, helped to shape and inspire this book. As a point of fact, several of the contributors to this book were

x *Acknowledgements*

themselves once students at Lancaster who have both benefited and bene-fited from the teachings of other fellow contributors.

Although the chapters contained within this book have been written exclusively by researchers at Lancaster University, it is by no means our intention to suggest that there are not a great many other leading figures in discourse analysis, affiliated to other institutions, who are equally or better qualified to have produced such a book. Working together in the same department, however, affords obvious logistical advantages when it comes to putting collections like this together. In all of the chapters contained herein, we hope to have been as inclusive and accurate as possible in repre-senting the works of the great many researchers around the world whose ideas have defined and continue to define the field of discourse analysis.

Finally, no book is produced without a debt of gratitude owed to friends and family. We would each like to thank the loved ones in our lives, near and far, lost and present, for all that they give. In particular, I, as always, must thank my parents, my partner Heather, and now my daughter Ivy. Discourse analysis is ultimately about finding meaning in contexts. In my own personal context, I have found my ultimate meaning in her.

While every effort has been made to trace copyright holders, this has not been possible in all cases. Any omissions brought to the publisher's attention will be remedied in further editions.

Editor's introduction

Christopher Hart

Discourse analysis is a rich and multifaceted, cross-disciplinary, field that is broadly concerned with the structures and functions of language in use – discourse. The term 'discourse analysis' has its roots in the work of Zellig Harris (1952), an American structuralist, who coined the term to designate a formal method for analysing language 'above the sentence'. That is, Harris saw discourse as the highest rank-level of linguistic organisation and discourse analysis as an area of descriptive linguistics akin to phonology, morphology, and syntax. However, Harris recognised two different ways of approaching discourse analysis:

> one can approach discourse analysis from two types of problems, which turn out to be related. The first is the problem of continuing descriptive linguistics beyond the limits of a single sentence at a time. The other is the question of correlating 'culture' and 'language' (i.e. non-linguistic and linguistic behaviour).
>
> (Harris, 1952: 1)

Harris's work focussed on the first of these issues and discourse analysis in this sense has since become an important part of linguistics (e.g. Brown and Yule, 1983; Schiffrin, 1994). Indeed, up until the 1970s 'discourse analysis' meant, almost exclusively, looking at the structural properties of linguistic units larger than the sentence (Reisigl, 2011). Since then, however, 'discourse analysis' has come increasingly to cover a broad range of scholarship addressing the second issue identified by Harris. Discourse analysis in this second sense is not concerned so much with the mechanics of discourse as it with the social actions performed in and through discourse, which are constitutive of the identities, relations, norms, values, institutions, conventions, and expectations etc. that define a given 'culture'. That is, with discourse as a form of social practice. Of course, the two issues are closely connected, as Harris observed, such that it is not possible to address one in isolation from the other (Coulthard, 1985; Johnstone, 2002). Rather, as always, the distinction is a matter of emphasis. Approaches to discourse analysis which emphasise the connections between discourse and social dynamics take many forms, coming from quite different academic disciplines, with different methods, perspectives, and epistemologies. Such approaches, for example, come from disciplines as far-ranging as sociology, anthropology, and psychology. However, approaches to discourse analysis in this broader 'social' sense have also been developed in linguistics as a form of *applied linguistics*, and this is where the present book is situated. The principle chapters in this book all outline approaches to discourse analysis which are based in linguistics but which go beyond the structural analysis of discourse to see discourse as indexical of, and constitutive of, structures and conditions in society. One particularly influential form of discourse analysis in the applied linguistics sense that developed in the late part of the twentieth century is *critical discourse analysis* (originally *critical linguistics*) (e.g. Fairclough, 1989, 1995; Fowler et al., 1979; Hodge and Kress, 1979). Critical discourse analysis (CDA) is not a single approach to discourse analysis – it is not, itself, homogeneous and is not associated with any specific method. Rather, what characterises CDA, as with other forms of critical social research, is a desire to transcend the standard academic tasks of describing and explaining, in the most objective way possible, and to instead adopt an openly political stance and seek social change through intellectual inquiry. Researchers in CDA therefore usually start from some perceived social problem, such as social inequality, and use the various tools afforded by discourse analysis to show how patterns of language use contribute to creating and sustaining that problem. A critical perspective is thus possible with any approach to discourse analysis and many, though not all, of the chapters in this volume do assume an explicitly critical stance toward the data they analyse.

There are many excellent and recent textbooks introducing linguistic and applied linguistics approaches to discourse analysis, including CDA (e.g. Bartlett, 2014; Blommaert, 2005; Bloor and Bloor, 2007; Gee, 2014a, 2014b; Georgakopoulou and Goutsos, 2004; Jones, 2012; Machin and Mayr, 2012; Paltridge, 2012; Simpson and Mayr, 2009). There are also several comprehensive handbooks (e.g. Flowerdew and Richardson, 2017; Gee and Handford, 2013; Hart and Cap, 2014; Jaworski and Coupland, 2006; Schiffrin, Tannen, and Hamilton, 2001; van Dijk, 2011). However, this book is neither intended as a textbook nor as a handbook. As suggested by its title, the book is intended to provide a practical guide for students of linguistics, whether undergraduate or post-graduate, who, perhaps for a taught module or as part of a dissertation or thesis, are embarking on an independent research project in discourse analysis (in the applied linguistics sense). It aims not only to provide an introduction to theoretical and analytical concepts in different approaches to discourse analysis but also to make explicit and explain the kind of decisions and practical steps involved in operationalising those concepts in a discourse analysis project. In other words, the book aims to make transparent those parts of the research process that researchers often take for granted in their writings and which, as a result, are not always immediately accessible to students.

Even discourse analysis in the more restricted sense of applied linguistics is multifaceted, consisting of various approaches that draw on and apply different models of linguistic description and different methods of linguistic inquiry, so that students can sometimes find it difficult to orient themselves. Common questions are: Which approach should I take? What kind of data should I analyse and how do I set about collecting it? What consideration should I give to ethics? How do I make my analyses systematic and rigorous? How do I report my findings? This book is intended to help students find answers to questions such as these. It therefore has a focus on issues of research design, methodology, and presentation throughout. Indeed, while the first chapter provides an overview of definitions, decisions, and debates in discourse analysis, all of the remaining chapters follow the same basic structure: (i) introduction; (ii) outline of approach; (iii) identifying research questions; (iv) data collection and ethics; (v) analysing and interpreting data; (vi) presenting findings and results; (vii) issues and limitations; and (viii) further reading. This places the book more in the vein of a research methods guide (e.g. Litosseliti, 2010; Podesva and Sharma, 2013) dedicated specifically to the subject of discourse analysis.

I hope that (prospective) students of discourse analysis will read the whole book in order to gain an insight into some of the different approaches that one can take toward a discourse analysis project, as well as to appreciate the connections between approaches and the recurrent themes and decisions involved in any research project. However, one or two chapters are always likely to stand out as most relevant for a given project and each chapter can be read independently of the others.

As a result of its practical focus, the book is organised around different analytical frameworks in discourse analysis rather than particular domains of language use (e.g. politics, law, health, literature). Alongside a general overview, each chapter, with the exception of the first and the final one, presents a particular case study by way of illustration. However, this should not be taken as implying that the approach in question is limited to only that data type. Although different approaches have been designed to account for specific phenomena in discourse – from turn-taking to transitivity, from metaphor to collocation and semantic prosody – and clearly lend themselves to analysing different quantities of data (e.g. large versus small samples), produced in different modalities (e.g. spoken versus written), the same or similar discourse phenomena occur across domains and genres, albeit where they may function differently and need to be analytically interpreted within their local context. Thus, while many of the chapters in this volume happen to focus on discourse topics and genres that can be characterised, more or less broadly, as 'political' (Chilton and Schäffner, 2002), the methods of linguistic analysis illustrated, including those based in systemic functional

4   *Christopher Hart*

linguistics, corpus linguistics, and cognitive linguistics, can also be applied to texts produced in other, e.g. literary or legal, contexts, as indeed they have been in the fields of stylistics (Jeffries and McIntyre, 2010; Simpson, 2014) and forensic linguistics (Coulthard and Johnson, 2016; Coulthard, Johnson, and Wright, 2013) respectively. Equally, methods of analysis such as conversation analysis, which in this volume is illustrated with reference to the literary setting of book groups, are equally applied in other interactional settings within 'political' realms (e.g. Hutchby, 2006).

The chapters contained within this book are all written by researchers currently working in the Department of Linguistics and English Language at Lancaster University in the UK. The approaches covered reflect the kinds of projects our students most frequently undertake. This, of course, may be down to the particular makeup of the department and the book, therefore, does not necessarily cover all approaches that could potentially have been included. But it does cover what we feel are currently the most interesting and popular of approaches, which have a firm footing in linguistics and whose models and methods are therefore likely to be familiar to students of linguistics and/or English language. This includes well-established approaches based in conversation analysis, ethnography, systemic functional linguistics, and corpus linguistics. However, it also includes newer and more nascent approaches based in cognitive linguistics, multimodal social semiotics, digitally mediated communication studies, and experimental methods. It is hoped, then, that as the field of discourse analysis continues to change and expand in new directions, the book will provide a valuable resource for students of discourse analysis for at least a few years to come.

References

Bartlett, T. (2014). *Analysing power in language: A practical guide*. London: Routledge.
Blommaert, J. (2005). *Discourse: A critical introduction*. Cambridge: Cambridge University Press.
Bloor, M. and Bloor, T. (2007). *The practice of critical discourse analysis: An introduction*. London: Routledge.
Brown, G. and Yule, G. (1983). *Discourse analysis*. Cambridge: Cambridge University Press.
Chilton, P. and Schäffner, C. (2002). Introduction: Themes and principles in the analysis of political discourse. In P. Chilton and C. Schäffner (Eds.), *Politics as text and talk: Analytic approaches to political discourse*. (pp. 1–44). Amsterdam: John Benjamins.
Coulthard, M. (1985). *An introduction to discourse analysis*. (2nd ed.). London: Longman.
Coulthard, M. and Johnson, A. (2016). *An introduction to forensic linguistics: Language in evidence*. (2nd ed.). London: Routledge.
Coulthard, M., Johnson, A. and Wright, D. (Eds.) (2013). *Routledge handbook of forensic linguistics*. London: Routledge.
Fairclough, N. (1989). *Language and power*. London: Longman.

Fairclough, N. (1995). *Critical discourse analysis: The critical study of language.* London: Longman.

Flowerdew, J. and Richardson, J.E. (Eds.) (2017). *The Routledge handbook of critical discourse studies.* London: Routledge.

Fowler, R., Hodge, R., Kress, G. and Trew, T. (1979). *Language and control.* London: Routledge & Kegan Paul.

Gee, J.P. (2014a). *An introduction to discourse analysis: Theory and method.* (4th ed.). London: Routledge.

Gee, J.P. (2014b). *How to do discourse analysis: A toolkit.* (2nd ed.). London: Routledge.

Gee, J.P. and Handford, M. (2013). *The Routledge handbook of discourse analysis.* London: Routledge.

Georgakopoulou, A. and Goutsos, D. (2004). *Discourse analysis: An introduction.* (2nd ed.). Edinburgh: Edinburgh University Press.

Harris, Z.S. (1952). Discourse analysis. *Language, 28*(1), 1–30.

Hart, C. and Cap, P. (Eds.) (2014). *Contemporary critical discourse studies.* London: Bloomsbury.

Hodge, R. and Kress, G. (1979). *Language as ideology.* London: Routledge & Kegan Paul.

Hutchby, I. (2006). *Media talk: Conversation analysis and the study of broadcasting.* Maidenhead: Open University Press.

Jaworski, A. and Coupland, N. (2006). *The discourse reader.* (2nd ed.). London: Routledge.

Jeffries, L. and McIntyre, D. (2010). *Stylistics.* Cambridge: Cambridge University Press.

Johnstone, B. (2002). *Discourse analysis.* Oxford: Wiley.

Jones, R.H. (2012). *Discourse analysis: A resource book for students.* London: Routledge.

Litosseliti, L. (2010). *Research methods in linguistics.* London: Continuum.

Machin, D. and Mayr, A. (2012). *How to do critical discourse analysis: A multimodal introduction.* London: Sage.

Paltridge, B. (2012). *Discourse analysis: An introduction.* (2nd ed.). London: Bloomsbury.

Podesva, B.J. and Sharma, D. (2013). *Research methods in linguistics.* Cambridge: Cambridge University Press.

Reisigl, M. (2011). (Critical) discourse analysis and pragmatics: Commonalities and differences. In C. Hart (Ed.), *Critical discourse studies in context and cognition.* (pp. 7–26). Amsterdam: John Benjamins.

Schiffrin, D. (1994). *Approaches to discourse.* Oxford: Blackwell.

Schiffrin, D., Tannen, D. and Hamilton, H.E. (Eds.) (2001). *The handbook of discourse analysis.* Oxford: Blackwell.

Simpson, P. (2014). *Stylistics: A resource book for students.* (2nd ed.). London: Routledge.

Simpson, P. and Mayr, A. (2009). *Language and power: A resource book for students.* London: Routledge.

van Dijk, T.A. (Ed.) (2011). *Discourse studies: A multidisciplinary introduction.* London: Sage.

1 Introduction to discourse
Definitions, debates, and decisions

Alison Sealey

Introduction

The chapters in this book will help readers to understand how a wide range of researchers have analysed discourse in different ways, and how you, as a student of discourse analysis, might plan a research project of your own investigating some particular aspect or area of discourse. The authors introduce various approaches to, and methods of, researching discourse. This opening chapter is therefore aimed at setting the scene by providing an overview of what is generally involved in the analysis of discourse. I begin with a brief survey of some of the ways in which the term 'discourse' is used within the study of language and linguistics, before presenting four elements which are core to the enterprise of discourse analysis: (i) the data that comprise discourse; (ii) the producers of discourse; (iii) the reception of discourse; and (iv) the perspective of the analyst.

Definitions

The conventional way to get a handle on what a term means is to consult a dictionary, and one trusted authority, the *Oxford English Dictionary*, informs us that 'discourse', like many words, has changed its meaning over time. (It also indicates that 'discourse' can be used as a verb, as in 'The early writers discoursed at some length ...', but that's not so relevant for us here.)

Among earlier definitions of 'discourse' as a noun are senses such as these: 'reasoned argument or thought'; 'the thread of an argument'; and 'a narrative or account of a particular subject'. More recently, 'discourse' has meant:

> The action or process of communicating thought by means of the spoken word; interchange of words; conversation, talk. Also: the words exchanged by this means; speech. In later use also: the written representation of this; communication in written form.

Introduction to discourse 7

The most current definitions are, in general contexts, (a):

> The body of statements, analysis, opinions, etc., relating to a particular domain of intellectual or social activity, esp. as characterized by recur-ring themes, concepts, or values; (also) the set of shared beliefs, values, etc., implied or expressed by this. Frequently with *of* or modifying word.

And in a more specifically linguistic sense, (b):

> A connected series of utterances by which meaning is communicated, *esp.* one forming a unit for analysis; spoken or written communication regarded as consisting of such utterances.

Since you are reading this book, you are probably already familiar with the concepts summarised by (a) and (b) above, but it is worth pointing out that the broad academic enterprise of discourse analysis may involve placing different degrees of emphasis on the different perspectives suggested by (a) and (b). Notice particularly the coda in (a): 'Frequently with *of* or modifying word'. This extra information indicates that 'discourse' often occurs in formulations such as these:

- the discourse of multiculturalism
- discourses of masculinity
- the discourse of colonialism
- political discourse
- feminist discourse
- dominant discourse

Now, these phrases would seem to relate more readily to definition (a) – i.e. to 'particular domain[s] of ... social activity' and their 'shared beliefs [and] values' – than to definition (b), which is more formal, concerned with 'series of utterances' or sentences and the way these are 'connected' linguistically. Yet many discourse analysts, including those who have contributed to this book, do research that bridges both senses of the term 'discourse'. That is, their linguistic training enables them to analyse the many ways in which the components of language (words, phrases, sentences, utterances) are linked together to form larger units, such as whole texts (written or spoken) and conversations. At the same time, they are interested in what these discursive choices indicate about individuals' thought processes, attitudes, and values, and also about broader social conventions, norms, and priorities. One analyst who draws attention explicitly to the link between these two senses of 'discourse' is James Paul Gee, who coined the use of 'little d' versus 'big D' discourse to distinguish between, on the one hand, the way language is used to enact activities and

8 *Alison Sealey*

identities, and, on the other hand, the way other non-linguistic 'stuff', such as gestures, material artefacts, values, and attitudes, are melded with language in situated communication practices (Gee, 2005).

You will notice different perspectives in the chapters that follow as well as in your wider reading about discourse analysis. I shall say a bit more about this later. For now, however, let us conclude this section with some definitions of 'discourse' sourced from the academic literature.

1. Discourse analysis examines how stretches of language, considered in their full textual, social, and psychological context, become meaningful and unified for their users (Cook, 1989: ix).
2. People in a variety of academic departments and disciplines use the term 'discourse analysis' for what they do, how they do it, or both ... Discourse analysts pose many different questions and propose many different sorts of answers (Johnstone, 2002: 1).
3. So abundant are definitions of discourse that many linguistics books on the subject now open with a survey of definitions ... They all, however, fall into ... three main categories ... (1) anything beyond the sentence, (2) language use, and (3) a broader range of social practice that includes non-linguistic and nonspecific instances of language (Tannen, Hamilton, and Schiffrin, 2015: 1).

As you read the chapters in this book, and in your wider reading, try to identify where the author(s) position themselves in relation to these definitions, and consider too where you would position yourself as a budding discourse analyst.

Discourse data

How many words do you think you have spoken this week? How many have you heard spoken? (And how do you define a word – do 'um'/ 'erm' count?) How many words have you read this week? (Including those you may have read inadvertently, like labels and signs you encounter in passing.) How much have you written? (Including online/on your mobile phone.) Now imagine multiplying all the linguistic communication you have been involved in during this one week by all the weeks of your life so far, and then by all the people alive now, and then by all the human beings who have ever left any records – written, recorded as audio signals, or in any digital form. If we assume that most of this communication could be classified as 'discourse', we get some idea of the 'universe' of data that might potentially be available to discourse analysts – and that is before we extend the range to include non-linguistic signs, such as photographs, soundtracks, emojis, and so on (see Chapters 8 and 9, this volume, which take stock of the 'multimodal turn' that discourse analysis has undergone in recent years

Introduction to discourse   9

to account for the wider range of semiotic modes used in contemporary communication and the interactions between these).

So, when you set out to design a research project around 'discourse', an early stage in the process will necessarily involve narrowing down your focus, and there are various ways that you might do this. Each chapter in this book takes a different approach to discourse analysis, and this often includes making different decisions about what kind of data to investigate. However, while such differences sometimes reflect contrasting perceptions about the very nature of discourse, in other cases the differences are more a matter of emphasis.

One way to set some boundaries around which data to collect is to identify some type or *genre* of communicative event or activity as your starting point. This could be, for example, informal conversations among friends, workplace meetings, political interviews or classroom interactions (e.g. Chapter 2, this volume), or it could be the virtual social gatherings enabled by digital media (e.g. Fester and Cowley, 2018). Data will then likely be restricted to detailed records of these interactions, in the form of recordings and transcripts of talk, or archives of messages exchanged, etc. More broadly, the starting point may not so much be a type of event, but rather a *social setting*, such as a school, small business, nursery, or community centre (e.g. Chapter 3, this volume), or even more formal institutional settings such as the Convention on the Future of Europe (Krzyżanowski and Oberhuber, 2007). In this kind of approach, the data may comprise a range of materials, including written texts, images, interviews with the people in the setting, field notes, and so on.

Some discourse analysts are particularly interested in the ways that different *modes* of communication influence the way it occurs. I know of several researchers who choose to explore exclusively written texts because of the challenges posed by working with speech. These include, for example, taking into account all the paralinguistic and prosodic features of spoken language which are very difficult to capture in transcriptions (see e.g. Cook, 1990). On the other hand, for some researchers, this is exactly what interests them – how the different components of face-to-face communication interact with one another. So if your interest lies primarily in one or more modes of communication, this could entail contrasting two kinds of data, such as, for example, both authentic informal conversation and scripted talk that aims to simulate casual interactions. Alternatively, your interest in a specific mode might lead you to restrict your data to one kind of mode, such as telephone conversations/emails/formal letters/Facebook posts/tweets: these are all examples of how a focus on the mode of communication leads to the selection of particular types of discourse from the vast range of potential data available for a discourse analysis project.

An aspect of discourse that intrigues some researchers is *how* it comes to take the forms it does. For some analysts, this line of research entails collecting very large quantities of data in order to reveal patterns in the

10   *Alison Sealey*

way words and phrases behave, including as they co-occur with one another (see Chapter 7, this volume). This is particularly interesting because users of language themselves are often not aware of these patterns. Other analysts look from the other end of the telescope, so to speak, zooming in on the internal processes that must be happening within the minds of language users to account for the formation of particular concepts (see Chapter 6, in this volume). As Hart explains, such 'cognitive' approaches tend to use as data texts that at least have the appearance of being 'monologic' (i.e. having been produced by one voice) rather than conversations, which are inherently 'dialogic' (i.e. produced in more interactional settings). I return to the issue of the production of data in the next section. Some analysts claim that these 'two ends of the telescope' are inevitably at odds with one another, but others believe that they need not be. For example, Hoey (2005) seeks to account for a central phenomenon associated with corpus analysis, namely 'the recurrent co-occurrence of words', and argues that it is a psychological concept, 'priming', that explains this. So his claim is that 'the mind has a mental concordance of every word it has encountered' which 'can be processed in much the same way that a computer concordance is' (2005: 11; see also Gries, 2005, 2006). These examples begin to point to another of the issues explored in this book: how much data is needed for different kinds of analysis, and does the analyst *measure* phenomena (quantitative analysis) or *interpret* them (qualitative analysis), or does the research, as is often the case, involve a combination of both?

Yet another point of departure in deciding on the kind of data to collect is the identification of a *social problem*, such as racism or gender inequality, which discourse plays a part in creating and sustaining. Again, this perspective and those summarised above are not mutually exclusive. The point is just that the primary motivations of the analysts may be different. That is, while one researcher investigates, say, casual conversations among friends in order to better understand turn-taking procedures in their own right, another may analyse the same data with a view to exploring gender dynamics and the way some speakers assert dominance over others. One form of discourse analysis directly concerned with issues of power and inequality is critical discourse analysis (CDA), a leading proponent of which is Norman Fairclough. Fairclough, and others working in this tradition, take care to point out that CDA is not a particular method or subdiscipline of discourse analysis, since a critical perspective is possible in any approach to discourse analysis. The relevance to us here is that CDA is discourse analysis that 'explicitly defines and defends its own sociopolitical position' (Van Dijk, 2001: 96). So, in this tradition, the starting point is a perceived social problem and the selection of data is guided by a concern to highlight and address 'the role of discourse in the production and reproduction of power abuse or domination' (Fairclough, 2001: 96). For this reason, many CDA projects select as data the discourse that is produced by 'elite' social actors, agencies, and institutions, such as politicians or the press, whose discourse, arguably, exerts the most influence over society. For many researchers in CDA the ultimate goal is to resist power and inequality as they are expressed in, and enacted through, discourse (see below for further discussion of what it means to take a critical stance).

Finally, for now, it is worth recognising that there has been a 'discursive turn' across the social sciences, and with this an increasing degree of collaboration between discourse analysts and researchers in other disciplines. For example, I gained access to a data set of transcriptions of parliamentary discourse (nearly 1000 sessions of Prime Minister's Questions) through a collaboration with a political scientist. His interests are primarily in political processes and how these are enacted in these events, and our joint analyses have focused sometimes more on these issues (Holden Bates and Sealey, 2019) and sometimes more on the pragmatics of the interactions (Sealey and Bates, 2016). Some other examples of where discourse analysis has been integrated with the concerns of other disciplines include collaborations with scholars who do research in disability studies (Grue, 2016), business and economics (Kelsey et al., 2016), and health policy (Evans-Agnew et al., 2016). In such cases, the data may well be similar to that in other discourse analysis projects, but the selection will be influenced by the specialist knowledge of collaborators from beyond linguistics.

The producers of discourse

This book is itself an example of one kind of written, published discourse, and, like nearly all the books you read, it contains at the beginning a copyright notice. This forbids anyone from making copies of the text without 'the prior permission in writing of the publishers', and each author whose chapters are included here has signed a 'contributor agreement' that 'asserts his/her moral right to be identified as the author', while at the same time we grant the exclusive copyright of our chapters to the publishers. Before the text reached the form you see it in now, there were lots of discussions about the content between the authors and editors, and correspondence by email with the publishers. Some changes were made to the drafts of the various chapters, first by the authors themselves and then by the book's editor, as well as by the 'copy editors' who work for the publishers and finalise matters such as the consistency of the layout and the accuracy and formatting of the references. This is because every chapter includes some quotations from other people's work and references to their ideas, which must, legally, be fairly acknowledged. So who, then, are the producers of this book as an example of discourse?

12 *Alison Sealey*

Some of the issues identified in the previous paragraph are technical and perhaps seem quite trivial – such as where to put the brackets, italics, and commas in a bibliographic reference. Another aspect of this area, though, is in the moral or even legal domain, usually identified in research projects as the consideration of 'ethics'. The chapters that follow include sections that discuss what is expected of researchers working with human participants, which often – although not always – applies to discourse analysis. Where relevant, each author explains how the procedures usually required within universities seek to safeguard both the collectors and the producers of data from causing or experiencing offence or even harm, for example, by intruding on privacy, breaching confidentiality, or triggering painful memories, etc.

So most examples of discourse cannot be thought of as produced by a single individual. Written texts often pass through the hands of several people; speakers draw on their prior experience of discourse as they produce utterances of their own, and the very process of speakers' interactions influences subsequent turns; texts that reach listeners as spoken, such as politicians' speeches, for example, may actually have been drafted and redrafted in writing by a number of different advisers (and as such are not truly monologic). This introduces the concept of *intertextuality* in discourse. Most published texts, in particular, are arrived at via a series of transformations that they undergo as they traverse an intertextual chain. Every text thus contains a 'trace' of previous texts. Other forms of intertextuality occur as texts directly reference other texts, as in the quotations characteristic of academic writing, or as texts like political speeches allude to other, well-known, texts by borrowing or creatively adapting memorable phrases. In other words, then, the ways in which discourse is produced are multifaceted, complex, and rarely, if ever, reducible to the intentions and actions of single individuals.

It is worth bearing all this in mind as you focus on the discourse data you choose to research. While, as I have said, the different approaches included in this book are not necessarily at odds with each other, there are conflicting views among discourse analysts about some matters concerning the producers of data. For example, the kind of large corpora with which Baker works (see Chapter 7, this volume) consist of texts produced by so many different people that it is not possible to consult each of them and interrogate them about the discourse they have produced. So some critics object to the omission from corpus studies of the viewpoint of discourse producers. Conversely, linguistic ethnographers often interview the producers of the texts they are analysing (see Chapter 3, this volume). However, a charge against the kinds of discourse analysis that works in depth on limited data is that findings cannot be generalised. As a result, there is a growing commitment in some quarters to approaches that combine methods and an example concerns the genre of news discourse. One team who research this area (Catenaccio et al., 2011) is very critical of the 'lack of attention to the news production process' that typifies many discourse studies of news texts which are analysed without any reference to how they come to take the form they do. Their criticism arises from their claim that '[t]he production process underlying the news text is an essential constitutive component of news contexts' (Catenaccio et al., 2011: 1845, see also Philo, 2007; Carvalho, 2008). These writers are not alone in drawing attention to 'the fluidity, complexity, and intricacies involved in jointly negotiating meaning' (Catenaccio et al., 2011: 1846), and this leads us to the third corner of what we might think of as the triangle of discourse – the audience, or reader, or 'receiver' of discourse. So, should discourse analysis encompass the perspective of readers and audiences, and if so, how?

Discourse reception

The term 'reception' presupposes a concern with certain modes of discourse rather than others. That is, when two or several participants in an interaction are co-producing discourse, as in the context of everyday conversations, for example, it is usually the case that each of them switches rapidly between the roles of speaker and hearer. In those cases, as various analysts have suggested, the concepts of 'production' and 'reception' of discourse are less relevant than that of collaboration (e.g. Coates, 1994; Jacoby and Ochs, 1995).

As noted above, some modes of discourse are more monologic than others, and it is when there is a clear distinction between producers and receivers that the notion of 'reception' may be most applicable, since, as another commentator on discourse analysis has observed, 'what a writer means by a text is not the same as what a text means to a reader' (Widdowson, 1995: 164). There is, of course, no infallible way to access the thought processes of discourse participants, but nevertheless several methods have been developed which seek to approach this goal.

At the intersection between discourse analysis and stylistics are studies of audience reception of literary texts. While stylistics conventionally examines the linguistic features of texts in order to understand, partly, how these features influence readers' interpretations, some researchers collect data from 'real readers'' discussions about the texts (Hall, 2009). Thus, discourse analytic studies of reading groups can shed light on how interpretations of texts are made and displayed in discourse (Peplow et al., 2015). Reading groups typically pre-date the arrival of the researcher, unlike the focus groups with which they otherwise have some features in common – and it is to this aspect of discourse reception research that I turn next.

One kind of discourse in which I am interested is the way that non-human animals are represented in language. Our research team compiled an electronic corpus of around 13 million words of text, from a variety of genres, which we explored in various ways from our own position as

14　*Alison Sealey*

analysts (e.g. Sealey, 2018, 2019; Sealey and Pak, 2018). In addition, though, we implemented an approach developed by the lead investigator on the project, Guy Cook (e.g. Cook, 2004; Cook and Ancarno, 2019), and incorporated into our analyses data collected from both discourse producers and receivers of the texts that made up our primary data. These took the form of interviews with people whose jobs involve communicating about animals (e.g. wildlife broadcasters, campaigners for the right to hunt foxes), and focus groups with various people who hold different views about animals (e.g. vegans, livestock farmers). Reactions to contrasting texts about animals and human–animal relations were elicited from members of these focus groups, who were also prompted to contribute their thoughts about examples of discourse about animals that they identified themselves.

Focus group interviews, which are not used exclusively for discourse analysis but also in various kinds of social research, are typically fairly open-ended. This means that, although the moderator of the focus group seeks to obtain the views of its members on a particular topic or issue, the participants can offer their own interpretations, in their own words. However, as mentioned above, no discourse is produced in a vacuum, and social interactions, including focus group interviews, are co-constructions, where factors such as imbalances of power and assumptions about what is expected or accepted can all influence what people say (see e.g. Edley and Litosseliti, 2018).

Taking a different approach to the reception of discourse, one chapter in this book is devoted to the use of experiments to test the analyst's hypotheses about how different versions of similar texts influence the way people interpret them (Chapter 10, this volume). Hart includes a thorough discussion of the methodological issues related to experiments in discourse analysis, so I don't cover those in detail here. In another of his chapters (Chapter 6, this volume), he explains how cognitive linguistics is concerned with the conceptual structures that texts evoke in the minds of readers, highlighting again how discourse analysts may choose to focus on responses and reception as well as the discourse itself.

Overall, then, while most discourse analysis focuses directly – and sometimes exclusively – on discourse as the data to be analysed, this section and the previous one serve as reminders that, where authentic language is concerned, there are always people – with their own interests, aims, attitudes and interpretations – involved in its production and reception.

The perspective of the analyst

Previous sections have discussed the 'triangle of communication' – discourse as data, the people and processes involved in its production, and those involved in its reception. Different approaches to analysis place different degrees of emphasis on each of these strands, while the tools and techniques associated with different approaches will also vary. The chapters that follow provide detailed examples of how these variations affect the practicalities of doing discourse analysis. All of this highlights how you, as someone intending to carry out a project of your own, will need not only to make some practical decisions, but also to think through your own position on some more theoretical and attitudinal issues. As Gee expresses it:

> any method always goes with a *theory*. Method and theory cannot be separated ... Any method of research is a way to investigate some particular domain. In this case, the domain is language-in-use. There can be no sensible method to study a domain, unless one also has a theory of what the domain is.
>
> (Gee, 2005: 6)

Theories about discourse have been developed from within different disciplines, including philosophy, psychology, sociology, anthropology, and computer science, as well as linguistics. Each of these ways of seeking to understand the world draws on contrasting, and sometimes conflicting, conceptions of what human beings are like, the nature of power and ideology, how language works, what constitutes an appropriate unit of analysis, and so on.

Even within linguistics, there are different degrees of emphasis on the issue of discourse as structural coherence ('What makes this stretch of talk or writing "discourse", as opposed to a random collection of sounds or letters?'), and as I indicated at the outset of this chapter for some discourse analysts the primary theoretical challenge lies predominantly within the language system itself. One of the pioneers of an early approach to understanding the patterns of spoken discourse, Malcolm Coulthard, identifies the following as the central questions:

> how does one characterize and label the basic unit of interaction; how many different functions are there; how are these functions realized lexicogrammatically and what structures do these basic units combine to form?
>
> (Coulthard, 2014: 9)

A somewhat different theoretical position is taken by another prominent discourse analyst, Ron Scollon, for whom 'Discourse is best conceived as a matter of social actions, not systems of representation or thought or values' (Scollon, 2002: 6). Thus, he argues that it is 'mediated action' that should be seen as the unit of analysis, rather than particular texts, genres or Discourses (like Gee, cited above, Scollon is interested in Discourses with a 'big D').

Scollon subscribes to the position that social action and discourse are inextricably linked, and it is the nature of this link that concerns many contemporary discourse analysts. One key point of controversy is the extent to which the social world is wholly constituted by discourse. So there are those who see language as 'a "machine" that generates, and as a result constitutes, the social world' (Jørgensen and Phillips, 2002: 9). Others suggest that the cause-and-effect might work the other way, so that discourses are themselves at least partly constituted by aspects of the social, while some theorists propose that this conundrum can be resolved by seeing discourse and social practice as mutually constitutive – each both reflecting and being reflected by the other. This is a neat formulation, but it doesn't clarify exactly how they can each simultaneously be both influencer and influenced. One way to resolve this is to invoke the concept of the 'dialectical' as the relationship between 'a particular discursive event and the situation(s), institutional(s) and social structure(s), which frame it: The discursive event is shaped by them but it also shapes them' (Wodak and Meyer, 2015: 6).

This orientation is usually associated with analysts whose central concern is with the *effects* of the kind of discourse being analysed, those who seek to answer the question of how particular discourses further the interests of some people rather than others. Where that concern is dominant, the modifier 'critical' is often inserted before 'discourse analysis', because practitioners recognise that there is no 'level playing field' in which people negotiate their respective interests. Therefore, since the most powerful typically further their own interests at the expense of the less powerful, the role of discourses in such exploitation is something to be exposed and challenged, rather than simply accepted and described. One of the founders of critical discourse analysis, Norman Fairclough, explains it like this:

> Critique brings a normative element into analysis ... It focuses on what is wrong with a society (an institution, an organisation etc.), and how 'wrongs' might be 'righted' or mitigated, from a particular normative standpoint. Critique is grounded in values, in particular views of the 'good society' and of human well-being and flourishing, on the basis of which it evaluates existing societies and possible ways of changing them.
>
> (Fairclough, 2013: 7)

Several – although not all – of the contributors to this book identify as critical discourse analysts, so that their epistemological standpoint is intertwined with their values as they approach the analysis of their selected data. Despite differences between their perspectives, all the authors here respect each other's positions, and the fact that there may be some areas of disagreement can be productive; a range of approaches can help to advance the field. I hope, then, that these initial reflections, in conjunction with the chapters that follow, will support you in your experiences of selecting, collecting, processing, and coding your data, and then in reporting the results of your own discourse analysis.

References

Carvalho, A. (2008). Media (ted) discourse and society: Rethinking the framework of critical discourse analysis. *Journalism Studies*, *9*(2), 6–18.

Catenaccio, P., Cotter, C., De Smedt, M., Garzone, G., Jacobs, G., Macgilchrist, F., Lams, L., Perrin, D., Richardson, J.E. and Van Hout, T. (2011). Towards a linguistics of news production. *Journal of Pragmatics*, *43*(7), 1843–1852.

Coates, J. (1994). No gap, lots of overlap: Turn-taking patterns in the talk of women friends. In D. Graddo, J. Maybin and B. Stierer (Eds.), *Researching language and literacy in social context.* (pp. 177–192). Clevedon: Multilingual Matters.

Cook, G. (1989). *Discourse, language teaching: A scheme for teacher education.* Oxford: Oxford University Press.

Cook, G. (1990). Transcribing infinity: Problems of context presentation. *Journal of Pragmatics*, *14*, 1–24.

Cook, G. (2004). *Genetically modified language.* London: Routledge.

Cook, G. and Ancarno, C. (2019). 'I do still love the taste': Taste as a reason for eating non-human animals. *Interdisciplinary Studies in Literature and Environment*, doi: 10.1093/isle/isy098.

Coulthard, M. (2014). *An introduction to discourse analysis.* (2nd ed.). London: Routledge.

Edley, N. and Litosseliti, L. (2018). Critical perspectives on using interviews and focus groups. In L. Litosseliti (Ed.), *Research methods in linguistics.* (pp. 195–226). London: Bloomsbury.

Evans-Agnew, R.A., Johnson, S., Liu, F. and Boutain, D.M. (2016). Applying critical discourse analysis in health policy research: Case studies in regional, organizational, and global health. *Policy, Politics, & Nursing Practice*, *17*(3), 136–146.

Fairclough, N. (2001). Critical discourse analysis as a method in social scientific research. In R. Wodak and M. Meyer (Eds.), *Methods of critical discourse analysis.* (pp. 121–138). London: Sage.

Fairclough, N. (2013). *Critical discourse analysis: The critical study of language.* Abingdon: Routledge.

Fester, M-T. and Cowley, S.J. (2018). Breathing life into social presence: The case of texting between friends. *Pragmatics and Society*, *9*(2), 274–296.

Gee, J.P. (2005). *An introduction to discourse analysis: Theory and method.* (2nd ed.). London: Routledge.

Gries, S. Th. (2005). Syntactic priming: a corpus-based approach. *Journal of Psycholinguistic Research*, *34*(4), 365–399.

Gries, S. Th. (2006). Corpus-based methods and cognitive semantics: The many senses of to run*. In S. Th. Gries and A. Stefanowitsch (Eds.), *Corpora in cognitive linguistics: The syntax-lexis interface.* (pp. 57–99). Berlin: Mouton de Gruyter.

Grue, J. (2016). *Disability and discourse analysis.* London: Routledge.

Hall, G. (2009). Texts, readers – and real readers. *Language and Literature*, *18*(3), 331–337.

Hoey, M. (2005). *Lexical priming: A new theory of words and language.* London: Routledge.

Holden Bates, S. and Sealey, A. (2019). Representing women, women representing: Backbenchers' questions during prime minister's questions, 1979–2010. *European Journal of Politics and Gender*, *2*(2), 237–256.

18 Alison Sealey

Jacoby, S. and Ochs, E. (1995). Co-construction: An introduction. *Research on Language and Social Interaction, 28*(3), 171–183.

Johnstone, B. (2002). *Discourse analysis.* Oxford: Blackwell.

Jørgensen, M.W. and Phillips, L.J. (2002). *Discourse analysis as theory and method.* London: Sage.

Kelsey, D., Mueller, F., Whittle, A. and KhosraviNik, M. (2016). Financial crisis and austerity: Interdisciplinary concerns in critical discourse studies. *Critical Discourse Studies, 13*(1), 1–19.

Krzyżanowski, M. and Oberhuber, F. (2007). *(Un)Doing Europe: Discourses and practices of negotiating the EU constitution.* New York: Peter Lang.

Peplow, D., Swann, J., Trimarco, P. and Whiteley, S. (2015). *The discourse of reading groups: Integrating cognitive and sociocultural perspectives.* New York: Routledge.

Philo, G. (2007). Can discourse analysis successfully explain the content of media and journalistic practice? *Journalism Studies, 8*(2), 175–196.

Scollon, R. (2002). *Mediated discourse: The nexus of practice.* London: Routledge.

Sealey, A. (2018). Animals, animacy and anthropocentrism. *International Journal of Language and Culture, 5*(2), 224–247.

Sealey, A. (2019). Translation: A biosemiotic/more-than-human perspective. *Target, 31*(3), 305–327.

Sealey, A. and Bates, S.R. (2016). Prime ministerial self-reported actions in prime minister's questions 1979–2010: A corpus-assisted analysis. *Journal of Pragmatics, 104,* 18–31.

Sealey, A. and Pak, C. (2018). First catch your corpus: Methodological challenges in constructing a thematic corpus. *Corpora, 13*(2), 229–254.

Tannen, D., Hamilton, H.E. and Schiffrin, D. (Eds.) (2015). *The handbook of discourse analysis.* Oxford: John Wiley & Sons.

Van Dijk, T.A. (2001). Multidisciplinary CDA: A plea for diversity. In R. Wodak and M. Meyer (Eds.), *Methods of critical discourse analysis.* (pp. 95–121). London: Sage.

Widdowson, H.G. (1995). Discourse analysis: A critical view. *Language and Literature, 4*(3), 157–172.

Wodak, R. and Meyer, M. (Eds.) (2015). *Methods of critical discourse studies.* London: Sage.

2 Conversation analysis

Greg Myers

Introduction

Conversation analysis is the study of the ways participants organise talk in interaction. For instance, think of a group of friends sitting around in a kitchen. There is no chair, no formal set of rules, no agenda of relevant topics. There is lots of noise and overlapping talk. But it is orderly, usually. You know it is orderly, because on the occasions when you can't get a word in, or someone's response doesn't seem to follow, it feels odd, and you look for an explanation. Conversation analysts look at how participants manage the taking of turns to talk, how one turn can set up expectations for the next turn, and how participants act when turns are, in some way, not expected. Discourse analysts have found the methods of conversation analysis useful, for instance, in looking at decision-making in business meetings (Boden, 1994), interactions in language teaching (Seedhouse, 2004), or adversarial styles in political news interviews (Clayman and Heritage, 2002). In this chapter, I go back to the origins of the approach that led to conversation analysis, then take a brief bit of data to illustrate the ways analysts might approach it, and finally consider some of the practical considerations for analysts, for instance, how much data one can present.

Outline of approach

In one sense, conversation analysis is the right place to begin a book on discourse analysis methods: talk is the central form of language use, and interaction is crucial in discourse (even much-written discourse). But in another sense, the academic approach called conversation analysis is an odd place to begin the book, because the people who developed this approach were not particularly interested in discourse as a level of linguistic analysis, or even, particularly in language.

Conversation analysis (CA) developed out of *ethnomethodology* (Garfinkel, 1967; Heritage, 1984), a sociological approach that turned away from testing out abstract, structural models of society, and instead focused on how social structure emerges in the course of people doing everyday practical actions. So, for instance, an ethnomethodologist might study queues (or in US English, lining up). There is no set of rules of the distance between people, body orientation, and direction that makes a group of people a queue; they make it a queue as they interact with the people around them. The queue may not be obvious to everyone. But the people in the queue have ways of showing they are in a queue, and when that doesn't work, dealing with such problems ('Hey, there's a queue here', 'Are you the back of the queue?', 'Is this the queue for registration?'). There are other practices that grow up where, for instance, there is check-in for a plane without a queue, but living in the UK I haven't had to figure out these practices. Other applications of ethnomethodology have included the maps people draw to show how to get to their house, the maintenance of clinical records, or something as complex as the organisation of an emergency centre.

When Harvey Sacks and his colleagues Emanuel Schegloff and Gail Jefferson began exploring conversation analysis (Sacks, Schegloff, and Jefferson, 1974), they saw talk as a particularly fertile area for developing this approach to studying society. Relatively inexpensive reel-to-reel tape recorders had become available, so they had rich, reproducible data that could be analysed in detail. They found even very small signals – a pause of half a second, a sudden intake of breath, a drawn-out word – could be crucial to the ways participants organised the talk, so the analyses became more and more detailed. But their focus was always on the way social organisation emerges in time as part of practical action – in this case, talking to someone. This focus made their approach different from the work of linguists, such as John Sinclair and Malcolm Coulthard (1975) who studied conversation as a level of linguistic organisation, modelled on grammar. It also makes their approach different from the work of philosophers, such as Paul Grice (Grice, 1989), who developed an approach starting deductively with what must be the assumptions of participants in conversation. And it makes their approach very different from that of corpus linguists studying patterns in large collections of speech data. All these approaches emerged in the same period, the 1960s and 1970s, but they had different aims.

Perhaps the greatest influence of Sacks on linguistics is that his work, with that of Goffman (1981), Hymes (1964), and others in the same period, started analysis with situated, specific interactions as they develop in time, rather than with language as a system.

CA asks us to look closely at what is going on, moment to moment, in time. Researchers look at the management of turn-taking, the way participants determine when one person speaks and then another. But there is much more to it; they look at the way one turn links to the next, the ways participants manage potential problems, and the ways talk is integrated with other kinds of action. The window of analysis can be very narrow, usually just two turns at a time, a few seconds of talk. And within this window, the assumption is that detail is worth attention. Since the devices participants use are so carefully calibrated, every pause or overlap, every marker such as 'um' or 'well', every intonation contour, every slight laugh, is potentially relevant.

Conversation analysts do not ask what is going on in participants' minds, and they do not explain an interaction by saying A was thinking this, or B was trying to do that (even when the analyst was one of the participants). They assume participants display to each other what is relevant in the course of their actions, and analysts can see these actions too. So, for instance, one might want to explain a pause as the time a speaker takes for cognitive processing, but what is relevant in this approach is how the other participant interprets it, and they may take it as a normal pause or as a pause indicating reluctance. Similarly, they do not ask whether a participant was motivated to say something by their position or identity or other social factors; again, they assume that participants 'orient to', that is, display and respond to, the positions and identities – as male or female, teacher or student, expert or novice – that are relevant in this specific interaction. This perspective does not mean that CA has to be uncritical or apolitical in its orientation; see for instance work by Kitzinger (2004), McIlvenny (2002), or Stokoe and Smithson (2001). Conversation analysts do not say there is no cognition, or is no social structure or categories, just that we should look first, in any bit of data, at just what the participants are doing.

The analysis begins by looking for patterns; for instance, what happens in the next turn after a question? But the test of a pattern is not statistical ('77% of the time the next turn is an answer, 12% of the time it is another question, so the hypothesis that a question is followed by an answer is proved'). Rather the test is to look at cases when participants do not follow the expected pattern. The interest is in how they manage the situation, moment to moment, not in the principle of what a question is, or in why someone might not want to answer, or how we can model the individual's process of interpretation. At its simplest, the CA approach is this: whatever you are looking at, look back to the previous turn, or on to the next turn, to see what it is.

Identifying research questions

As you might guess from this background to the approach, conversation analysis asks *how* research questions.

- How do participants collaboratively present something as an error and correct it?
- How do doctors and patients talk during physical contact in an examination?

22 Greg Myers

- How do participants get out of talk about their troubles and into talking about other matters?
- How does laughter start and end in a group?

As suggested above, conversation analysts do not ask *why* questions, such as:

- Why do men dominate business meetings?
- Why are students reluctant to answer questions?
- Why do people laugh at jokes?

And they don't ask questions of value, of what should be rather than what is:

- When is a broadcast interview biased?
- What is the best way to correct students in class?
- What's the most effective to conduct a cross-examination in court?

But they could say that a good place to start the study of these practical questions is to look at how people do what they do, in specific cases. An analyst can then show that these processes are probably more complex and delicate than one would have thought, and that the answers to the big questions may involve going back to these specific interactions.

Data collection and ethics

There is no substitute, in conversation analysis, for starting with a detailed recording of the interaction. A CA researcher cannot use someone's recollection of what was said, even of what they said themselves, because in remembering it they have already edited out the kind of detail we would need to construct their own interpretation. A researcher cannot make up plausible or generic examples, because those smooth out the detail of the processes one gets in any real example.

There are, of course, readily available media examples of lively conversations. One can study broadcast interactions, for instance from a talk show, but they are not examples of people doing ordinary talk; they are examples of people performing something that they think will seem like ordinary talk to an overhearing audience (Tolson, 2001). Scripted examples, as in soap operas, are even more complex; they present what the writers, actors, directors, and editors thought would sound like ordinary talk (Richardson, 2010).

What about interactions produced for institutional purposes, such as business meetings, research interviews, courtroom recordings, social work sessions, or police interviews? They are, of course, conversations, and one needs to know how people organise ordinary conversations to make sense of how they talk in these specific contexts, but these interactions are also strongly constrained on such matters as who speaks when, what sorts of turns are preferred, and how topics shift. It works best to start with everyday conversation, and then move on to the ways it is transformed in institutional contexts.

If one is collecting one's own data, one must, of course, get prior permission from everyone involved. This means it is very hard to gather naturalistic data of some situations, such as customers coming up to the bar in a pub, or racial abuse on campus, or sexual harassment at work. One can gain valuable insights by analysing people talking about these situations, but those conversations are not at all like the original situations one wants to know about. Often, one has to use data that has already been recorded and transcribed. My examples all come from the Santa Barbara Corpus of American Spoken English, collected in the 1990s.

Perhaps the best-known aspect of CA, to those outside the approach, is the very detailed transcripts filled with symbols indicating such features as timed pauses, brackets to show overlapping talk, underlines to show stress, degree signs to show quietness, angle brackets to show speeded up talk, and so on. (For a demonstration of why this is all needed, see Antaki, 2002). The original purpose was to show what was on the audio, so that readers could see evidence for one's argument, but also so that other analysts could use the same passage to make arguments different from those of the first person to publish it. There is some benefit to this work; if one transcribes the talk oneself, one often notices much more about the passage than one did in just listening to it. But it is a lot of work; one rule of thumb is that detailed transcription takes about 20 hours for one hour of audio (and it takes me much longer). Even with all this work, one gets a rough version of the talk; different readers would add more detail and read it in different ways. One could argue that such detail is less necessary now, when in many contexts one can just attach the audio file. The basic principle is that one should use as much detail as you need to make the talk clear to your readers.

CA began with audio recordings. More recent studies are likely to use video, to capture such aspects as gaze, gesture, and movement. But video can be problematic; it can be harder to get permission, it requires choosing which angles will get the relevant visual data, and all that wonderful visual information produces an even more unwieldy transcript. But one can see that many of the mechanisms of, for instance, selection of the next speaker, involve visual as well as auditory cues. When a colleague and I did a paper on laughter (Myers and Lampropoulou, 2015), one reviewer said that they wouldn't consider any study that didn't have video. And we could see their point.

Let us take one example, chosen from the 60 recordings of talk in the Santa Barbara Corpus of Spoken American English (Du Bois et al.,

24   *Greg Myers*

2000–2005). SBC023 is a half-hour recording of a reading group, with 11 women between 46 and 85, discussing E.M. Forster's 1910 novel *Howards End* (and sometimes the 1992 movie based on it, which had then been recently released). I have chosen a 30-second section about six minutes into the recording, where they are talking about where the characters were in the ending. Let's look at it first in the simplified form that will be more familiar to many readers, as a kind of playscript.

Example 1

KIM: What did, it seems to me XX in the movie, they were looking at this big house, interior of this big house, did they move to a big house? Where did they live

JANICE: I think they lived in the big house, they ended up living in Howard's End didn't they?

KIM: They did live in the big house,

LINDA: for a while

PATTY: No

LINDA: Yeah, at the end, they were in Howard's End.

LORI: Who was at Howard's End] at the end? I thought it was Helen and the little boy.

LINDA: No, all of them were at Howard's End, Henry, Margaret, Helen, they were all one big happy family

DIANE: they all lived in Howard's End,

LORI: whole family,

PATTY: Oh my God.

LINDA: [laughs]

KIM: When

JANICE: That was kind of unbelievable, wasn't [laughs]

PATTY: Tell me another one

EVELYN: and Margaret brought em all together.

LINDA: Well,

KIM: and when they married

LINDA: and the other thing

KIM: and when they married, did what was his name, the wimpy little son

X: Tibby?

KIM: the bro-

SUE: Tibby?

KIM: did Tibby and the young girl come and live with them?

That is easy enough to read, and gives something of a sense of the group, but if one listens to the recording, one finds it is missing a great deal. The transcription in the corpus uses its own symbols to record some of the way the talk unfolded. Here I convey some of the same information using conventional symbols from conversation analysis transcription.

Conversation analysis   25

Example 2

1. KIM: .(h) What- . uh did uh: . it seems to me () in the movie . they were looking at this bi:g house . in:terior of this big house . did they move to a big house? . Where did they live?
2. JANICE: . I think they lived in the big house
3. KIM: (they did) live in the big [house],
4. JANICE: [they] ended up [living in Howards] End
5. LINDA: [for a while]
6. JANICE: didn't they?
7. PATTY: [No].
8. LINDA: [Yeah] at the end. They were . [in Howard's End].
9. LORI: [Who was at Howard's End] at the end? I thought it was Helen and the little boy.
10. LINDA: . No . all of [em were at Howards] [End].
11. JANICE: [I thought all of em] –
12. DIANE: () [they all lived in How]ards [End],
13. LINDA: [Henry] . Margaret
14. DIANE: ()
15. LINDA: . Helen, [they were all] one big happy family h.
16. LORI: [(whole family)],
17. PATTY: Oh [my] God.
18. LINDA: [h]
19. KIM: W- . [when uh] –
20. JANICE: [That was kind of] unbelievable [h wasn't h it h h [h h h] [h]
21. LINDA: [h]
22. PATTY: [Tell me] [an][other one].
23. JANICE: [h] [h]
24. EVELYN: [and Margaret brought em all:] together.
25. LINDA: h: [well],
26. KIM: [and when they married and]
27. LINDA: [and the other thing] –
28. KIM: when uh: . they married . did uh: . uh what was his name. the uh: . wimpy little son?
29. X: . [Tibby]?
30. KIM: [the bro-] –
31. SUE: [Tibby]?
32. KIM: [did Tib]by . and the young girl come and live with them?

Most researchers in conversation analysis use a similar set of symbols, developed by Gail Jefferson, originally on typewriters (for one example, see Atkinson and Heritage, 1984).

[ ]	overlaps (The brackets are lined up to show the beginning of the overlap. In the Santa Barbara Corpus system, these overlaps are indexed with numbers, so you can tell which brackets go with which.)
.	short pauses (longer pauses are usually timed by tenths of a second)
___	stressed syllable
:	lengthened sound

26   *Greg Myers*

wor-	broken off
WORD	louder than surrounding talk
° word °	quieter than surrounding talk
h	audible breath
h h h h	laughter
( )	unintelligible or uncertain words

Punctuation marks are not used in their conventional grammatical meanings; a comma is sometimes used to show level pitch at the end of an intonation group, and a question mark to show rising pitch, not a grammatical question (more detailed transcriptions of pitch are sometimes used now). Any approach to transcription needs some symbols (perhaps not these) to show these features, as well as many other symbols for intonation, voice quality, and other features.

Analysing and interpreting data

Conversation analysis deals with many aspects of talk, but there are three kinds of organisation that are central to the approach: turn-taking, adjacency pairs, and preference structure.

Turn-taking

The central observation made by Sacks and others is simply that people have complex, precise ways of taking turns in conversation, avoiding overlaps and silences. The example I have chosen may seem a strange one to make this point, since all but three of the turns have some overlapping talk. The point is that such overlaps do not, generally, continue for long, so participants are dealing with them. The orderliness is striking, with 11 participants wanting to say something, and, in this group, no leader or chair to assign turns. In a few cases, the overlap is a bid to speak and perhaps change the topic, as when Linda overlaps with Kim:

Example 3

26. KIM: [and when they married and]
27. LINDA: [and the other thing] –
28. KIM: when uh: . they married . did uh: . uh what was his name. the uh: . wimpy little son?

Kim has been trying to get a turn since 19. Here she and Linda talk at the same time. What happens here is what usually happens with longer overlaps: one of the participants, Linda here, stops talking and lets the other continue.

Not all overlaps are presented as problematic. They can be taken as support for the speaker, not as bids for a turn, as in 15–16:

Example 4

15. LINDA: Helen, [they were all] one big happy family h.
16. LORI: [(whole family)]

Linda has listed all the members of the Wilcox family, and Lori chimes in saying this is the whole family, therefore agreeing, and Linda acknowledges this by repeating a version of what Lori just said.

Another key observation about turn-taking is that participants do not generally leave long silences. Again, this doesn't mean silences don't happen (though they are rare in this particular group) but that they are treated as potentially meaningful when they do happen.

Adjacency pairs

So far, then, we have a string of turns, in which speaker selection follows an orderly pattern, even in this lively and informal example. The next central aspect of CA is the observation that one turn often makes a certain kind of response relevant in the next turn, for instance a question leading to an answer. In the quoted example, there are four question–answer pairs, in turns 1–3, 4–8, 9–12, and 28–31. These two-part structures are called *adjacency pairs*.

It may seem obvious that questions are followed by answers, but the observation leads to details that show us how the interaction is developing.

Example 5

1. KIM: [earlier part of turn omitted] . did they move to a big house?. Where did they live?
2. JANICE: I think they lived in the big house
3. KIM: (they did) live in the big [house],
4. JANICE: [they] ended up [living in Howards] End

Kim's first question is followed by a pause. Kim treats it as meaning that they can't answer her question phrased this way. She follows it with a more open form of question about the same information, 'where did they live?' This time there is a short pause and then an answer from Janice in 2, which Kim echoes in 3. But Janice does not treat this as the answer to the question in 1; instead she overlaps Kim to give a different answer, with a tag question ('didn't they?') inviting agreement. She thus makes a distinction between 'a big house' (they lived in several) and the house Howards End in particular.

28   Greg Myers

Even if what follows is not directly an answer, and it may be presented as and taken as an answer, as in this exchange later in the book group recording, after the example I have given:

Example 6

1. DIANE: ((earlier part of turn deleted)) h was England the strong world power in nineteen ten? still? the: w- . empire English the sun never sets on the English empire?
2. EVELYN: tha- that was where uh: . a- a- Wilcox made his money . wasn't it?

(SBCASE 23: 552–563)

Evelyn does not directly answer Diane with yes or no. She points out that a family in the novel made large amounts of money in the Empire, with the implication that England must still have been a world power then. It is the adjacency, not some formal fit with the question, that makes a turn an answer. The same patterning is explained in a different way in pragmatics, as following from a *conversational maxim of relevance* (Grice, 1989). Since questions set up an expectation of an answer, they can be used in a range of contexts to control the interaction, whether it is by a child asking repeated questions, an interviewer in academic research, a cross-examiner in a courtroom, or a therapist in a session.

Greeting/greeting, question/answer, and invitation/response seem obvious to most people as pairs. It is probably less obvious how the expression of an opinion or evaluation sets up a relevant response. Anita Pomerantz (1984) calls these turns *assessments*, and shows they lead to specific kinds of next turns, *second assessments*. This kind of pair is particularly useful in analysing the book group, where participants often put forth their view of something in the set book. Here Janice is talking about the ending:

Example 7

20. JANICE: [That was kind of unbelievable [h wasn't h it h h [h h h] [h]
21. LINDA: [h]
22. PATTY: [Tell me] [an][other one].

Janice gives her assessment of the ending. Patty responds with a turn that also expresses that it was unbelievable, quoting the kind of response typically given to a story one doubts, 'tell me another one'. Janice goes on, and Patty's response is taken as agreeing with her.

Another example of an adjacency pair is *repair*, where one turn contains a potential source of trouble, and the next prompts a correction.

Conversation analysis 29

Example 8

28. KIM: when uh: . they married . did uh: . uh what was his name. the uh: .
          wimpy little son?
29. X: . [Tibby]?
30. KIM: [the bro-] –
31. SUE: [Tibby]?
32. KIM: [did Tib]by . and the young girl come and live with them?

Kim starts a question, but first needs to know the name of a character, whom she calls 'the uh; . wimpy little son' with a pause before the description. Someone gives the name but uses a question intonation, and at this point Kim repairs her own turn, to say it is the brother of Margaret and Helen she is looking for, not the son. She then restarts her question in 32, with the right name now inserted. This is typical of processes of repair, in that they often involve the person who recognises the problem prompting the first speaker to correct it themselves, rather than saying directly, for instance, 'Tibby is not her son' (Schegloff, Jefferson, and Sacks, 1977).

Preference

For some adjacency pairs, there is only one possible second part; for instance, a greeting typically leads to a greeting in the same form. But for other pairs, there are two kinds of second parts that are treated differently by participants. For instance, an invitation can be accepted or rejected. If it is accepted, the response is typically quick and brief. If it is rejected, the response may be delayed, or be prefaced by a particle such as 'well', or by a statement about their desire to accept, before it is rejected. The unmarked, simple, more typical response is called *preferred*, while the marked form is called *dispreferred*. (The terms don't say anything about whether the person invited really prefers to accept or not, just that the preferred response is presented in this unmarked way.)

In Example 7, we saw how quickly another speaker chimes in when they want to agree. We can also see in the next turns an example of what happens when a participant follows with a second assessment that does *not* agree:

Example 9

23. EVELYN: [and Margaret brought em all:] together.
24. LINDA: h: [well],

Evelyn is giving a positive evaluation of the role of the character Margaret in bringing about this ending. We don't know what Linda was going to say, because she is cut off by others. But we do know that she

30   Greg Myers

starts with a long breath, and then the particle *well*. So we can tell that, whatever she was going to say, it wasn't something presented as agreement.

Second assessments are common in book groups; one has to say something when someone has ventured an opinion about the book. So we can find some very complex examples of how friends disagree. This example comes in the same group, after the example I have quoted:

Example 10

1. LORI: you know he . I mean Mister Wilcox is: a charming. man
2. EVELYN: [hm]
3. LINDA: [yeah]
4. JANICE: [hm] . well [as long as things are going his way]
5. LINDA: [h I guess I couldn't see any charm]

(SBC023: 246–250)

Evelyn uses a *filled pause*, 'hm', that just acknowledges what Lori has said. In a context in which agreement is preferred, a neutral response is often taken as disagreement. She is overlapped by Linda, who says 'yeah'. But as we will see, when she continues, even 'yeah' does not always signal agreement. Evelyn is also overlapped by Janice, who starts with the same neutral response, 'hm', and a particle, 'well', that is often the preface to a dispreferred turn. Janice qualifies Lori's statement by completing it with 'as long as things are going his way'. Linda continues her turn with a direct disagreement. But this disagreement is prefaced with a weakening 'I guess'. She does not say he has no charm, but that she 'couldn't see any'. Her turns 3 and 4 in this example are a very common structure of a second assessment, something like 'yes but ... ' So the participants in this group (and participants in any conversation) have quite elaborate and carefully timed devices for signalling whether their assessment aligns with what has just been said or diverges from it.

I have focused on question/answer and assessment/second assessment adjacency pairs. In some other kind of interaction, we might be looking at other conversational features. In a meeting we might look at turn assignment. In an interaction between friends we might look at invitations and acceptances or rejections. In an interview one might look at the ways one party uses *reformulations* – turns that are presented as repeating, in other words, what the other person just said. In a group where someone is telling stories, we might get questions from the listeners about the events, showing who knows about the events already, and who is taken to be the audience. All these would have their own structure and analysis.

Though book group members have usually read the same book (or in this case, have at least seen the movie), they have different experiences and memories. So questions are a central way people define their relations to each other. One person admits not knowing something; others offer themselves as knowing, and define what they know and how. The other way people in a book group relate is by offering their opinions on what they have read, in the form of assessments. Others then respond with their own opinions. And we have seen that these second assessments are presented very carefully to show just how they diverge from the assessment, and how their turn is still relevant to what the previous speaker said. Book groups make good data for conversation analysis, because they show how a group without a leader or fixed rules organises itself, and brings out responses to the book in ways that (mostly) allow participants to come back next month (for discourse analyses of reading groups, see Benwell, 2012; Swann and Allington, 2009).

Presenting findings and results

Conversation analysis findings focus on showing how social order (such as a that of a functioning book group) emerges as participants manage interaction) for instance in asking questions and making assessments) as a practical activity – that is, they are doing it as part of acting normally in everyday activities. This focus has implications for the amount of data, the process of development, the form of presentation, and the kind of argument one can make.

CA researchers analyse a large amount of data, but they usually present a very small amount, in detail, to show their findings. For instance, a study of questions might show several ways the question/answer adjacency pair works in the data, and then look at an example where the participants do *not* follow the expected pattern, to see how they respond to it. One case cannot show what participants always or typically do, but it is enough to show what participants can do – because they do it. Usually, a researcher starts writing up with many examples, and in the final version, they have just a few examples that make the points they need to make. In CA, it is generally better to do more with less.

The process of conversation analysis is usually collaborative. It is a craft, not a science, and the best way to develop an analysis is not by reading more textbooks, or tightening up the argument in a finished paper, but by having data sessions in which you wrestle with making sense of all the details. Others pitch in; they might point out how an in-breath in the previous turn could suggest a bid for a turn, or how the level intonation of one turn end suggests a continuation, or how the overlap begins a syllable earlier that you said, which shows the speaker is presenting the response in a different way. There may be questions about laughter, asides, gestures, gaze. Of course, it is educational to do this with seasoned CA researchers, but it works just as well with anyone who is committed to the same aims of analysis. Any data session results in a more fine-grained analysis, and challenges your assumptions as an analyst.

32   Greg Myers

The form usually used for conversation analysis transcription puts off some researchers outside the tradition, and puts off almost all non-academics (such as professionals or group members or clients) to whom one is presenting the data. As I have noted, the principle is that you need to put in enough detail for other researchers to question or challenge your reading as they would in a data session. But for many presentations, you will need to simplify, just so you don't put off your intended audience. In some cases you can play the sound file, so they will have the original data themselves. Use of an elaborate transcription system is not the defining characteristic of conversation analysis.

The focus of CA on the emergence of social order means that researchers make some kinds of argument and not others. For instance, if the analyst was a participant themselves, this does not give them special insight into what was going on in the minds of the participants; for the purposes of analysis, everything they need to show to each other is shown in the interaction itself. Similarly, interviews with other participants about their recollection adds other data that can be analysed in other ways, but it does not help with the analysis of the interaction itself. And it is not useful to do conversation analysis if you are going to assume that you, as analyst, already know what social categories are relevant here, institutional role or gender or race or social class. Of course, lots of social categories may matter in any interaction, but the task of this particular kind of analysis is to see how they emerge for the participants. If you want to start with your theory of the social order, and see how the talk fits into it, you can certainly take a different approach, but you will miss some of the insights possible in conversation analysis.

Issues and limitations

I have focused on some of the foundations of CA, but researches over the years have broadened its remit. Of the many new developments, three might be particularly relevant here, dealing with the relation to grammar, the analysis of members' categories, and the analysis of talk as part of embodied action.

I have stressed that conversation analysis never set out to be a kind of grammar. But analysts have seen ways in which participants establish and interpret linguistic constructions in the course of turn-taking. An early example is the work of Ford and Thompson (1996) on how speakers in next turns interpret the completion point of a turn, the place where they can speak. In a more recent example, Stivers, Mondada, and Steensig (2011) collect studies of interaction with differences in knowledge, giving a new take on the linguistic topic of evidentiality.

In the lectures in which Harvey Sacks developed conversation analysis (Sacks, 1992), he also developed membership categorisation analysis, or MCA. An example that might interest him comes later in the book group I have analysed, when Patty talks about 'people who are so knowledgeable. it wasn't . certainly it wasn't any of us' (SBC02: 1125).

She says this with aspiration marking a sort of laughter in her voice. Others start laughing as soon as she said the first two syllables of 'knowledgeable'. She offers this as a recognisable category, and others do recognise it, and suggest candidate names for who might have provided the list in question. The attributes or actions of the people in this category don't need to be spelt out, because everyone knows the sort of person she is talking about, even if this phrase hasn't been used before; the talk shows that they share this category as a resource for conversation. This kind of analysis was neglected for many years, as a kind of fuzzy side of Sacks' legacy. But recently there has been a great interest in how MCA can be used in social research, with Stokoe (2012) providing a good short guide and Housley and Fitzgerald (2015) ringing together a collection of studies.

Conversation analysis was always about social action, not just about talk. But for many years the most accessible data was from audio recordings. Now with video recordings, analysts can consider gestures and movement as part of the communicative act, still within a framework of detailed sequential analysis, rather than the broad semiotics of most multimodal analysis. Early examples can be found in Christian Heath's (Heath, 1987) work on the medical interview; more recent examples are Ford and Stickle (2012) on the ways bids for turns are signalled in business meetings, and Lorenza Mondada's (Mondada, 2014) witty article on tour guides, and her other studies of movement and talk.

I have stressed that conversation analysis started with quite different questions from those of linguistics. But its analyses have proved useful in a range of approaches to discourse, including Interactional sociolinguistics, critical discourse analysis, and multimodal discourse analysis. It has provided insights into a range of social interactions. As often happens, academic boundaries that were once fought over fiercely are now open to some negotiations and trade back and forth.

Further reading

Two widely-used textbooks of conversation analysis are Hutchby and Woofitt (1998) and Ten Have (2007). A broader intellectual background for ethnomethodology and CA can be found in Heritage (1984) and Silverman (1998). If you take up CA as a central part of what you are doing, it is worth reading some of Sacks' lectures (Sacks, 1992); they are wider ranging and more accessible than the publications he completed in his short lifetime, and they give a wonderful sense of a mind at work (they have a very detailed index, so you can pick out some lectures relevant to what you are doing). One journal that consistently publishes quite specialised CA is *Research on Language and Social Interaction*; applications are often found in such journals as *Language in Society* and the *Journal of Pragmatics*.

References

Antaki, C. (2002). An introductory tutorial in Conversation Analysis. Retrieved 15/2/2018, from http://ca-tutorials.lboro.ac.uk/sitemenu.htm%3E.

Atkinson, J.M. and Heritage, J. (Eds.) (1984). *Structures of social action: Studies in conversation analysis*. Cambridge: Cambridge University Press.

Benwell, B. (2012). Common-sense anti-racism in book group talk: The role of reported speech. *Discourse & Society, 23*(4), 359–376.

Boden, D. (1994). *The business of talk: Organizations in action*. Cambridge: Polity Press.

Clayman, S. and Heritage, J. (2002). *The news interview: Journalists and public figures on air*. Cambridge: Cambridge University Press.

Du Bois, J.W., Chafe, W.L., Meyer, C., Thompson, S.A., Englebretson, R., and Martey, N. (2000–2005). *Santa Barbara corpus of spoken American English, Parts 1–4*. Retrieved 15/2/2018, from Linguistic Data Consortium, http://linguistics.ucsb.edu/research/santa-barbara-corpus.

Ford, C. and Stickle, T. (2012). Securing recipiency in workplace meetings: Multimodal practices. *Discourse Studies, 14*(1), 11–30.

Ford, C.E., and Thompson, S.A. (1996). Interactional units in conversation: Syntactic, intonational, and pragmatic resources for the management of turns. In E. Ochs, E.A. Schegloff and S.A. Thompson (Eds.), *Interaction and grammar*. (pp. 134–184). Cambridge: Cambridge University Press.

Garfinkel, H. (1967). *Studies in ethnomethodology*. Englewood Cliffs, NJ: Pentice-Hall.

Goffman, E. (1981). *Forms of talk*. Oxford: Basil Blackwell.

Grice, J.P. (1989). *Studies in the ways of words*. Cambridge, MA: Harvard University Press.

Heath, C. (1987). *Body movement and speech in medical interaction*. Cambridge: Cambridge University Press.

Heritage, J. (1984). *Garfinkel and ethnomethodology*. Cambridge: Polity Press.

Housley, W. and Fitzgerald, W. (Eds.) (2015). *Advances in membership categorization Analysis*. London: Sage.

Hutchby, I. and Wooffitt, R. (1998). *Conversation analysis: Principles, practices and applications*. Malden, MA.: Polity Press.

Hymes, D. (1964). Introduction: Toward ethnographies of communication1. *American Anthropologist, 66*(6, 2), 1–34.

Kitzinger, C. (2004). Feminist approaches. In J.G. Giampietro Gobo, C. Seale and D. Silverman (Eds.), *Qualitative research practice*. (pp. 125–140). London: Sage.

McIlvenny, P. (Ed.) (2002). *Talking gender and sexuality*. Amsterdam: John Benjamins.

Mondala, L. (2014). Bodies in action: Multimodal analysis of walking and talking. *Language and Dialogue, 4*(3), 357–403.

Myers, G. and Lampropoulou, S. (2015). Laughter, non-seriousness and transitions in social research interview transcripts. *Qualitative Research, 16*(1), 78–94.

Pomerantz, A. (1984). Agreeing and disagreeing with assessments: Some features of preferred/dispreferred turn shapes. In J.M. Atkinson and J. Heritage (Eds.), *Structures of social action*. (pp. 57–101). Cambridge: Cambridge University Press.

Richardson, K. (2010). *Television dramatic dialogue*. New York: Oxford University Press.

Sacks, H. (1992). *Lectures on conversation*. Oxford: Oxford University Press.

Sacks, H., Schegloff, E.A. and Jefferson, G. (1974). A simplest systematics for the organization of turn taking for conversation. *Language, 50*, 696–745.

Schegloff, E.A., Jefferson, G. and Sacks, H. (1977). The preference for self-correction in the organization of repair in conversation. *Language, 53*, 361–382.

Seedhouse, P. (2004). *The interactional architecture of the language classroom: A conversation analysis perspective*. Oxford: Blackwell.

Silverman, D. (1998). *Harvey Sacks: Social science and conversation analysis*. Cambridge: Polity Press.

Sinclair, J. and Coulthard, M. (1975). *Towards an analysis of discourse: The English used by teachers and pupils*. Oxford: Oxford University Press.

Stivers, T., Mondada, L. and Steensig, J. (Eds.) (2011). *Knowledge, morality and affiliation in social interaction*. Cambridge: Cambridge University Press.

Stokoe, E. (2012). Moving forward with membership categorization analysis: Methods for systematic analysis. *Discourse & Society, 14*(3), 277–303.

Stokoe, E.H. and Smithson, J. (2001). Making gender relevant: Conversation analysis and gender categories in interaction. *Discourse & Society, 12*(2), 217–244.

Swann, J. and Allington, D. (2009). Reading groups and the language of literary texts: A case study in social reading. *Language and Literature, 18*(3), 247–264.

Ten Have, P. (2007). *Doing conversation analysis*. (2nd ed.). London: Sage.

Tolson, A. (Ed.) (2001). *Television talk shows*. Mahwah, NJ: Lawrence Erlbaum Associates.

3 Discourse analysis and ethnography

Karin Tusting

Introduction

This chapter will describe how to go about discourse analytic research from an ethnographic perspective. It will briefly outline two complementary research traditions which have informed each other in this area, ethnographic approaches in critical discourse analysis, and the emergence of linguistic ethnography as an independent research paradigm. It will then describe how, within this approach, research questions can be identified, data collected, interpreted and analysed, and findings and results can be presented. Issues and limitations around adopting an ethnographic approach to discourse analysis will also be addressed.

To illustrate the points made in this chapter, a sample of written data has been taken from an ethnographic project of my own which explored the impact of paperwork demands in a nursery, an information poster displayed on a wall outside one of the rooms, designed to inform parents about the curriculum and about children's activities.

Outline of approach

Discourse analysis is sometimes seen as an approach which focuses primarily on the analysis of texts. As the chapters in this collection show, however, many discourse analysis approaches – e.g. conversation analysis, or analysis of digitally mediated communication – work with texts which arise from, and are clearly located in, a social interactional context. Placing discourse analysis within a broader ethnographic perspective puts the practices and experiences of people interacting in a social context at the heart of the research.

The term *ethnography* originally referred to the primary data collection methodology used in anthropology, the discipline which studies human cultures. Etymologically rooted in 'ethnos', meaning 'peoples' or 'cultures', and 'graph', denoting writing, it refers to an approach in which the principal means of data collection is, indeed, writing about people; systematically keeping records of what people do in a particular setting through writing detailed observational fieldnotes, which then form the basis of an analysis of cultural practices.

A prevailing myth of anthropological history is that of the typical student anthropologist in the early twentieth century, whose training might consist simply of being given a notebook and a pen before being sent off to live in a distant village for an extended period of time. They would keep careful fieldnotes recording their attempts to learn enough of the culture (and language) in order to try and belong, noting the mistakes they made in doing this and what they learned from these, and eventually being able to provide something close to an insider account of local cultural practice. Atkinson, Okada, and Talmy (2011: 85–86) define ethnography as having initially been the '*up-close, intensive, long-term, holistic* study of small-scale, non-Western societies'. For a European anthropologist, these settings were often in places which had been colonised by the anthropologist's home country. Many US anthropologists would do similar work with Native American groups, and the development of linguistic anthropology as a discipline in the US was very much informed by scholars such as Boas and his students who made serious attempts to produce respectful and non-reductive accounts of their cultural practices (Scollon & Scollon, 2007). A key influence on the development of ethnography was the work of Bronislaw Malinowski (1922), who was interned on the Trobriand islands during the First World War. He used this experience to develop both an anthropological account of exchange practices on the islands, and a more conceptually-informed account of the participant-observation approach.

Later in the twentieth century, ethnographic methods were drawn on in other areas of the social sciences, particularly sociology, to explore settings closer to home (at least in geographical terms) for the scholars who engaged in this research. Most famously, researchers from what became known as the 'Chicago school' explored the cultural practices of urban settings, often choosing those seen as 'deviant' in some way, like dance halls, gang culture, and 'street corner society' (see Becker, 1999 for a fuller account).

In the present day, ethnography normally still entails participant-observation and fieldnote writing. But over time, the term ethnography has come to signal much more than just a data collection method. Ethnography has become associated with a particular perspective, which seeks to understand a social setting holistically, taking account of the culture, history, and meanings of that setting for those who are involved in it. Developing understandings of research participants' own perceptions and experiences is known as developing an *emic* perspective (Copland & Creese, 2015: 29).

It is clear from this account that to describe ethnography as simply a method of data collection does not do it justice. What ethnographies have in common is a particular perspective on the world, a set of beliefs about what is important, and what we need to focus on, in order to

38 Karin Tusting

understand what is going on. This is why Blommaert and Jie (2010) and Lillis (2008) describe ethnography as a perspective, theory, or epistemology – that is, a set of beliefs about what it is possible to know about the (social) world, associated with a set of beliefs about the best way to go about generating this knowledge. These include:

- Studying what is happening in the 'real world' as much as possible, through direct observation, rather than setting up artificial experimental settings.
- Adopting a holistic perspective which tries to understand how multiple factors interact in a particular setting, rather than pulling out and isolating a limited number of influences.
- Trying to develop an 'emic' (insider) understanding of the meanings of the context for those who live in it, through listening to participants in the setting and through adopting a 'participant-observer' stance: becoming involved in what is going on in an attempt to understand it as a member of the community would.
- Reflecting carefully on what this insider role as a researcher means for the knowledge constructed by the research: 'researcher reflexivity'.

This account has not, so far, focused very much on language, because it is important to understand the ethnographic perspective before exploring what ethnography can bring to discourse analysis. However, some branches of ethnographic work have indeed focused very particularly on language and on other aspects of communication such as gesture, gaze and posture (see also Chapter 8, this volume, on multimodality).

In the US tradition of linguistic anthropology, mentioned above, developing knowledge of the language of Native peoples was an intrinsic part of developing an understanding of their culture (Duranti, 2003). This informed the development in the 1960s and 1970s of the *ethnography of communication*, associated particularly with the work of Hymes and Gumperz (e.g. Gumperz & Hymes, 1972). This was an approach to language, resistant to the then-dominant perspectives of generative grammar, which insisted that the development of *communicative competence* in a given social and cultural context was reliant on developing both an understanding of the structure of a language and of how it should appropriately be used in *speech events* in speech communities.

And in a broader sense, all analysis of ethnographic data can be seen as a kind of text analysis. Fieldnotes, interview transcripts, recorded interaction, and documents collected from the setting are all texts which the researcher may work with. Some ethnographic discourse analysis does indeed draw on analysis of all of these texts, for instance combining them to understand the prevailing discourses around a particular topic in a given setting. Other approaches will make an analytic separation between the text in focus for discourse analysis, and the understandings of the broader context generated by the ethnographic data. Whatever the perspective adopted on the relationship between text and context, though, ethnographic research on discourse is, by definition, research which incorporates, to some degree, participant-observation, long-term engagement with a context, researcher reflexivity, and a holistic and emic perspective, rather than focusing on texts or transcripts alone.

As an example of how text can be drawn on as part of an ethnographic analysis, I will be drawing on a specific piece of written data. The poster reproduced in Figure 3.1 was placed on the wall of a nursery I was researching, outside the baby room, which catered for children aged from three months up to one year. (Photographs which reveal children's faces have been blanked out for ethical reasons, to maintain their anonymity.)

The project exploring the dataset which included this poster sought to understand how bureaucratic paperwork shaped practices in different educational settings. I spent several months engaged in participant-observation in the various rooms of this nursery, writing fieldnotes, taking photographs, and interviewing staff. This piece of data illustrates how the *Birth to Three Matters* framework for nursery provision (DfES, 2002), which had been recently introduced in this nursery at the time of the research, shaped both the daily workplace routines and practices and the representations of the children's lives which emerged from these. (This framework has now been superseded and replaced by the *Early Years Foundation Stage* statutory framework, DfE, 2017.)

To explain the poster a little: the centrality of the framework in shaping the organisation of the poster is evident in the phrase 'Birth to Three Matters', which is used as the main title of the display, centred, in large letters and roughly at eye height. Above this, photographs of the children are displayed with the smaller headings 'A skilful communicator'; 'A competent learner'; 'A strong child'; 'A healthy child'. These phrases directly replicate the titles of sub-sections of the framework. Below the main heading are displays of the planning carried out for activities with the children, on different timescales – long-term, medium-term, weekly, and daily 'focused activities' – by the staff working in the room. The floor plan explains the layout of the room, and at the foot of the poster can be found detailed accounts of the room's daily routines.

The local purpose of the display was to inform parents about the activities and practices of the room, although I rarely observed parents reading the boards; their information about their children's activities came principally from discussions with the staff and individual written records of observation of their own child. However, while parents were generally not overtly concerned with the curriculum framework on

Figure 3.1 Birth to three matters

a day to day basis, the display also served to publicly demonstrate the explicit connections between the nursery activities and the national framework for pre-school education.

Throughout this chapter, I will refer back to this piece of discourse data, set in the context of the broader project it was drawn from, to illustrate the points I am making about the potential of locating discourse analysis within an ethnographic approach to research.

Discourse analysis and ethnography 41

Critical discourse analysis and ethnography

Ethnography has provided a useful perspective in various forms of discourse analysis, including interactional sociolinguistics and critical discourse analysis. The historical development of critical discourse analysis (CDA) has been influenced by the fact that it arose from a group of text-focused linguists who sought to extend linguistic analysis to engage with social questions around power and ideology. The birth of CDA, as a sub-discipline is often traced back to a meeting in 1991 between Fairclough, Wodak, van Dijk, van Leeuwen, and Kress, all of whom were, in different ways, starting from the analysis of text and looking to extend this to address critical social questions (Wodak, 2001), building on the nascent discipline of critical linguistics (e.g. Fowler, Hodge, Kress, & Trew, 1979). Developing a sound theoretical model of how text and context relate to one another has therefore often been an issue of concern within CDA.

CDA has developed systematic ways of conceptualising this, often by separating out different layers of context. Fairclough's three-dimensional model of discourse practice (Fairclough, 1995: 97–98), for instance, takes the view that any given text can be interpreted variously as text, as discourse practice, and in terms of how it is embedded in sociocultural practice at various levels. Reisigl and Wodak (2009: 93) divide context into four different levels: the immediate context; the intertextual context; the context of situation; and the broader sociopolitical and historical context.

Both of these approaches have, in fact, been shaped by ethnographic perspectives. In both, the influence can be traced of Malinowski's division of context into *context of situation*, the immediate context of the act in focus, and *context of culture*, the broader social and cultural norms, expectations, values, and history within which the act takes place (probably mediated through Halliday's interpretation of these ideas, see e.g. Halliday, 1999). Nevertheless, the tendency within CDA is to begin with the text(s) in focus placed centrally and then develop an understanding of context in relation to those texts. The starting point of ethnography is different. Ethnography begins by focusing on social and cultural practices, and analysis of text and discourse – even the choice of which texts will be analysed – arises from the understandings of those practices.

Having said that, from a theoretical perspective, there is consonance between CDA and ethnography. The notion of understanding discourse as 'language as social practice' has been central to CDA from its origin (Fowler, 1996: 3). It follows that an attempt to understand the social practices within which texts are embedded is indeed absolutely necessary when analysing discourse data. As Krzyżanowski (2011b: 233) says:

> a potential for a more thorough inclusion of context and its explor-
> ation via fieldwork and ethnography in critical-analytic research has
> always been 'there' [in discourse analysis] yet was often left unexplored

42   *Karin Tusting*

due to previous preoccupation with texts as the only objects of CDA-based or CDA-inspired examinations.

There has been a move in recent years towards developing more ethnographic approaches within CDA, particularly among those who identify with the *discourse historical approach* (see for instance Krzyżanowski, 2011a, which brings together a collection of studies which have adopted this approach; Krzyżanowski & Oberhuber, 2007, which used ethnographic observation of the European Convention to explore its inner workings). But there is more to do to explore the potential of ethnography for a more sensitive engagement with text in a social context in discourse analytic research.

Linguistic ethnography

Another approach developed more recently which seeks to bring together ethnography and analysis of language is known as *linguistic ethnography* (Copland & Creese, 2015; Maybin & Tusting, 2011; Snell, Shaw, & Copland, 2015). Where CDA developed from a group of text-focused linguists extending their work outwards, linguistic ethnography developed from a group of socio- and applied linguists whose work was already drawing on ethnographic perspectives. From an initially small group of around 30 researchers in 2001 seeking to build a network for more coherent theoretical and methodological discussions, linguistic ethnography has grown rapidly. Researchers who identify with this approach have carried out research in many domains, including classrooms (Karrebaek, 2014; Lefstein & Snell, 2011), teacher training (Copland, 2011), youth language (Madsen, 2013), English as a *lingua franca* (Cogo, 2012), health (Swinglehurst, 2014), critical policy studies (Shaw, Russell, Parsons, & Greenhalgh, 2015), and multilingual urban contexts (Blackledge, Creese, & Hu, 2016), to name but a few.

Linguistic ethnography is influenced by the ethnography of communication (discussed above) and indeed by CDA, but also by literacy studies, ethnographic studies of classroom discourse and interactional sociolinguistics. It seeks to bring together key aspects of ethnography with the analytic tools and understandings of language developed within linguistics. Key characteristics of ethnography explicitly oriented to in this work include maintaining a holistic focus on local settings while also untangling the complex interrelationships between local and broader levels of social organisation; looking for patterns and structures without quashing the particularities of individual instances; and recognising the role of the researcher in the construction of knowledge. Useful aspects of linguistics in this context include the capacity to precisely describe and analyse structural patterns of language while locating them in relation to the human social communities in which these patterns of language use arise.

(See Rampton, Maybin, & Roberts, 2015 for further development of these relationships.)

Although much of the work in linguistic ethnography develops complex theoretical anthropological concepts such as *heteroglossia*, *indexicality*, or *enregisterment*, mastery of the full theoretical range of the area is not required to implement an ethnographic approach to discourse analysis. There is still value in incorporating an ethnographic perspective into the analysis of discourse data. The rest of this chapter will focus on some of the more concrete aspects of adopting an ethnographic approach to discourse analysis which are useful for beginner researchers to think about, illustrating them using the discourse data sample above.

Identifying research questions

In keeping with the holistic perspective, the initial research questions in an ethnographic project are often fairly broad. While usually informed by some theoretical understandings which have shaped the initial interest in that area, the research questions that one begins with normally need to be open enough to enable fieldwork to be sensitive to local realities, so that understanding can develop as the research goes on. As the fieldwork continues, the research questions usually become more focused and specific.

In the study of paperwork in the nursery which included the discourse sample in Figure 3.1, the aim in the original research proposal was a broad and exploratory one: 'to understand more about how changing textual processes are transforming the nature and experience of work in contemporary society'. The work was informed by an existing interest in 'audit society' (Power, 1997) and how this was shaping people's experiences of work, but the question was open enough to enable me to explore how this might be manifesting itself in the experiences and engagements with texts I was observing in that setting.

There were also some more specific questions. The first was: what are the literacy practices of workers in educational environments, particularly in relation to paperwork generated by external demands? Answering this question required detailed observational fieldwork and attention to the realities of the local setting. The second was: what are the effects of these paperwork demands on workers' experiences, identities, and social practices, from their perspectives? This required interviews and informal conversations with the participants over the year I spent carrying out fieldwork in the setting. The third was: how had these demands changed in recent years, and what was the impact of these developments? This was a question which both provided me with a specific focus in the setting, and took my attention outward to make connections with the broader structural issues and policies that shaped what was going on.

44   *Karin Tusting*

Over time, I was able to frame more focused and specific questions which drew on my developing ethnographic knowledge, for instance: what was the role of text in mediating the national framework in the local setting? The national framework was supported by a large investment in training and materials, and every aspect of the framework was supported by multi-coloured textual resources, posters, and cards, displayed around the walls of the nursery as a constant reminder and support for staff. Figure 3.1 is just one example of this visible textual mediation (Smith, 1990) of the framework. Part of the focus of the research therefore became much more specific, exploring through observation and interview how the texts associated with the framework shaped the staff activities, their engagement with time and planning, their relationships with parents and their identities as nursery professionals. Ethnographic work showed clearly how the carefully thought-through organisation and planning laid out in the poster in Figure 3.1 could be overturned at any point by the realities of working with babies and small children, and how a key aspect of the work of the nursery staff was to negotiate this tension (see Tusting, 2010 for an account of the 'eruptions of interruptions' which characterised everyday work).

Data collection and ethics

The key methods of data collection for an ethnographic project have already been introduced. Participant-observation and the writing of detailed observational fieldnotes have always been central to the ethnographic approach (see Emerson, Fretz, & Shaw, 2011 on writing ethnographic fieldnotes). Many other methods of data collection may also now be used, including interviewing, document collection, photography, and audio- and video-recording, while ethnographies in digital settings may draw on a range of data including screenshots, downloaded audio and video files, and interviews, carried out either face to face or at a distance (see Chapter 9, this volume). Since understanding participants' perspectives is crucial, building up relationships with participants is important. Ethnographers' understandings come not only from interviews, but also from all the informal conversations and interactions which arise naturally over the course of fieldwork. Krzyżanowski (2011b: 233) prefers to talk about ethnography not purely as participant-observation but rather using what he calls 'the very broad idea of "fieldwork"', which can include a wide range of different methods of data collection. Since ethnography is dependent on the researcher's interpretation of data, triangulation – collecting data in different ways, and deliberately trying to explore multiple perspectives – is a very important aspect of ethnographic research.

In the project from which the data in focus here was taken, data collection consisted of participant-observation in all the rooms of the nursery, audio-recording, and taking detailed written fieldnotes; informal

Discourse analysis and ethnography 45

conversations with many of the staff; document collection, both the local documentation and the national framework documents; many photographs; semi-structured interviews with most of the staff and with the nursery management; presentation and discussion of initial analysis to the staff meeting; and regular participation in the parent–staff forum.

Fieldnotes can include both observations of practice and notes from informal conversations. My fieldnotes from observing the baby room, which informed my analysis of the poster in Figure 3.1, include both of these. Notes on what was happening in the room show how the daily work responding to the immediate demands of the children can be unexpectedly interrupted by demands from outside, here by a request for longer-term planning to be quickly completed (staff names are pseudonyms and children are referred to with initials):

> 10.15 – Louise changing J. Lm and La lying down playing with the toys. Nicola cuddling Ae.
> 10.25 – Lm has his bottle. La is with Louise waiting for his bottle.
> 10.30 – Louise, Lm, Ae playing with toys, J watching, Nicola with La.
> 10.35 – Centre manager comes in with brainstorming sheets for the next theme. She apologised, she needs them back by next Friday, had forgotten to bring them in before now. Member of staff complains ironically: 'We'd only just got the Teddy Bear's Picnic up!!'

Notes from conversations with staff provided insight into the planning process.

> Enid talked me through the paperwork that they have to deal with. Planning for the week is one of the major things. Every month, one of the staff becomes Team Leader for the month. They plan activities for each week, and circulate them to everyone.
>
> Daily observation sheets: each day, they aim to note something specific relating to each child, linking it to the Birth to Three Matters framework. These observation sheets are taken away and used for planning activities, helping them to decide which area to focus on. There should be ticks in each box representing a main section of the Birth to Three framework (a strong child, a skilful communicator, a competent learner, a healthy child), and they can then get an overview and see which boxes need more ticks …
>
> To do the planning, they will look at the observation sheets. If something is repeated for a few children, they will write it down as something to do … They plan one activity for each morning and afternoon. They mark with a * when something has been written down for one of the children specifically, and mark with initials which child it corresponds to …
>
> They were given Birth to Three matters cards, and had to figure out from the cards what to write down. To start off with it was hard, you

46 *Karin Tusting*

had to look at the aspect and find the component, or vice versa, and that took a long time. They still refer to the cards every day – they are up behind the highchairs. The aspects are also put in the books, on the wall, with photos, and outside on the parents' board. But the more they do it, the quicker they get.

These notes record a very important conversation that made it clear to me how the everyday, messy, immediate work with children in the room, recorded in daily observations, fed into the controlled, systematised planning (immediate, medium, and long term) seen in the poster in Figure 3.1. The conversation explained the importance of the daily observation sheets in co-ordinating responsiveness to the needs of each child with the demands of the framework; how the framework mediated very directly the activities planned for each room; and how the poster and postcard displays of the framework in the room were drawn on by staff to support this process.

The ethical challenges of ethnographic research can be very complex. Gaining informed consent at the very start of the research project is both important from an ethical perspective and is usually required by university ethics committees. However, ethnographic methods may not be a good fit with participants' understandings of social scientific research. Long conversations may be necessary to ensure consent is really informed, explaining what the research is about, what commitment is needed from participants, and how the research will create knowledge. Given the open, exploratory nature of ethnographic research, it is possible that, even taking this care at the start, informed consent at the outset will not be enough, and consent may need to be re-negotiated over the course of the research as the focus changes and becomes more specific. Ongoing attention to ethical issues is an important part of an ethnographic researcher's reflexivity and self-awareness.

Ethical dilemmas can be uncomfortable, but can also serve as important learning points for the researcher. In the project in focus here, as I said above, as fieldwork progressed I began to develop an understanding of how challenging it was for staff to respond to the planning and recording requirements of the framework, and the tensions they faced in trying to keep on top of the associated paperwork while at the same time taking care of the children. This reflected the broader theoretical issue which was driving the research, my prior interest in the bureaucratisation of work and the unintended negative impacts of accountability in a range of different educational settings. This was the aspect I focused on when presenting initial results at the staff meeting and inviting responses.

After the meeting, the nursery manager (who was very supportive of the project in general, and to whom I owe a great debt of gratitude) invited me to meet her to discuss the findings, and, in the gentlest possible way, expressed her discomfort at the predominantly critical stance I had taken.

Discourse analysis and ethnography 47

Thinking this through, I realised that she had made an important point. In my presentation of the more challenging facets of the analysis, I had failed to balance this with both the positive aspects of the framework, and the hard work that the nursery management and staff had put in to mediating the national framework and making it work in their setting. This felt like an ethical misstep on my part. However, while it was difficult to come to terms with this, this uncomfortable conversation did lead me in the longer term to a more complex and rounded understanding of what was going on, highlighting the positive as well as the negative aspects of textual mediation in this particular workplace.

Analysing and interpreting data

There is no single approach to interpreting and analysing data in ethnographic research. The approach chosen depends on what research questions the researcher is trying to answer, and may also be influenced by developing understandings of what is significant about the research setting. Because of the extended time commitments and multiple approaches to data collection outlined above, ethnographic research generates a rich and complex dataset. It is important to have systematic and explicit ways of approaching this, tracking the insights that are generated and drawing different kinds of data together in analysis to illuminate the purposes and meanings of discourse in a social context.

For rigour and systematicity, coding approaches influenced by *grounded theory* may be used. Qualitative researchers have developed systematic approaches to coding data in order to evidence and track emerging patterns. This involves working through the data, labelling up short chunks of data with short, meaningful phrases, or 'codes', and re-using these codes as appropriate. Codes which are re-used frequently identify patterns in the data which can provide answers to research questions and can become themes in the writing up of the research. Researchers can code data for content, but also to identify other kinds of patterns and regularities, including linguistic features. (See Saldaña, 2009 for a comprehensive account of different approaches to coding.) This process can be supported by computer-assisted qualitative data analysis software. In the project from which the data above was taken, the computer software ATLAS.ti was used to code the data systematically (see Tusting, 2015 for more detail on this). The coding of the whole dataset enabled me to see patterns across the interview data, the observational fieldnotes, and documents and images collected like the poster in Figure 3.1.

However, some researchers and scholars feel that this systematic coding is too mechanistic an approach to research which ultimately seeks to understand cultural practice. For some, analysing ethnographic data involves a process of reading, re-reading, and writing about the dataset in the light of theoretical understandings, enabling understandings and answers to research questions to emerge in a more organic way through the

48 *Karin Tusting*

researcher's in-depth engagement with the meanings of the data. While this can still be a rigorous approach to the analysis of a complex ethnographic dataset, it is less directly systematic than the coding process described above.

The place of linguistic analysis in ethnographic projects varies too. As is clear from the description of linguistic ethnography above, some linguistic ethnographers draw extensively on the tools of one or other subfield of linguistics, perhaps some of those represented in other chapters of this book – conversation analysis, systemic functional linguistics, multimodality, or metaphor analysis, for instance – to analyse in detail some or all of the texts in an ethnographic dataset.

It is not uncommon for different texts in the dataset to be analysed in different degrees of detail, with the broader fieldwork enabling the researcher to identify and select key texts for more detailed linguistic analysis. Rampton (2006: 395–396), for instance, describes his approach to the analysis of interaction in an urban school as a 'long, slow immersion in the recordings of specific episodes, repeatedly replaying a given sequence, carefully following its turn-by-turn development' and a 'slow, close look at the moment-by-moment unfolding', informed by a range of linguistic perspectives including conversation analysis and Goffmanian interactional analysis, which at first glance seems quite different from the systematic coding for patterns described above. However, he also goes on to explain that the selection of episodes to analyse at this intense level of engagement was motivated by a particular interest in aspects of them which arose through noticing patterns during fieldwork, and that the episodes had already been categorised according to broader categories which had emerged as relevant.

In relation to the example of discourse data introduced at the start of this chapter, at first glance, it is relatively straightforward to interpret it as an instantiation of the *Birth to Three Matters* framework. The title and sub-headings make the role of the framework in the organisation of the poster clear. A more detailed multimodal analysis of the poster itself could make these connections more explicit. But setting this analysis within observation of everyday practice in the nursery, and interviews and conversations with the staff and manager provided much greater insight into the meaning of this piece of discourse data in context. In order to really understand the meaning of this poster in its place, how and why it was there and what its role was in the broader processes of nursery life, I had to draw on my knowledge, developed through longer-term fieldwork, of:

- The system which was then in place for observations and photography of individual children on a daily basis, driven by the framework
- The processes of production of the posters, including the division of labour between different members of staff in the long- and short-term planning processes

Discourse analysis and ethnography 49

- How time and resources were provided for staff to do planning and produce visual records and displays, and the challenges of balancing this time with maintaining the inviolable correct levels of staff–child ratio
- How the managerial practices and systems of the nursery ensured that this system was followed by the nursery staff
- The location of the poster within broader national systems of accountability, particularly the Ofsted inspections which could happen at any time. The poster served as a material, physical display that the nursery was using the framework appropriately in its planning and organisation.

Presenting findings and results

When writing about research, the aim of the researcher must always be to convey the answers to the research questions posed in the study as clearly as possible, and to provide the reader with a clear understanding of the evidence on which these answers are based. Given the complexity of an ethnographic project, and the commitment required to approaching social practice in a way which takes account of multiple interacting factors, it may be difficult to present the researcher's emerging understandings in a linear form which can be usefully accessed by a reader. A combination of means have been developed to achieve this. Ethnography may be presented in the genre of the traditional research report, using the introduction – methods – results – discussion – conclusion format; but other means may also be used to convey understanding in a different way.

Within the ethnographic community more broadly, since the 1980s there has been active debate around the appropriate ways of representing ethnographic work. There has been extensive critique of earlier ethnographic work which tended to portray a single 'truth' about the cultures which were studied, written from the perspective of the Western observer. Clifford and Marcus (1986) highly influential book *Writing Culture* examined this issue closely, critiquing the traditional model of ethnography as a book about 'them' written by 'us' which occluded the role of the ethnographer in the writing. This opened up the space for exploration of other possibilities (from van Maanen, 1988; Atkinson, 1990 onwards), and there now exists a much wider range of possibilities for writing about ethnographic work. For instance, vignettes and narratives may be used to convey a more 'storied' account of the context and to try and evoke the emic experience more directly.

Writing up ethnographies which use linguistic analysis of discourse data raises a particular challenge. On the one hand, carefully presenting close analysis of language data can provide the research with an evidential and analytic support base that can provide a clear warrant for the claims which

50 Karin Tusting

are made. Rampton (2006) claims that linguistics can serve an important purpose in this regard, 'tying ethnography down' by providing this kind of systematic evidence. On the other hand, it can be misleading to position the language data in focus as providing privileged access to the 'truth' of the situation, when a moment of researcher reflexivity makes clear the potential multiplicity of interpretations one can make of most social situations. Ultimately, the best way to develop an understanding of how ethnographic discourse research can be presented is to read a range of discourse and language-focused ethnographies such as those cited in this chapter and thereby get a sense of the possibilities available in writing up this kind of research.

Issues and limitations

Ethnographic work does raise challenges. It can be difficult to negotiate access in a setting where a relatively open-ended commitment may be required. It may require a more significant investment of time from the researcher than some approaches which start from the collection of texts – though that rather depends, of course, on how many texts need to be collected and how accessible they are; building a large corpus can take just as much time as ethnographic fieldwork.

More significantly, perhaps, as implied by the mentions of researcher reflexivity above, an ethnographic approach can place significant interpersonal and emotional demands on the researcher. A commitment to 'being there' in a context and trying to understand it from the insider perspective can open the researcher to a degree of personal vulnerability that other approaches to discourse analysis do not usually entail.

Other difficulties include the challenges of finding patterns and answers within a mass of data where these may not be readily evident. This challenge is part of all research, of course, but the complexity of an ethnographic dataset highlights the difficulty of this. However, if one seeks to understand the complexities of how discourse really operates in a given social context, I would argue that an ethnographic approach to data collection can provide a depth of explanatory warrant that analysis of texts or transcripts alone can rarely achieve.

Ethnographers tend to be sensitised to complexity and aware of the limitations to our knowledge. While the presentation of findings and results always needs to put a case and make an argument, the epistemological orientation of ethnography recognises too the limitations of our knowledge. We can try and capture the emic perspective, we can make connections between the local discourse data and the broader social context, we can connect our longer and wider historical knowledge of the context over time with specific discursive instances, but the claims to knowledge that we can make on these bases can only ever be provisional and are open to contestation, discussion, and differing interpretations of the data. Appreciating these limitations to our knowledge, sharing data, and sharing the analysis which has been carried out to form the basis for an interpretation, is crucial in making the rhetorical case, so that the reader can make a meaningful assessment of the strength of the case which is being made.

Further reading

Copland and Creese (2015) is a useful book focusing on how to approach doing a linguistic ethnographic project, using case studies to illustrate how research is carried out from this perspective, and addressing the practicalities of working with data, ethics, transcription, and writing up. Krzyżanowski (2011a) brings together several articles reporting on research within critical discourse analysis which has adopted an ethnographic approach, showing the range of ways in which researchers have done this in different contexts, including long-term ethnographic ethnography, mental health settings, language policy, and media reports. Snell et al. (2015) can be seen as complementary to the Copland and Creese volume above. While Copland and Creese focus on methodological questions, Snell, Shaw, and Copland's edited collection showcases the wide range of settings and questions addressed in contemporary linguistic ethnography.

References

Atkinson, D., Okada, H. and Talmy, S. (2011). Ethnography and discourse analysis. In K. Hyland and B. Paltridge (Eds.), *Continuum companion to discourse analysis.* (pp. 85–100). London and New York: Continuum.

Atkinson, P. (1990). *The ethnographic imagination: Textual constructions of reality.* London: Routledge.

Becker, H. (1999). The Chicago school, so-called. *Qualitative Sociology, 22*(1), 3–12.

Blackledge, A., Creese, A. and Hu, R. (2016). The structure of everyday narrative in a city market: An ethnopoetics approach. *Journal of Sociolinguistics, 20*(5), 654–676.

Blommaert, J. and Jie, D. (2010). *Ethnographic fieldwork: A beginner's guide.* Buffalo, NY: Multilingual Matters.

Clifford, J. and Marcus, G. (Eds.) (1986). *Writing culture: The poetics and politics of ethnography.* Berkeley: University of California Press.

Cogo, A. (2012). ELF and super-diversity: A case study of ELF multilingual practices from a business context. *Journal of English as a Lingua Franca, 1*(2), 287–313.

Copland, F. (2011). Negotiating face in feedback conferences: A linguistic ethnographic analysis. *Journal of Pragmatics, 43*(15), 3832–3843.

Copland, F. and Creese, A. (2015). *Linguistic ethnography: Collecting, analysing and presenting data.* London: Sage.

DfE (Department for Education) (2017). *Statutory framework for the early years foundation stage.* London: DfE.

DfES (Department for Education and Skills). (2002). *Birth to three matters.* London: DfES.

52 *Karin Tusting*

Duranti, A. (2003). Language as culture in US anthropology – Three paradigms. *Current Anthropology*, 44(3), 323–347.

Emerson, R.M., Fretz, R.I. and Shaw, L.L. (2011). *Writing ethnographic fieldnotes*. (2nd ed.). Chicago: University of Chicago Press.

Fairclough, N. (1995). *Critical discourse analysis: The critical study of language*. London: Longman.

Fowler, R. (1996). On critical linguistics. In C. Caldas-Coulthard and M. Coulthard (Eds.), *Texts and practices: Readings in critical discourse analysis*. (pp. 3–14). London: Routledge.

Fowler, R., Hodge, B., Kress, G. and Trew, T. (1979). *Language and control*. London: Routledge and Kegan Paul.

Gumperz, J.J. and Hymes, D. (1972). *Directions in sociolinguistics: The ethnography of communication*. New York: Holt, Rinehart and Winston Inc.

Halliday, M.A.K. (1999). The notion of 'context' in language education. In M. Ghadessy (Ed.), *Text and context in functional linguistics*. (pp. 1–24). Amsterdam: John Benjamins.

Karrebæk, M.S. (2014). Rye bread and halal: Enregisterment of food practices in the primary classroom. *Language & Communication*, 34, 17–34.

Krzyżanowski, M. (Ed.) (2011a). Ethnography and critical discourse analysis. Special Issue of *Critical Discourse Studies*, 8(4).

Krzyżanowski, M. (2011b). Ethnography and critical discourse analysis: Towards a problem-oriented research dialogue. *Critical Discourse Studies*, 8(4), 231–238.

Krzyżanowski, M., and Oberhuber, F. (2007). *(Un)doing Europe: Discourses and practices of negotiating the EU constitution*. Brussels: Peter Lang.

Lefstein, A. and Snell, J. (2011). Promises and problems of teaching with popular culture: A linguistic ethnographic analysis of discourse genre mixing in a literacy lesson. *Reading Research Quarterly*, 46(1), 40–69.

Lillis, T. (2008). Ethnography as method, methodology, and "deep theorizing": Closing the gap between text and context in academic writing research. *Written Communication*, 25(3), 353–388.

Madsen, L.M. (2013). "High" and "low" in urban Danish speech styles. *Language in Society*, 42, 115–138.

Malinowski, B. (1922). *Argonauts of the Western Pacific*. New York: Dutton.

Maybin, J. and Tusting, K. (2011). Linguistic ethnography. In J. Simpson (Ed.), *Routledge handbook of Applied Linguistics*. (pp. 229–241). London: Routledge.

Power, M. (1997). *The audit society: Rituals of verification*. Oxford: Oxford University Press.

Rampton, B. (2006). *Language in late modernity: Interaction in an urban school*. Cambridge: Cambridge University Press.

Rampton, B., Maybin, J. and Roberts, C. (2015). Theory and method in linguistic ethnography. In J. Snell, S. Shaw, and F. Copland (Eds.), *Linguistic ethnography: Interdisciplinary explorations*. (pp. 14–50). Basingstoke: Palgrave MacMillan.

Reisigl, M. and Wodak, R. (2009). The discourse–historical approach. In R. Wodak and M. Meyers (Eds.), *Methods of critical discourse analysis*. (2nd ed., pp. 87–121). London: Sage.

Saldaña, J. (2009). *The coding manual for qualitative researchers*. London: Sage.

Scollon, R. and Scollon, S.W. (2007). Nexus analysis: Refocusing ethnography on action. *Journal of Sociolinguistics*, 11(5), 608–625.

Shaw, S.E., Russell, J., Parsons, W. and Greenhalgh, T. (2015). The view from nowhere? How think tanks work to shape health policy. *Critical Policy Studies*, *9*(1), 58–77.

Smith, D.E. (1990). Textually mediated social organization. *International Social Science Journal*, *34*, 209–224.

Snell, J., Shaw, S. and Copland, F. (Eds.) (2015). *Linguistic ethnography: Interdisciplinary explorations.* Basingstoke: Palgrave Macmillan.

Swinglehurst, D. (2014). Displays of authority in the clinical consultation: A linguistic ethnographic study of the electronic patient record. *Social Science & Medicine*, *118*, 17–26.

Tusting, K. (2010). Eruptions of interruptions: Managing tensions between writing and other tasks in a textualised childcare workplace. In D. Barton and U. Papen (Eds.), *The anthropology of writing: Understanding textually mediated worlds.* (pp. 67–89). London: Continuum.

Tusting, K. (2015). Workplace literacies and audit society. In J. Snell, S. Shaw, and F. Copland (Eds.), *Linguistic ethnography: Interdisciplinary explorations.* (pp. 51–70). Basingstoke: Palgrave Macmillan.

van Maanen, J. (1988). *Tales of the field: On writing ethnography.* Chicago: University of Chicago Press.

Wodak, R. (2001). What CDA is about – A summary of its history, important concepts and its developments. In R. Wodak and M. Meyer (Eds.), *Methods of critical discourse analysis.* (pp. 1–13). London: Sage.

4 Discourse analysis and systemic functional linguistics

Veronika Koller

Introduction

Discourse analysts, especially those of a critical persuasion, are interested in how speakers and writers use language to represent the world and negotiate social identities and relationships. In other words, they want to know what functions language has in particular contexts and how its use helps to create particular meanings. Critical discourse analysts are also interested in how language use and discourse practices contribute to, or help solve, social problems. While this, by definition, involves wider situational, institutional, and social contexts, language and discourse are the entry points to critical social analysis, and any claims and interpretations are grounded in textual analysis. Hence, (critical) discourse studies needs a detailed linguistic methodology that is grounded in a functional theory of language.

Systemic functional linguistics provides just that: as Fairclough, one of the founders of critical discourse analysis, notes, '[t]here is much in SFL which is of value ... including a longstanding concern with socially-oriented analysis of text and a linguistic theory which is itself socially oriented and informed' (2010: 299). Martin (2000: 275–276) agrees with this assessment, noting as the strength of SFL

> its ability to ground concerns with power and ideology in the detailed analysis of texts ... in real contexts of language use ... SFL ... make[s] it possible to look very closely at meaning, to be explicit and precise in terms that can be shared by others, and to engage in quantitative analysis where it is appropriate.

Given this fit between SFL and (critical) discourse analysis, it is not surprising that systemic functional approaches have informed a number of studies looking at different discourse domains, including organisational discourse (Lockwood and Forey, 2016), history (Martin and Wodak, 2003), and education policy (Bloor and Bloor, 2018), to name only a few.

This chapter introduces SFL as a theory of language which provides concrete methods for analysing discourse. SFL views language as a set of rule-governed sign systems – sounds, words, and grammar – from which speakers and writers make motivated choices to create particular meanings. In this chapter, I introduce the concept of ideational, interpersonal, and textual metafunctions, and map these onto the notions of field, tenor, and mode. Focusing on lexicogrammar, I provide an overview of transitivity as a grammar system that can be analysed to identify ideational meaning and discuss basic categories of social actor representation to show how participants in a clause can be analysed in more detail. I illustrate this approach to discourse analysis through a comparative analysis of the leaflets distributed by a range of British parties during the 2019 EU elections. In this illustration, I show how political contexts can be expressed through particular lexico-grammatical choices to represent participants, processes, and circumstances.

Outline of approach

Systemic functional linguistics is a theory of language and language use that was originally developed by the late Michael Halliday from the 1960s onwards, culminating in his book *Introduction to Functional Grammar* (1985), which is now in its fourth edition (Halliday and Matthiessen, 2014). Despite its name, the book is much more than an introduction; in fact it presents a detailed 789-page overview of Halliday's complex theory. If that sounds daunting, note that Suzanne Eggins and Geoffrey Thompson have made SFL accessible to intermediate learners and beginners, respectively, with their treatments of the theory now in subsequent editions themselves (Eggins, 2004; Thompson, 2013). Whichever presentation of the theory we consult though, the authors all articulate the following fundamental understanding of language:

- Language [is a] resource – choices among alternatives. (Halliday and Matthiessen, 2014: 20)
- Language is a semiotic system ... organised as a set of choices. (Eggins, 2004: 3)
- '[R]ules' in Functional Grammar are expressed as sets of possible options, as systems of choices. (Thompson, 2013: 263)

This basic definition captures the idea that speakers and writers choose from options at various levels of language (phonology, morphology, lexicogrammar, and discourse semantics) to make meaning. As such, it combines the notion of language as a system and selections from it as having a purpose or function, giving us the phrase 'systemic functional linguistics'.

The purpose of language is to make meaning, and according to the theory, every clause that a speaker or writer comes up with simultaneously realises three different kinds of meaning, or *metafunctions*, to use the more technical term (Halliday and Matthiessen, 2014: 30–31). These metafunctions are known as the *ideational metafunction*, which conveys an aspect of human experience, the *interpersonal metafunction*, i.e. 'enacting our ... social relationships with other people' (Halliday and Matthiessen, 2014: 30), and the *textual metafunction*, which organises discourse and lends it cohesion as it unfolds in speech or writing, thereby making the ideational and interpersonal metafunctions possible in the first place. The three metafunctions make different kinds of meanings and therefore also view the clause – as the smallest unit of analysis – in different ways: to the extent that it makes ideational meaning, the clause can be seen as a representation of human experience, but when creating interpersonal meaning, it acts as a kind of exchange between language users and their audience. What is being 'exchanged' is information, offers, and requests as well as appraisals, attitudes, and stances, and, ultimately, relations and identities. Finally, the textual meaning construed by a clause is what makes it a coherently structured message. The following example helps illustrate how a single clause can be representation, exchange, and message at one and the same time, i.e. realise the ideational, interpersonal, and textual metafunctions of language:

(1) Will you help us end this Brexit mess? (Liberal Democrats, 2019 European Parliament election leaflet)

This clause has a topic or focus (or *field*, as it is known in SFL) – Brexit – which is ideationally presented from a particular viewpoint, featuring as it does as part of the evaluative noun phrase 'Brexit mess'. The negatively evaluated topic is linked to an action as well, namely 'end[ing] the mess'. However, the clause does more than represent a topic and an activity; it also enacts relations of power and solidarity (the *tenor* variable, to use the technical term). The reader is directly addressed as 'you' in a question that on the face of it seems to ask them for information ('will you help us?'). In pragmatic terms though, the question is a request for action and also assumes that the reader shares with the writer the evaluation of Brexit as a 'mess'. As such, the clause construes solidarity between the sender and the receiver, and also puts the latter in a position where they have the power to help the former. Lastly, the clause in example (1) is also grammatical and coherent, e.g. in how it uses a demonstrative pronoun to refer to 'this Brexit mess' and thereby point to the perceived 'Brexit mess' as given information known to both writer and reader. In the technical terminology of SFL, the clause thus has a *rhetorical mode* (Halliday and Matthiessen, 2014: 33).

The three metafunctions (ideational, interpersonal, and textual) with their associated views of the clause (as representation, exchange, or message) and respective variables (field, tenor, and mode) can be mapped onto different systems of lexis and grammar. (There are also systems for the levels of phonology, morphology, and discourse semantics, but we will here focus on the mid-range level of lexicogrammar.) The ideational metafunction can be explored through the system of *transitivity*, which investigates 'processes involving participants in certain circumstances' (Thompson, 2013: 92) or, put simply, who does what to whom in a clause. SFL theory sees processes as the central element of a clause, but SFL-inspired frameworks have also been developed to examine how participants are represented.

Moving on for now, the interpersonal metafunction that every clause also realises can be analysed by employing the grammar systems of *mood* and *modality*. Descriptions of mood and modality, as well as transitivity, provide the analyst with entry points to the interpersonal and ideational metafunctions, respectively, because these are the lexico-grammatical systems through which those metafunctions are enacted. Mood relates to different speech functions of clauses; in a reworking of *speech act theory* (Searle, 1969), clauses can be phrased as statements with *declarative mood* (e.g. 'This Brexit mess needs to end'), questions with *interrogative mood* (see example (1): 'Will you help us end this Brexit mess?') or commands with *imperative mood* (e.g. 'Help us end this Brexit mess!'). There are a number of other speech functions (see Eggins, 2004: 147) and speech acts can show atypical moods as well; for instance, example (1) could also be analysed as realising a command function using the interrogative mood, in order to lessen the imposition that a direct command would have. The second related grammar system realising the interpersonal metafunction is modality. Different forms of it occur depending on what is being 'exchanged' in the clause: when information is being exchanged, the speaker or writer presents a proposition and can, through various modal markers, indicate their stance on how probable or usual it is that the proposition is true (Thompson, 2014: 70). (In other theories of modality, this is known as *epistemic modality*.) To use example (1) once more, this would give us clauses like 'You *may* help us end this Brexit mess' or 'You have *often* helped us end a mess'. If, on the other hand, the metaphorical currency exchanged in the clause is requests and offers, then we are dealing with a proposal that conveys a measure of obligation – other accounts of modality refer to this as *deontic modality* – or willingness. Examples would be 'Please help us end this Brexit mess' or 'I'll help you end this Brexit mess'. Although we do not have the space to go into detail here, it is worth noting that James Martin and Peter White, two systemic functional linguists, have developed another more lexically oriented system to analyse interpersonal meaning: *appraisal theory* (Martin and White, 2005) provides a detailed account of the linguistic resources that speakers of English can use to evaluate people and their behaviours, appraise objects, concepts, and processes, and express and ascribe emotion, in addition to (de) intensifying and (de)concretising their stance, and bringing the voices of others into their own discourse.

58   *Veronika Koller*

Table 4.1 Metafunctions, clause types, variables, and grammar systems in SFL

metafunction	clause type	variable	grammar system(s)
ideational	representation	field	transitivity
interpersonal	exchange	tenor	mood and modality, appraisal
textual	message	mode	cohesion, theme/rheme

Finally, the textual metafunction can be investigated through the grammar systems of *cohesion* (Halliday and Hasan, 1976) and *theme/rheme* (Halliday and Matthiessen, 2014: 88–96). While cohesion is about the way that conjunctions, pronouns, lexical substitutions, and lexical semantics can be used to make a text hang together syntactically and semantically, theme/rheme organises information in a clause, with given information usually placed as theme at its beginning and new information following as rheme.

Table 4.1 provides an overview of the categorisation of language into metafunctions, clause types, variables, and grammar systems.

Again, it needs to be remembered that all three aspects of language are simultaneously present in each and every clause; it is merely the analytical focus that shifts between them. In the remainder of this section, the focus will be on the ideational metafunction as conveying aspects of human experience and on transitivity as the grammar system that goes with it.

Transitivity

As mentioned above, the grammar system of transitivity governs the ideational metafunction, and its analysis shows what choices text producers have made in representing a domain of experience, with its processes, participants, and circumstances, from a particular viewpoint. This is obviously a functional understanding of transitivity; in formal grammars, the same term is used to denote if the subject in a clause takes no, one, or two objects, i.e. if the verb is intransitive, transitive, or ditransitive. The difference between formal and functional understandings of transitivity is best illustrated with an example, again from the data analysed in this chapter. (In the following examples, the subject/actor is underlined once and the object/goal twice, while the verb/process is set in italics.)

(2a) <u>We</u> need to *change* <u>politics</u> for good. (Brexit Party, 2019 European Parliament election leaflet)

In formal terms, 'we' is the subject, 'change' is the verb (here used alongside the modal verb phrase 'need to' and the adverbial phrase 'for good'), and 'politics' is the object. When the construction is changed from active to passive, subject and object switch roles:

Discourse analysis and SFL 59

(2b) <u>Politics</u> need to *be changed* for good by <u>us</u>.

In functional terms, by contrast, example (2a) features 'change' as a so-called *material process* (see below), 'we' as the *actor* and 'politics' as the *goal* of the action, with 'for good' being a *circumstance of manner* (for different types of circumstance, see Halliday and Matthiessen, 2014: 313–314). Crucially, when we change the active to a passive construction, these functional roles remain the same:

(2c) <u>Politics</u> need to *be changed* for good by <u>us</u>.

The following discussion will first address processes, before redirecting the focus to participants.

Process types

Transitivity as understood in SFL centres on the process, which determines what roles participants have. According to the theory, there are three major and three minor process types: material, mental, relational and behavioural, verbal, and existential. *Material processes* denote outward actions that require some input of energy to occur and where one participant is likely to undergo a change, whereas *mental processes* concern inward perceptions, thoughts, desires, and feelings. Mental processes therefore involve a participant endowed with consciousness and typically a participant entering into or created by that consciousness, such as a sight, an idea, a wish, or an emotion. *Relational processes* are a complex category, but in the main can denote attributes and identities. Attributive relational processes denote class membership, e.g. 'My son is tall' places him in the category of tall people. By contrast, identifying relational processes indicate a unique identity, such as 'My son is the tallest in the group'. To test which of the two relational process types is expressed in a particular clause, we can try to reverse its parts: it is perfectly grammatical to change 'My son is the tallest in the group' to 'The tallest in the group is my son', but '*Tall is my son' is not possible other than in poetic language (or if you want to sound like Master Yoda in Star Wars). To complicate matters further, both attributive and identifying relational processes can also come in a possessive form. In this kind of relational process type, 'Emily has a piano' (but not '*A piano has Emily') is attributive while 'The piano is Emily's' (or 'Emily's is the piano') is identifying. There is more detail, but for the purposes of this chapter, we can now leave the major process types and turn to the three minor ones.

Where material processes denote outward action and mental processes inward action, *behavioural processes* are halfway between the two, denoting an outward manifestation of an inner state, e.g. smiling, staring, or waiting. As Halliday and Matthiessen state,

60   Veronika Koller

[t]hey are the least distinct of all the six process types because they have no clearly defined characteristics of their own, rather, they are partly like the material and partly like the mental … The boundaries of behavioural processes are indeterminate.

(2014: 301)

By contrast, *verbal processes* are clearly delineated and easy to identify, denoting communicative actions such as talking and speaking. Finally, *existential processes* simply indicate that a participant in a clause exists. To avoid confusion with relational processes, consider the difference between 'The picture on the wall is amazing' (relational-attributive) or 'The picture on the right wall is the largest in the whole gallery' (relational-identifying) on the one hand and 'The picture is on the wall' (existential) on the other. Table 4.2 summarises the six process types and also details the terms for the participants engaged in each of them.

It is to the second element of the clause, i.e. participants and especially social actors, that we now turn.

Participants

The central element of transitivity as understood in SFL is the process, and Table 4.2 shows how process types determine participant roles. Nevertheless, it can be useful to look in more detail at how actors are represented. This is especially true for social actors, i.e. people being represented to carry out different processes: investigating how groups and individuals are constructed in discourse can tell us a lot about the text producer's ideological viewpoint and what image of a social actor they seek to project to the recipient. (There is also an interpersonal component – represented in Figure 4.1 – in that the writer or speaker may seek to, for instance, create solidarity with the reader or hearer against a third party who is represented as [belonging to] an out-group.) Therefore, and next to analysing what idea about social actors is conveyed through the processes ascribed to them, a framework for categorising social actors will be helpful.

Such a framework was developed by van Leeuwen (1996, 2008: 23–54), whose 'sociosemantic inventory of the ways in which social actors can be represented' (2008: 23; emphasis omitted) was inspired by SFL and has found widespread traction in discourse-analytical studies. His taxonomy is very complex though, including 6 levels and 50 categories, and it is usually not necessary to refer to all of them in an analysis. The following overview therefore relies mostly on the simplified account provided by Darics and Koller (2019). Their three-step model of social actor analysis is represented in Figure 4.1.

In the following, I will focus on the first step of the model. The questions to begin with when identifying social actors are who is present in the text, how frequently they are referred to, and who is excluded. The

Table 4.2 Process types and participant roles in SFL

Process types	Participant roles	Example(s)
material	actor + process + goal (+ recipient)	'She handed the book to him'.
mental	senser + process + phenomenon	
• perceptive		'He could see trouble ahead'.
• cognitive		'I don't understand the question'.
• desiderative		'Do you still want the job?'
• affective		'I just loved that film'.
relational		
• attributive	carrier + process + attribute	'My son is tall', 'Emily has a piano'.
• identifying	token + process + value	'My son is the tallest in the group', 'The piano is Emily's'.
behavioural	behaver + process (+ circumstance)	'She was smiling all the way home'.
verbal	sayer + process + verbiage (+ receiver)	'The leaflet will talk you through the dangers associated with smoking'.
existential	existent + process (+ circumstance)	'There have been no problems with the new software so far'.

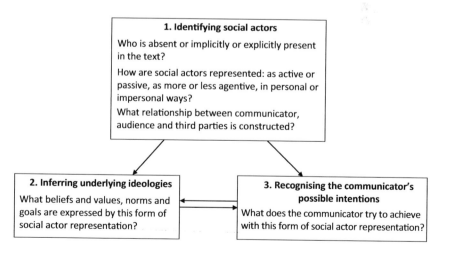

Figure 4.1 A three-step model of social actor analysis (adapted from Darics and Koller, 2019: 222)

latter is not as clear-cut as it sounds: sometimes the social actor may not be mentioned, but the audience can be assumed to know who they are or they may be mentioned elsewhere in that text. In that case, the social actor is said to be *backgrounded*. If they can neither be known nor inferred, however, the social actor is *suppressed*, and there are a number of grammatical ways to achieve such radical exclusion. Perhaps the most obvious way is *agentless passives*, as in the classic example 'Workers were made redundant'. Other ways include using *non-finite* verb forms that function as a grammatical participant (e.g. 'To maintain/maintaining any enthusiasm is hard under the circumstances') and *nominalisations* (e.g. 'support for immigration was at an all-time high'). The latter way of avoiding social actor reference – nominalisation – takes us to another category, namely *impersonalisation* and, more specifically, *abstraction*. As Darics and Koller elaborate, abstraction 'can be achieved through a grammatical twist by which social actors are turned into non-social actors by changing word classes' (2019: 224). Apart from nominalisation, i.e. turning verbs into nouns (to support → support, to immigrate → immigration), we also find adjectives (indicated by a broken line) being turned into nouns (underlined) and vice versa, as demonstrated in examples (3a) and (3b):

(3a) That new plant manager seems singularly incompetent.
(3b) Proceedings at the plant have suffered from managerial incompetence.

This abstraction not only sounds more formal but also avoids any reference to the social actor in question. Another means of impersonalising social actors is to turn them into objects, often – but not always – through *metonymy*, where a part or aspect of the whole stands for the whole. Thus, a text can take the place of its producer or a country can stand for the people living in it. The following example is taken from the data analysed in this chapter:

(4) 'Theresa May's Brexit strategy has humiliated Britain.' (Liberal Demo-crats, 2019 European Parliament election leaflet)

Critical discourse analysts have long debated what ideological functions such impersonalisation has (e.g. Fairclough, 2003: 143–150). While the aim often seems to be to divert blame or responsibility away from a social actor, lack of reference to social actors can also be done for stylistic reasons, e.g. to avoid repetition, to save space or time, or for legal or ethical reasons, e.g. when suspects must not be named or anonymity needs to be protected.

The opposite of impersonalisation is the *personalisation* of social actors. The most obvious way of achieving this is to refer to individuals by their name, be that formally by last name only, semi-formally with their given and last name, or informally by first name only. Additionally, speakers and writers may or may not include any titles and honorifics. (The different forms of nomination, of course, have implications for interpersonal meaning.) Other than that, social actors can be categorised in terms of what they *do* or what they *are*, two forms of representation known as *functionalisation* and *identification*, respectively. The former is perhaps the easier one to identify: when the term referring to a social actor can be traced back to a verb, we are dealing with functionalisation (e.g. manager > manage, student > study, voter > vote). This casts the social actor in question as more dynamic than when they are identified as what they are, including in terms of what socio-demographic class (age, gender, ethnicity etc.) they belong to, what physical characteristics they have, or what other social actors they are related to (e.g. friend, niece, employee).

In between personalisation and impersonalisation, we find what is known as *specification*. We have already seen that social actors can be referred to as individuals, but they can also be represented as particular groups of people. One way of doing this is to categorise them by means of plural nouns (e.g. 'linguists'), mass nouns (e.g. 'staff at the linguistics department'), or a noun denoting a group of people (e.g. 'the linguistics community'). Alternatively, social actors can be represented as numbers or statistics, which specifies how many of them there are – which may or may not be presented as a threat – but arguably takes away the humans behind the figures. However, such *aggregation*, as it is known, can also serve to lend credibility and importance to the actions of the group thus referred to, as in the following two examples from the data analysed below:

(5) 17.4m of you voted to leave the EU. (UKIP, 2019 European Parliament elections leaflet)
(6) Labour will put 10,000 bobbies back on the beat. (Labour, 2019 European Parliament elections leaflet)[1]

Considering that UKIP wants the UK to leave the European Union as soon as possible, and by all means necessary, example (5) uses aggregation to bolster their stance (and create solidarity with the reader), while example (6) constructs Labour as making a substantial effort benefitting people in Britain.

The various forms of social actor representation are summarised in Figure 4.2.

Of course, the different ways of referring to social actors can be combined in noun phrases, e.g. in example (6), which combines aggregation and categorisation in its reference to '10,000 bobbies'. What is especially interesting though is to look at how references to social actors, or lack thereof, compound one another in longer stretches of text to create a particular ideational meaning. Example (7) is part of an internal email that 'management' sent to all staff at Lancaster University on a day when students staged a protest over rent increases for on-campus accommodation.

64 *Veronika Koller*

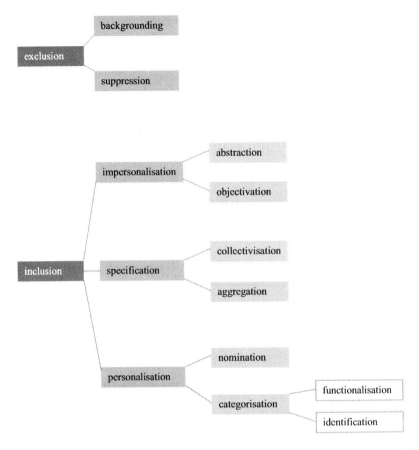

Figure 4.2 Forms of social actor representation (adapted from van Leeuwen, 2008: 52)

(7) At around 11.30am this morning a group of approximately <u>30 to 40 students</u> staged a protest in Lancaster University's main administration building University House. The protest is ongoing. <u>University management</u> are talking to <u>students</u> about their concerns and additional security measures have been put in place on campus. Until further notice, the main doors to University House will remain closed.

The first thing to notice is the dearth of social actors. There are only two: students and management. The former are functionalised twice, in one instance with added aggregation ('approximately 30–40'); in the first instance, they have one material process ('staged') ascribed to them while in the second mention, they feature as recipients of what management – an abstracted actor – has to say to them in a verbal process. More often, social actors are excluded – through a metonymy in which a nominalised action stands for the actors in a relational process ('[t]he protest is ongoing'), through an agentless passive ('security measures have been put in place'), and through a non-social actor featuring in another relational process ('doors ... will remain closed'). As an effect, students are not presented as very active, managers have largely taken themselves out of the text – and nowhere does the reader learn what the protests are actually about.

The last aspect in identifying social actors, *activation* and *passivation*, takes us back to processes. Table 4.2 shows how different types of process feature participants in different roles, both when they instigate an action, e.g. as actor, and when they are at the receiving end of it, e.g. as goal. Semantically, passivated social actors can also be beneficiaries of an action, as in the following example from the data:

(8) We must ... restore our coastal communities. (Brexit Party, 2019 European Parliament elections leaflet)

There is another distinction we need to draw though, and that is between grammatical action and semantic agency. The former is a binary category – a participant is either active or passive – while the latter is graded, i.e. a participant can be more or less semantically agentive. Semantic agency is linked to process types, in that the more dynamic, outward-oriented material and verbal processes make actors and sayers appear more agentive than behavers, sensers, carriers/tokens, and existents.[2] This entails that a social actor can be grammatically active but semantically relatively non-agentive.

Having introduced the SFL approach to analysing discourse, especially the system of transitivity with its processes and participants, I will now reflect on how to best formulate research questions that are suitable to an SFL analysis.

Identifying research questions

Before delving into the detail, we need to formulate some research questions (RQs) to guide the analysis. In doing so, it is important to avoid two common pitfalls in discourse analysis, namely to either fail to advance beyond description or, conversely, to disregard descriptive analysis altogether and jump straight to interpretations before we have established a basis for them. Instead, we need to ask ourselves what we want to know of the data and what our findings will tell us. That is, we need to identify both a descriptive and an interpretative research question.

Say you are interested in why a particular party was successful in an election. You have collected some suitable data and have familiarised yourself with the SFL framework, but you are not sure how your interest can be formulated as a research question that you can actually answer through SFL analysis, i.e. how your interest can be operationalised. Clearly, a question like 'What made the party successful?' is too broad to begin with, while a question like 'How are process types used in the data?' is too narrow to ultimately say something about the reasons for the party's strong performance in the elections. Suitable mid-range questions could be based on the assumption that how the party presents itself and its competitors to potential voters in its communications, and what relationship it forges with voters, has an impact on the election result. This can be translated into a number of descriptive RQs: 'How does Party X use language in the data to present itself?', 'How does it use language to present other parties?', 'What linguistic features are employed in the data to construct a relationship between the text producer and the reader?'. These are questions that can be answered using an SFL approach to identify ideational and interpersonal meaning. We still need to make the jump to the party's electoral success though. Here it could be helpful to compare the findings with those from similar data for other parties. This leads to the same RQs for the comparison data, i.e. 'How does Party Y use language to present itself?' etc. After such a comparative analysis, we would know the differences between the respective parties' language use and be a step closer to answering an interpretative question. Such a question could, for instance, be 'How might the parties' different use of language have influenced their performance in the elections?' Note that this question is hedged ('*might* ... have influenced'): first, discourse is only ever one of many factors contributing to how a party fares with voters, and second, text analysis alone cannot tell us how the communications were received by voters and if they swayed their voting decision. Investigating that question would need an additional approach, such as ethnography or experimental methods (see Chapters 3 and 10, this volume, respectively).

For the purposes of this chapter, I address the following two, somewhat less ambitious, research questions:

RQ1 (descriptive): How are social actors represented in the leaflets by British parties for the 2019 European Parliament election?
RQ2 (interpretative): In what ways does this representation reflect UK political actors, concerns, and conflicts at the time?

These RQs deviate from the SFL grammar system of transitivity in that they do not centre on processes but on human participants. However, political discourse is very often pre-occupied with actors at least as much as with processes and events and it can therefore be useful to make that aspect of ideational meaning the focus of the investigation. Accordingly, the analysis will address the following questions in the order below:

- What social actors are present?
- How many different social actors are mentioned in the text?

- How often are the different social actors mentioned?
- Is there an image, or even several images, of them?
- How can we group social actors, especially as in- and out-groups?
- How are the social actors referred to?
- What processes are ascribed to them?

Data collection and ethics

We have seen in the previous section that a question as to why a particular party was successful in elections can only be partially answered through analysing texts. Nevertheless, what textual data should we choose? During election campaigns, political parties and politicians produce a great number of texts, from speeches and TV debates to manifestos and leaflets. SFL work has been done on both written and spoken data (for the latter, see e.g. Bullo, 2014), and there is no reason to prioritise one or the other. It is true that spontaneous spoken discourse will include more incomplete, ungrammatical, and non-cohesive clauses and sentences, but in whatever form people use language they will always construct experiences and build relations with others. So what data to collect will often be a question of what is available and practical: printed written materials are often also available online and need little preparation for further analysis. A party's website may also include transcripts of speeches, but it is advisable to check the transcript against a video of the speech being delivered, if one is available. Radio interviews and TV debates usually have to be transcribed by the researcher, which can pose some difficulty when discussants talk over each other (as politicians seem wont to do). On the plus side, interpersonal meanings in particular can be thrown into sharper relief in dynamic interactions.

Data that are in the public domain typically do not raise ethical concerns, although different social media platforms have different data protection policies that need to be adhered to. As mentioned above though, the SFL approach is suitable for spoken and written texts from a number of discourse domains, including e.g. healthcare and workplace discourse, which are sensitive and where confidentiality is important. In those cases, it is necessary to obtain informed consent from discourse participants, regardless of whether the data are pre-existing or specifically elicited for a research project.

The data that make up the case study for this chapter comprise leaflets distributed in the South West of England, although most of them, with the exception of the Green Party leaflet, make no special reference to that region. The parties included are the Brexit Party, the Green Party, Labour, the Liberal Democrats, and the UK Independence Party, but neither the short-lived Change UK Party nor the Conservatives, who did not reply to my request for materials. In the interest of space, I will restrict myself to the two parties that were most successful in the elections, namely the

68 *Veronika Koller*

Brexit Party, which secured 31.6% of the vote, and the Liberal Democrats, whom 20.3% of voters opted for (BBC, 2019).

Analysing and interpreting data

There are two things to consider before embarking on an analysis of transitivity, specifically process types: what verb forms will you include and how will you deal with metaphoric expressions (see Chapter 5, this volume)? As for the former, all finite verb forms should be part of a transitivity analysis, while auxiliary and modal verbs and constructions and negations should not be included. It further makes sense to code phrasal verbs (e.g. 'stand up for') as a whole process. However, I, for one, would leave it up to the analyst whether to also consider non-finite forms and nominalisations. Consider the following example from the data analysed in the next section:

(9) She's pushed for rapid investment in renewables and helped shape a Green New Deal. (Green Party, 2019 European Parliament election leaflet, South West)

Clearly, 'pushed' is a material process type expressed by a finite verb form, but there is also the non-finite (here: infinitive) form 'shape', which if included, would be another material process.[3] In addition, example (9) also features 'investment', which could be analysed as a nominalised form of 'invest'. Whatever decision an individual analyst takes, it should be made explicit and applied consistently.

Looking at example (9) again, we can note that the first process, 'pushed', is actually a metaphoric expression: it is clear from the co-text that the MEP referred to here has not engaged in a literal material process of exerting force on an object or person to move it or them. Rather, she is likely to have used verbal actions such as arguing to achieve her political objective. Material processes can also be employed to metaphorically refer to mental processes, as in 'They'll need some time to digest that proposal', or one sub-type of mental process can be used metaphorically to denote another sub-type, e.g. 'Do you see what I'm saying?', where a mental-perceptive process stands in for a mental-cognitive one. In some cases, it may not be possible to establish the literal process type beyond doubt. For example, it is ultimately not clear whether the material process in 'Let's just return to your previous point for a moment' stands in for a mental or a verbal process. There is a pattern though that more outward processes metaphorically represent more inward ones, which is in line with one of the main functions of metaphor, namely to make the abstract or subjective more concrete or objective (see Chapter 5, this volume). What are the implications for transitivity analysis, however – should we analyse the metaphoric process, the literal one, or both? Given the fundamental idea in

SFL, i.e. that all language use represents a motivated choice from the set of resources that is the language system, the use of a metaphor by a speaker or writer is functional. If, for instance, a particular social actor is frequently represented as engaging in metaphorical material processes rather than literal mental ones, that actor will appear dynamic and outgoing rather than introspective. My advice, especially for a quantitative analysis, would therefore be to include the metaphoric process but also to comment on any patterns in the figurative representation of social actors.

Keeping the above issues in mind, this section presents an illustrative analysis of how ideational meaning is created by the linguistic choices evident in a set of election leaflets that British parties published in the 2019 European Parliament election campaign. The analysis of the leaflets disregarded peripheral text such as small print about the text producer and printer, the recipient's address on direct mail, legally required information, and website addresses, but did include hashtags and words in images, e.g. placards. No multimodal analysis was carried out, however, other than to ascertain whether a social actor mentioned in the text was also represented in an image (see Chapter 8, this volume, for multimodal discourse analysis).

Table 4.3 contrasts the Brexit Party leaflet with that by the Liberal Democrats to provide answers to the first four questions: What and how many different social actors are present, how often are they mentioned and are they also represented in images?

It can be useful to start with a quantitative analysis, as frequencies and variety can give a first indication as to what participants and processes are salient. Likewise, patterns of how particular social actors are predominantly referred to and what processes they have ascribed to them most are often a good pointer toward the ideational meanings created in the text. The particular aspects that need to be considered when presenting numerical findings will be discussed below. The leaflets analysed in this section are composed of a number of images and text elements that, while coherent, do not follow on from each other in the manner of a run-on text. For such texts, e.g. editorials or news reports, van Leeuwen reminds us that 'frequencies often shift with the stages in the writer's argument and may not be an overall characteristic of the text' (2008: 31).

In quantitative terms then, the two leaflets do not show major differences: the ratio of different actors to words is almost identical (0.069 for the Brexit Party and 0.07 for the Liberal Democrats), and the percentage of words taken up by social actor references is also similar, with 13.21% for the Brexit Party and an only slightly higher figure (15.56%) for the Liberal Democrats. If we divide the number of different actors by the number of overall occurrences, we get a measure of the variety of social actor references, which in this case is slightly higher for the Brexit Party (0.523) than the Liberal Democrats (0.45). Overall though, the results are not strikingly different.

Table 4.3 Frequency of different social actors in the Brexit Party and Liberal Democrats leaflets

Brexit Party (333 words)	Liberal Democrats (257 words)
in-group: party, leaders, and candidates	
we (all) (7)	we (6)
Brexit Party (8)	Liberal Democrats (6), the biggest party (1)
I (4)	
Brexit Party Leader, Nigel Farage (1 + image)	Vince Cable (1)
Claire Fox, writer (1 + image) June Mummery, fishing industry (1 + image) Joel Chilaka, medical student (1 + image) Ben Habib, CEO (1 + image) Annunziata Rees-Mogg, journalist (1 + image) Richard Tice, CEO and entrepre neur (1 + image) James Glancy CGC, decorated Royal Marine (1 + image)	
extended in-group: voters and supporters	
17.4m (of us) (2), Brexit voters (1)	fellow Remainers (1), more and more people (1)
wider in-group: country and its people	
our great nation (1), our country (2), our coastal communities (1)	our country (1), Britain (3), UK (1), people (3)
out-group: government, other parties and politicians	
MPs, government and MPs Labour MPs (1), Conservative Party (1)	Labour (1), Conservatives, Labour, UKIP and Brexit Party (1), all these parties (1) Theresa May (2 + image), Nigel Farage (1), Boris Johnson (1), (Jeremy) Corbyn (2 + image)
miscellaneous social actors	
the EU (3)	the EU (3) EU citizens (1)
left-wing democrats (1)	
you (1)	you (3)
23 actors, 44 occurrences	**18 actors, 40 occurrences**

Where we can see differences is in what social actors are present. While both leaflets refer to a collective 'we' and directly address the reader ('you'), only the Brexit Party makes use of the first person singular, in statements attributed to their leader and two of their candidates. The Liberal Democrats leaflet does not include any statements from candidates, opting instead for quotes from various media to provide evidence that the UK is in a 'mess'. The Brexit Party, by contrast, quotes media sources for numbers and statistics (e.g. '92% of Brexit voters feel betrayed'). Both parties mention other, rival parties, but only the Brexit Party refers to the government. On the other hand, only the Liberal Democrats refer to specific politicians from other parties. Taken together, the strategy of the Brexit Party seems to be to foreground its own leader and candidates in the text and images, alongside constructing an out-group of the government and rival parties as those who have 'betrayed Brexit', whereas the Liberal Democrats use text and images to focus more on the out-group, i.e. groups and individuals whom they perceive to be responsible for the 'Brexit mess'.

In qualitative terms, the forms of social actor reference further corroborate this difference. Looking at noun phrases and pronouns that unambiguously refer to a specific social actor, we can see that the two parties' self-reference is done through objectivation ('the Brexit Party', 'the Liberal Democrats') and that the first-person plural occasionally refers to politicians of the party, albeit only for the Liberal Democrats. Party leaders are referred to by semi-formal nomination, but only Nigel Farage is functionalised as 'Brexit Party leader', whereas his counterpart is mentioned along with party members ('[t]he Liberal Democrats and Vince Cable'), making him appear as less authoritative and more like a first among equals. The Brexit Party also has images of, and quotes from, no fewer than seven candidates who are nominated, even titulated ('James Glancy CGC'),[4] and either functionalised ('student') or identified ('journalist'). Both parties refer to the extended in-group of voters and supporters by means of aggregation ('17.4m', 'more and more people') to appear powerful. It is noteworthy though that Brexit Party supporters are referred to in more dynamic terms: 'Brexit voters', a functionalisation, can be contrasted with 'fellow Remainers', a collectivisation. An even wider in-group is referred to as 'our country' by both parties, but apart from that objectivation, the Brexit Party also includes two collectivised actors with emotional associations ('our great nation',[5] 'our coastal communities') whereas the Liberal Democrats represent 'Britain' and the 'UK' as further objectivations. The lack of the possessive pronoun makes the party seem more distant from the country than the Brexit Party.

Both leaflets also construct out-groups, but the focus here is inward rather than outward: it is not the EU that is represented as Other but other parties and their MPs as well as the UK government (see also Koller and Ryan, 2019). Other parties are referred to either by name, i.e. through objectivation, or are, in the case of the Liberal Democrats, collectivised as 'all these parties'. Although only the Brexit Party includes 'government and MPs' as a combined

72   Veronika Koller

abstraction and collectivisation, the Liberal Democrats' stronger focus on the out-group is expressed through nomination of a number of politicians from other parties.

So far, we have identified a focus on the in-group and a tendency to represent in-group members in ways that signal closeness, authority, and dynamicity for the Brexit Party, which can be contrasted with a focus on the out-group and a more detached, egalitarian, and static representation of social actors on the part of the Liberal Democrats. The last part of the analysis will look at whether these findings are corroborated by the use of process types in the leaflets.

Limiting ourselves to finite verb forms (unless the non-finite form is the main process, e.g. 'trying to deliver'), we can see that both parties feature as goals in a material process when readers are asked to vote for them. Beyond that, however, there are notable differences: whereas the Brexit Party is represented as an actor only (' ... will restore trust in politics'), the Liberal Democrats are likewise cast as actor (e.g. 'we've led the opposition') but also as sayer (' ... demand better'), token (' ... are the biggest party fighting to stop Brexit') and senser (' ... want to stop Brexit'). The Liberal Democrats' leader is part of the latter process. Nigel Farage, however, the leader of the Brexit Party, is represented visually and through a quote, making him an implicit sayer. In the quote, the first-person singular refers to him as senser in a mental-cognitive process ('I believed we had won'). Brexit Party candidates, too, are included through images and quotes, in which they feature not only implicitly as sayer but also explicitly as actor (e.g. 'I fought for our country ... ') and carrier (' ... and I'm not prepared to see it humiliated'). Thus, while both parties refer to themselves mostly as grammatically active, the Brexit Party also presents itself, its leader, and its candidates as semantically more agentive than the Liberal Democrats do.

The extended in-group of supporters is represented as senser by both parties ('Brexit voters feel betrayed', 'more and more people are realising how important EU membership is'), but only the Brexit Party additionally casts them as actors ('17.4m voted to leave the EU'), while the Liberal Democrats include them only as a circumstance ('on behalf of fellow Remainers'). We have already seen that the wider out-group of the country is represented as somewhat distant by the Liberal Democrats, and the use of processes makes it passive and relatively non-agentive as well: 'our country', 'Britain', and the 'UK' feature as grammatical actor only once, in a relational process ('UK [is] "embarrassed", "powerless" and "frustrated"'), while the Brexit Party casts it as actor ('We must leave the EU') and token ('our country deserves better leadership'). Both leaflets also passivate the country as value or phenomenon ('what kind of country we are', ' ... want Britain to remain in the EU'), respectively, and construct it as a beneficiary of the parties' action (e.g. 'restore our coastal communities', 'give people the final say'). However, the Liberal Democrats additionally relegate it to a circumstance (' ... how important membership is to our country').

Finally, when it comes to the out-group, both parties represent rival MPs and parties as grammatically active and therefore as a threat to be prevented by voting for the Brexit Party or Liberal Democrats, respectively. MPs and other parties are presented as actors in material processes, but again, they are more semantically agentive in the Brexit Party leaflet, where they are sayers ('MPs promised to honour the result'). This contrasts with their role as senser in the Liberal Democrats' text ('a disastrous Brexit that only Nigel Farage … wanted').

To sum up, the analysis has shown that while the quantitative results are fairly similar, and both parties represent themselves as mostly grammatically active, the Brexit Party foregrounds its own leader and candidates, who are represented as close, authoritative, dynamic, and agentive. They also set up an out-group of the government and rival parties but by comparison, the Liberal Democrats focus more on that out-group. Both leaflets construct the wider in-group that is the country as benefitting from the respective party's action; the Liberal Democrats also represent it as rather non-agentive. As for the out-group, both parties cast it as grammatically active, but the Brexit Party leaflet ascribes a more semantically agentive role to it.

While this answers the first research question as to how social actors are represented in the leaflets, we still have to address in what ways this representation reflects UK politics at the time. Apart from the obvious differences in the political goals of the two parties, it is worth noting that the Brexit Party had existed for only a few weeks when the leaflet was published. As its name indicates, it is a one-issue party and as such has succeeded UKIP, which seems like a spent force at the time of writing (July 2019). The Brexit Party enjoyed considerable momentum during the election campaign, not least because of its well-known and controversial leader. This dynamic and agentive nature of the newest party in the UK is also reflected in its language use. By contrast, the Liberal Democrats had seen their poll ratings and electoral success collapse after five years as junior partner in a coalition with the Conservatives. Reinventing themselves as the party of 'Remain' – next to the Green Party, who is conspicuously absent from the out-group – has given the Liberal Democrats a new lease of life, as demonstrated in their success in the 2019 European elections. A stronger focus on itself and a less cautious, more dynamic tone of voice might have contributed to an even stronger performance.

Presenting findings and results

Depending on how many research questions there are, how much data has been collected, and in how much detail it has been analysed, the number of findings can easily become overwhelming. It is important therefore to have a clear structure for presenting them. To go back to the example from the 'Identifying research questions' section above, let us assume you have analysed the manifestos of three political parties for how the text producer has used language to represent the party in question as well as other

74   *Veronika Koller*

parties, and to construct a relationship with the voter/reader. In that case, you could either present the results of the analysis by going through texts X, Y, and Z, and pointing out the relevant linguistic features in each. Alternatively, it is possible to structure the presentation by the different linguistic features and compare the use of, say, modality in the three texts. Whichever way you choose, you want the findings section to be detailed but not repetitive, concise but not sketchy. Crucially, RQs need not only to be stated clearly before the presentation of findings, but also answered explicitly at the end.

While cognitive linguists often use circles and lines to present their findings (see Chapter 6, this volume) the diagram of choice for systemic functional linguists is the tree diagram. As those can get rather unwieldy though, I have in this chapter refrained from using tree diagrams to present findings from the analysis, including only one to give an overview of forms of social actor representation (Figure 4.2). For the findings, I have opted for a mixed presentation of both quantitative and qualitative results in Table 4.3, combining frequencies for social actors with categorising them into in- and out-groups. (That table is in fact a simplified and tidier version of a much more elaborate collection of findings, drawn up as the analysis progressed.) Other than that, I have presented results in prose form, making sure to give relative frequencies and ratios rather than absolute numbers: the two leaflets I compared differ in word length, so it would not be very informative to say that a feature occurred, e.g. three times in one text and five times in the other. For the qualitative findings, a written-up rather than tabular version seemed more suitable.

Issues and limitations

Hopefully, the illustration above has shown that an SFL (here: transitivity) analysis can be a powerful tool to investigate how speakers and writers use language to convey experience from a particular viewpoint, and project identities and relations. A systemic functional analysis can be a strong foundation on which to base broader interpretations about social and political configurations and processes. Despite this potential of SFL though, it is not as widely applied in discourse studies as one might think. Part of the problem is its complexity: this chapter has only presented one simplified part of the whole framework and still introduced a large number of categories and terms. There is no doubt that SFL-inspired taxonomies have a tendency to proliferate, adding ever finer sub-categories to their tree diagrams. Such differentiation brings anther problem with it, suggesting as it does that every part of a clause can unambiguously fit into a box. Yet, SFL is ultimately a theory of meaning, and meaning is never unambiguous. Worse still, novices might think that slotting processes and participants into boxes constitutes a complete analysis when in fact, detailed description needs to be followed by interpretation in discourse analysis.

My advice is therefore to take a pragmatic approach to SFL: focusing on those parts of any framework that help answer a specific research question, acknowledging that there may sometimes be more than one possible categorisation, and combining SFL with other methods. This chapter should therefore be read together with other chapters in the book, in order to build up a comprehensive toolkit for researching discourse.

Further reading

For anyone new to SFL, Thompson's (2014) accessible introduction is very much recommended. The book covers the most important aspects of SFL, but with a student rather than an expert reader in mind. It also includes useful exercises with an answer key. Bloor and Bloor (2013) is another commendably accessible introduction to the SFL approach, with somewhat more detail than Thompson's book and an additional historical overview, glossary, and companion website. In Darics and Koller (2019), my co-author and I have sought to make van Leeuwen's (1996, 2008) framework of social actor representation accessible to a wider community of interested professionals. There was no space in this chapter to more than mention appraisal theory, but the appraisal website contains introductions at various level of detail, along with some key texts for download. Available at http://grammatics.com/appraisal/.

Notes

1 For non-British readers, 'bobbies on the beat' are police officers patrolling the streets.
2 In her analysis of media representations of female party leaders in Scotland, Barty-Taylor (2020) has integrated the gender aspect of semantic agency, in that dynamic, outward processes are culturally associated with masculinity.
3 Example (9) is rather complex in that the non-finite verb '(to) shape' is preceded by a verb denoting semantic aspect ('helped shape'), which can be omitted.
4 CGC stands for Conspicuous Gallantry Cross, a medal that is awarded to military service personnel who have distinguished themselves in operations against an enemy.
5 Interestingly, the Green Party leaflet makes no reference to the UK as a country or nation, but instead mentions Europe as 'our great continent'. This can be interpreted as a focus on the European nature of the election, but possibly also as a wish to distance the party from any nationalism.

References

Barty-Taylor, M. (2020). *The gender politics of politicians online: How Scottish young people discuss constructions of women leaders*. PhD thesis, Lancaster University.
BBC (2019). The UK's European elections 2019. Available at https://bbc.co.uk/news/topics/crjeqkdevwvt/the-uks-european-elections-2019, accessed 19 July 2019.

Bloor, T. and Bloor, M. (2013). *The functional analysis of English*. (3rd ed.). Abingdon: Routledge.

Bloor, M. and Bloor, T. (2018). Systemic functional linguistics. In J. Flowerdew and J. E. Richardson (Eds.), *The Routledge handbook of critical discourse studies*. (pp. 151–164). Abingdon: Routledge.

Bullo, S. (2014). *Evaluation in advertising reception: A socio-cognitive and linguistic perspective*. Basingstoke: Palgrave.

Darics, E. and Koller, V. (2019). Social actors 'to go': An analytical toolkit to explore agency in business discourse and communication. *Business and Professional Communication Quarterly*, 82(2), 214–238.

Eggins, S. (2004). *An introduction to systemic functional linguistics*. (2nd ed.). London: Continuum.

Fairclough, N. (2003). *Analysing discourse: Textual analysis for social research*. London: Routledge.

Fairclough, N. (2010). *Critical discourse analysis: The critical study of language*. (2nd ed.). London: Longman.

Halliday, M.A.K. (1985). *Introduction to functional grammar*. London: Edward Arnold.

Halliday, M.A.K. and Hasan, R. (1976). *Cohesion in English*. London: Pearson Education.

Halliday, M.A.K. and Matthiessen, C.M.I.M. (2014). *Halliday's introduction to functional grammar*. (4th ed.). Abingdon: Routledge.

Koller, V. and Ryan, J. (2019). A nation divided: Metaphors and scenarios in media coverage of the 2016 British EU referendum. In C. Hart (Ed.), *Cognitive linguistic approaches to text and discourse: From poetics to politics*. (pp. 131–156). Edinburgh: Edinburgh University Press.

Lockwood, J. and Forey, G. (2016). Discursive control and power in virtual meetings. *Discourse & Communication*, 10(4), 323–340.

Martin, J.R. (2000). Close reading: Functional linguistics as a tool for critical discourse analysis. In L. Unsworth (Ed.), *Researching language in schools and communities: Functional linguistic perspectives*. (pp. 275–303). London: Cassell.

Martin, J.R. and White, P.R.R. (2005). *Evaluation in English: The language of appraisal*. Basingstoke: Palgrave.

Martin, J.R. and Wodak, R. (Eds.) (2003). *Re/reading the Past: Critical and functional perspectives on time and value*. Amsterdam: Benjamins.

Searle, J.R. (1969). *Speech acts: An essay in the philosophy of language*. Cambridge: Cambridge University Press.

Thompson, G. (2014). *Introducing functional grammar*. (3rd ed.). Abingdon: Routledge.

van Leeuwen, T. (1996). The representation of social actors. In C.R. Caldas-Coulthard and M. Coulthard (Eds.), *Texts and practices: Readings in critical discourse analysis*. (pp. 32–71). London: Routledge.

van Leeuwen, T. (2008). *Discourse and practice: New tools for critical discourse analysis*. Oxford: Oxford University Press.

5 Analysing metaphor in discourse

Veronika Koller

Introduction

Metaphor continues to be a source of fascination, not just for speechwriters or scholars of literature, but also for a range of linguists and students in linguistics. It is perhaps the sheer breadth of subjects for which metaphor is relevant – spanning from natural sciences such as neuroscience and psychology to social sciences like organisational studies and education research, all the way to the humanities including literary criticism and art, and even theology – that makes metaphor studies such a popular and growing endeavour. (For overviews of metaphor in language and thought, see Gibbs, 2008; Semino and Demjén, 2016.) In this chapter, I will focus on the analysis of metaphor in discourse, outlining how identifying, systematising, and interpreting the phenomenon of metaphor in language use can help recognise the often covert ways in which text producers construct particular versions of reality. To this end, I will briefly present the main tenets of what is arguably still the dominant approach to metaphor, namely conceptual metaphor theory, before introducing the origins and applications of critical metaphor analysis as an approach that combines critical discourse studies with cognitive semantics, including recent work on *metaphor scenarios*. I illustrate how to analyse and interpret metaphor in discourse by presenting a short case study of RESTRAINT metaphors as used in British parliamentary debates on Brexit (e.g. 'free from the shackles of the EU', 'trapped in the backstop'). The sample analysis will also include advice on how to harness corpus linguistic methods for analysing metaphor in discourse.

Outline of approach

The key to understanding metaphor lies in the term itself: the English word 'metaphor' derives from the Ancient Greek verb μεταφέρειν (*metapherein*), meaning 'to carry across'. What is being carried across is meaning, which is transferred[1] from one domain of experience to another. Rather remarkably, 'metaphor' is itself a metaphoric expression and as

78 Veronika Koller

such can be traced back to a conceptual metaphor MEANING IS OBJECT.[2] The Western tradition of metaphor studies goes back to Aristotle, who in his *Poetics* defined metaphor as 'an application of an alien name by transference' (ca. 350 BC a), adding in the *Rhetoric* that 'it is from metaphor that we can best get hold of something fresh' (ca. 350 BC b).

The latter quotation refers to one of the many functions of metaphor in language use, namely to explain things and concepts that are new to the hearer. Other important functions of metaphor in discourse are to express abstract ideas in more concrete terms, to convey subjective experiences (e.g. emotions), to elicit emotional reactions from an audience, to persuade, to amuse and entertain, and to structure and set the scene for narratives. I will return to the last function when I discuss metaphor scenarios below; for now, it is important to introduce a pivotal theory in contemporary metaphor research, namely *conceptual metaphor theory*.

Conceptual metaphor theory

Although Lakoff and Johnson's (1980) conceptual metaphor theory (CMT) was not conceived in a vacuum (for an overview of some precursor theories, see Koller, 2003: 14–23), their contribution was ground-breaking in making the argument that metaphor is first and foremost a cognitive phenomenon. In their own words, metaphor is 'understanding and experiencing one thing in terms of another' (1980: 5). For them and later proponents of CMT, metaphor structures thought, starting in pre-lingual children, and is only later realised in language – or indeed other semiotic modes – as *metaphoric expressions* (see Chapter 8, this volume, for discussion of metaphor as it realised visually as well as verbally). Relying on native speaker intuition, Lakoff and Johnson (1980) provide a wealth of examples from American English to illustrate their point. Due to the fact that mental processes are highly abstract, they take recourse to metaphor themselves when explaining metaphor as a *mapping* of semantic features from a *source domain* to a *target domain*. To cite their well-worn illustration, examples (1) and (2) would be taken as evidence for a conceptual metaphor LIFE IS A JOURNEY, in which features of the JOURNEY source domain, i.e. our structured knowledge about journeys, are transferred to the LIFE target domain.[3]

(1) A graduate is at his or her first major <u>crossroad</u> in life.
(2) As you're <u>approaching end</u> of life, you may hear your medical team using many different expressions.[4]

According to CMT, conceptual metaphor has a number of defining characteristics (see Jäkel, 2002). We can here identify seven: first off, because metaphor structures thought, it is ubiquitous, used not just in oratory, poetry, or fiction, but in everyday language as well. This point was already made by Aristotle, who observed in his *Rhetoric* that 'these two classes of terms, the proper or regular and the metaphorical... are used by everybody in conversation' (ca. 350 BC b). Second, CMT sees the mapping from source to target domain as unidirectional, arguing that life may be conceptualised as a journey, but journeys are not understood as life. This sets the theory apart from interactional approaches, which claim that metaphor arises when semantic features are mapped between two domains and that the emerging metaphor is more than the sum of its constituent parts. While this view has a long history, it has found its most recent manifestation in the theory of conceptual integration or blending (Fauconnier and Turner, 2002). CMT, however, is a comparison approach, stipulating that metaphor is motivated by a perceived similarity of the source to the target. In other words, we understand life as being similar to journeys in some respects, but not vice versa. This leads to the third feature of conceptual metaphor, namely that the mapping from source to target is *invariant*, with target domain features overriding those of the source domain but not the other way round. To once more use the LIFE IS JOURNEY example, life is like a journey in that it has a beginning, a duration, and an end. Additional semantic features of the source domain, such as obstacles and crossroads, can also be mapped onto certain aspects of the target domain, like difficulties and decisions. So while certain features of the source domain, such as obstacles, detours, crossroads, mode of transport etc. have corresponding elements in the target domain, other features of journeys such as the need for a passport or checking into a hotel do not have corresponding elements in the LIFE domain and so are not mapped across.

The fourth characteristic of metaphor according to CMT is its systematicity. At the level of language, the same underlying conceptual metaphor can give rise to a number of metaphoric expressions. For example, the expressions 'I am ruthless in using every <u>bullet</u> I have', '[he has] <u>lost ground</u> to rivals on ... international <u>fronts</u>' and '[s]he barked out new <u>marching orders</u>' (cited in Koller, 2004a) can all be traced back to a metaphor EXECUTIVES ARE MILITARY PERSONNEL. Metaphor is systematic at the conceptual level as well, in that specific conceptual metaphors are related if they elaborate a more general conceptual metaphor. Systematicity at the linguistic and conceptual levels is represented in Figure 5.1.

We have already seen that according to CMT, mappings are unidirectional and invariant. To this we can now add a fifth important feature of metaphor, namely the selective nature of mappings. Not only does the target domain block certain elements of the source domain from being mapped, but speakers and writers also make motivated choices in which aspects of the source domain they select for mapping in order to highlight particular features of both source and target domains, while ignoring others. Looking again at the BUSINESS IS WAR conceptual metaphor, we saw that both the violent and strategic nature of war are appealed to in the examples above. However, other, less palatable aspects of war, such as

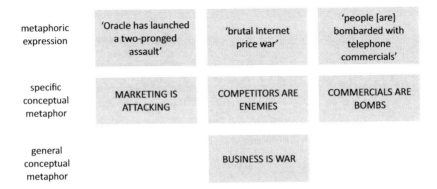

Figure 5.1 Metaphor systematicity at the linguistic and conceptual levels (examples cited in Koller, 2004b)

civilians fleeing their homes, do not feature. As metaphor leads to understanding the target domain in a particular way, business is here conceptualised as a violent, strategic activity, but not as one that brings suffering. And while semantic mappings may be unidirectional, the ideological effect of exploiting only certain elements of the source domain is that both the unethical nature of war and problematic elements of business, as the target domain, remain hidden.

The aspect of selective mapping is related to the notion of *metaphoric entailments*, as the sixth defining characteristic of conceptual metaphor. In mapping only certain aspects of the source domain, writers and speakers direct readers and hearers toward specific entailments among a greater number that are potentially triggered by the wider frame. (This explains why, in the examples above, the metaphor BUSINESS IS WAR does not give rise to entailments relating to death and destruction etc.) To return to the LIFE IS JOURNEY metaphor, we can state that if life is indeed conceptualised as a journey, it follows that it has a beginning, a duration, and an end, and features forward movement[5] that can be impeded. Which entailments are promoted by text or talk depends on what the writer or speaker wants to highlight; however, which entailments are actually inferred by the reader or hearer is outside of the text producer's control. For example, many companies like to present themselves as a 'family' of employees or customers (e.g. 'the IKEA Family is for everyone').[6] Given the promotional nature of most, if not all, externally oriented corporate discourse, there is no doubt that text producers use that metaphor to evoke notions of closeness and nurturing, but another possible entailment would be the power asymmetry between parents and children.

The final characteristic of conceptual metaphor is one that has received a large amount of attention, namely the dual nature of metaphor as being grounded both in physical and in socio-cultural experience. In this context, the theory of *primary metaphors* (Grady, 1997) holds that pre-lingual children learn to associate concrete physical sensations with abstract emotional experiences and mental states. This would, for example, explain the primary metaphor EMOTIONAL INVOLVEMENT IS PHYSICAL PROXIMITY, which is then reflected in expressions such as 'a close friend'.[7] Other common primary metaphors include SEEING IS UNDERSTANDING (e.g. 'her point wasn't <u>clear</u> to me') and EMOTION IS FORCE (e.g. 'he <u>burst</u> into tears'). Because such primary metaphors are theorised to emerge from infants moving and experiencing their bodies in three-dimensional space, the metaphors are said to be embodied and universal. However, emotion metaphors in particular have been studied in a number of languages and have been found to exhibit considerable variation across cultures. Both English and Chinese, for instance, conceptualise anger as heat, but while English speakers specify this to ANGER IS HOT FLUID (e.g. 'she was <u>boiling</u> with rage'), Chinese speakers draw on a conceptual metaphor ANGER IS HOT GAS instead (Yu, 1995). Similarly, while anger can be a growing organism in both English and Akan, one of the main languages in Ghana, only the latter specifies anger to a weed growing on the angry person's chest (Ansah, 2011).

In view of such cultural variation next to embodied universality, Kövecses (2000) introduces the concept of 'body-based constructionism' (p. 183), which, although developed with regard to emotion language, applies 'possibly not only [to] emotion language' (p. 182). This synthesis combines views from theories of embodiment with social constructionism, concluding 'that some aspects of emotion language and emotion concepts are universal and clearly related to the physiological functioning of the body' while 'the very significant remaining differences in emotion language and concepts can be explained by reference to differences in cultural knowledge and pragmatic discourse functions' (p. 183). Another important development in metaphor theory that likewise reconciles constructivism and embodiment, or critical and cognitive approaches, is *critical metaphor analysis*.

Critical metaphor analysis

We saw in the previous section that one of the defining characteristics of conceptual metaphor is selective mapping, meaning that some aspects of the source domain are foregrounded while others are backgrounded, resulting in highlighting and hiding effects in the target domain. The examples given above showed that such selective mappings may serve the ideological agenda of text producers in that it enables them to represent an aspect of experience from a particular viewpoint (see Chapter 4, this volume, on this so-called ideational meaning). As Lakoff and Johnson (1980: 156–157) put it: 'metaphors ... highlight and make coherent certain aspects of our experience ... metaphors may create realities for us,

82 Veronika Koller

especially social realities'. This becomes particularly important when it is 'people in power [who] get to impose their metaphors' (p. 157).

Although they have never acknowledged each other's work, this quote is remarkably close to Fairclough's view that 'dominant metaphors construct domains in a way which helps marginalize other constructions from the perspective of oppositional groups' (1995: 71–72; see also Chilton, 1996: 74). Despite this clear theoretical overlap, it took until the early 2000s for critical discourse studies and conceptual metaphor theory to be combined in what has since come to be known as critical metaphor analysis (CMA). 2004 saw the publication of three books initiating this paradigm: in their analysis of metaphor in various discourse domains, Charteris-Black (2004), Musolff (2004), and I (Koller, 2004b) all sought to bring together insights about metaphor from cognitive semantics, including CMT, with critical approaches to discourse, thereby further developing earlier work by Chilton (1996), among others. In my own formulation of the theory underpinning CMA, I wrote that

> [e]ach individual has a dynamic pool of shifting complex metaphors and concomitant expressions at his or her disposal. However, access to that pool ... [is] restrained by the interplay of social and personal cognition ... Through discourse and text production, particular metaphors can rise to hegemonic prominence to establish, reify or challenge social relations ... [S]ocial cognition in the form of ideology is at work at every stage after the formation of primary metaphors.
>
> (Koller, 2004b: 42)

The main aim of CMA is to establish, through discourse analysis, what role metaphor use plays in serving ideological goals. Ideology is here defined as 'a network of beliefs that gives rise to expectations, norms and values about events, ideas and people', with 'ideologies ... giving sense to encounters between people and ... being shared among people' (Koller, 2014: 239–240). Metaphors can help build that 'network' by representing actors and events from a particular perspective, by creating in-groups and out-groups, and by presenting social processes as natural and common sense, thereby creating and maintaining unequal power relations. To quote two instances from media discourse on politics, examples (3) and (4) (quoted in Koller and Ryan, 2019) use elaborations of spatial UP–DOWN and CENTRE–PERIPHERY metaphors, respectively, to comment on the result of the 2016 British referendum on EU membership:

(3) The quiet people of our country <u>rise up</u> against an out-of-touch political class and a contemptuous Brussels elite.
(4) 'Many communities ... feel very angry about the way they have been betrayed and <u>marginalised</u>.'

Analysing metaphor in discourse   83

Both examples represent 'people' or, in more abstract terms, 'social communities' (see Chapter 4, this volume, for forms of social actor representation) as disadvantaged, but the first sees them as being subdued by two other named groups, while the second constructs them as being relegated to the margins by an unnamed actor. However, the focus in both examples on a particular social actor group suggests that 'people' may be positioned as the in-group. The fact that example (3) was taken from the *Mail Online*, a British news website that had strongly supported a Leave vote, while example (4) is a quote from the leader of the British Labour party, Jeremy Corbyn, supports this interpretation: the *Mail Online* writer represents Leave voters as an in-group taking back power from a negatively evaluated out-group, while Corbyn empathises with traditional Labour voters in the face of negative actions by more powerful actors. The use of spatial metaphors reinforces this representation by linking it to embodied and universal schemata, and hence to common sense. And finally, while the 'people' are represented as relatively powerless in both examples, the particular elaboration of the UP–DOWN metaphor in example (3), in the form of an upwards movement, constructs them as more agentive than the CENTRE–PERIPHERY metaphor combined with an agentless passive and mental process (see Chapter 4, this volume, on process types) in example (4).

As mentioned above, one function of metaphor is to set the scene for narratives. This function is captured and further theorised by the notion of *metaphor scenarios* (Musolff, 2004), which have been defined as '[f]igurative mini narratives that carry an evaluative stance' (Musolff, 2004: 3) and as

> a set of assumptions made by competent members of a discourse community about 'typical' aspects of a source-situation, for example, its participants and their roles, the 'dramatic' storylines and outcomes, and conventional evaluations of whether they count as successful or unsuccessful, normal or abnormal, permissible or illegitimate, etc.
>
> (Musolff, 2004: 28)

Clearly, metaphor scenarios include, at least implicitly, actors, actions, and motivations. We can think of the source domain of a metaphor as a stage, complete with props and backdrops, on which the scenario can play out once the actors come on stage. The way the stage is set up makes certain actions more possible or likely than others, impacts who can take part in activities, raises expectations as to what will happen, and favours particular plots as desirable and valuable. Taking the source domain of MARRIAGE as an example, the different metaphor scenarios it gives rise to will include a certain number of actors who have a romantic and/or sexual relationship and share domestic life.[8] The actors may be expected to have children and fidelity is usually seen as desirable while divorce is negatively evaluated. Semino, Demjén, and Demmen (2016) clarify the difference between conceptual metaphor and metaphor scenario with the following example

84   *Veronika Koller*

from health discourse relating to cancer: 'My consultant said that I was a born fighter'. The authors argue that the underlying conceptual metaphor is BEING ILL WITH CANCER IS A VIOLENT CONFRONTATION WITH THE DISEASE, while the metaphor scenario is about engaging in a fight.

CMA is a paradigm for linking the cognitive nature of metaphor to its discursive manifestation, an aim that it shares with Kövecses' (2017) four levels of schematicity in metaphor. In that framework, conceptual richness increases as schematicity decreases across levels. To illustrate, the source domain JOURNEY is based on a less conceptually rich SOURCE–PATH–GOAL schema on the one hand and can be further enriched by being framed as driving, for example, on the other. (On metaphor and framing, see Ritchie, 2013.) Even less schematic would be the specification of driving to, for example, a car being driven through difficult terrain. Kövecses calls this level of specification a mental space but acknowledges that it is at least similar to what is elsewhere called metaphor scenario. Such mental spaces or scenarios are then expressed in 'instances of semiosis', i.e. in specific examples of language and/or visuals. One such example is the lead article of *The Economist* newspaper from 8 October 2016,[9] which had the following to say about Britain leaving the EU:

(5) The destination was decided in June … The journey, however, will be complex and perilous, beset by wrong turnings, chicanes and elephant traps.

The article was accompanied by a drawing of then Foreign Secretary and Prime Minister, respectively, Boris Johnson and Theresa May, in a car, with a landscape of winding paths, cliffs, loops, and mountains stretching out before them. This realisation of the metaphor scenario not only features certain actors and actions, and evaluates particular aspects, but also does ideological work in foregrounding the dangers rather than possible pleasures of the journey ahead, and indeed selectively highlighting aspects of the journey rather than the destination. In employing this particular scenario, the text producers foreground problematic aspects of both journeys and the process of Britain leaving the EU.

After introducing both conceptual metaphor theory and critical metaphor analysis in this section, I will now address possible research questions that can be addressed by the latter approach, comment on how and where to collect suitable data, and what to consider in terms of ethics.

Identifying research questions

As discussed in the previous section, CMA addresses what role metaphor as used in discourse has in expressing, reinforcing, and challenging the socio-cognitive phenomenon that is ideology. This means that research questions (RQs) should likewise seek to enquire about the conceptual, discursive, and ideological functions of metaphor use, without prioritising one over the others. Apart from being purely descriptive, questions about what metaphoric expressions are used in news articles or other genres on a specific topic (e.g. 'What metaphors do Twitter users employ to talk about climate change?') fail to account for metaphor's cognitive dimension. Conversely, RQs asking how a certain social actor group metaphorically conceptualises an event, process, entity, phenomenon, or another social actor group (e.g. 'What conceptual metaphors about global warming guide the actions of climate activists?') ignore how such conceptualisations are realised in language use as social practice, i.e. in discourse. An integrated question would e.g. be 'What conceptual metaphors for global warming are suggested by the language use of climate activists on Twitter?'. Although it still needs to be operationalised, such a question accounts for both the discursive and the cognitive aspects of metaphor – we will turn to metaphor's ideological functions shortly – and is neither too broad nor too specific.

Note that the final RQ above included the phrase 'as suggested by ... ', rather than 'as shown/demonstrated by'. Importantly, conceptual metaphors cannot be read off texts. In discourse studies, we can analyse metaphoric expressions at the level of language and treat them as 'windows to the mind' (Handl and Schmid, 2011), but discourse analysis alone cannot ascertain cognitive structures and processes. (See Chapter 10, this volume, on experimental methods.) RQs about the conceptual aspect of metaphor therefore need to be appropriately hedged, just as any claims about it need to be based on textual evidence and again be suitably modalised. Moreover, to the extent that ideology is a network of beliefs engendering attitudes and expectations, and as such partly cognitive in nature, it, too, cannot be directly derived from texts. To further elaborate the question above, then, we can include the ideological aspect of metaphor by reformulating it as 'What conceptual metaphors for global warming are suggested by the language use of climate activists on Twitter and what ideologies do the relevant metaphoric expressions indicate?'.

The next two sections will discuss how suitable RQs can be operationalised through data collection and analysis.

Data collection and ethics

Given that metaphoric thought and hence language is ubiquitous, ultimately any kind of data is suitable for analysing metaphor in discourse. However, different types of data each require certain considerations.

First of all, particular genres favour particular metaphors (Deignan, Littlemore, and Semino, 2013), as do different discourses. For instance, we have seen above that marketing discourse favours a WAR/VIOLENCE source domain, but it should also be noted that relevant conceptual metaphors are realised in genres such as media articles and possibly internal meetings

86 *Veronika Koller*

rather than, say, companies' press releases. Findings from the analysis of such data that show atypical use of metaphor therefore deserve special attention. In addition, some metaphoric expressions have acquired the status of (semi-)technical terms in some discourses, with examples including 'clinical care pathways' in health discourse or 'balance sheet' in accounting discourse. While it is interesting to see what conceptual metaphors become highly conventionalised in language and why, claims about whether such metaphoric expressions activate the related source domains should be treated with due caution.

Second, metaphor is not restricted in its articulation to the linguistic mode but finds expression also in non-linguistic forms of communication, such as visual communication, where it is realised quite differently. Identifying and analysing instantiations of conceptual metaphors in visual modes and genres therefore requires its own particular set of tools and skills. Multimodal metaphor is dealt with in Chapter 8, this volume.

Third, metaphor use and development differs between dialogic and monologic data, where the former comprise conversations and online interaction, while the latter are exemplified by speeches and magazine articles. For instance, Cameron (2003: 117–119) shows how a highly specific metaphor is co-constructed and developed by the teacher and pupils in a stretch of classroom discourse, while I have elsewhere (Koller, 2004b: 79, 130–131) pointed out that journalists often use variations of the same metaphor at the beginning and end of their articles in order to 'bracket' them. Analyses of different data therefore need to account for such specific dynamics of metaphor use.

There are no specific ethical issues to be considered when collecting data for metaphor analysis, but the usual caveats apply: informed consent needs to be sought and obtained before collecting and working with data that is not in the public domain and all such data needs to be fully anonymised. In addition, the usage guidelines for online platforms and media outlets need to be consulted even when they are publicly accessible.

The next section will demonstrate how to analyse and interpret metaphor in discourse by presenting a concise case study of RESTRAINT metaphors as used in parliamentary debates on Brexit.

Analysing and interpreting data

The case study through which I will demonstrate how to analyse and interpret metaphor in discourse addresses British parliamentary debates on Brexit. Specifically, it seeks to answer the following research question, which comprises both a descriptive and an interpretative part:

Analysing metaphor in discourse   87

How do Conservative members of parliament discuss Brexit and what does their language use suggest about divisions within the party?

The focus is on the Conservative party because it has arguably shown the deepest divisions of all parliamentary parties over how to effect Brexit. To operationalise the question, I collected data from both the House of Commons (HoC), which is made up of 650 members of parliament (MP) who have been elected by voters in their respective constituencies, and the House of Lords (HoL), which is the upper chamber of British parliament and home to 776 peers and bishops who are either appointed by the Queen, as advised by the Prime Minister, or hold a hereditary position. During the period covered by the data – 12 February to 12 May 2019 – both chambers had a Conservative majority. I chose those three months for data collection because they encompass a crucial vote, and preceding debate, to ask the European Council to extend the original date for leaving the EU (29 March 2019), as well as debates on the withdrawal agreement between the EU and the UK government, and a further extension of the Brexit date.

To gather the data, I searched Hansard, the parliamentary record including transcripts of votes and debates,[10] for debates including the words 'Brexit', 'European Union', 'referendum', and 'withdrawal' in the title. Given the high number of relevant debates, those on specific aspects of Brexit (e.g. energy and environment, campaign expenditure) were disregarded. The search resulted in 14 debates each for the HoC and the HoL. Contributions by Conservative MPs and lords were manually copied and pasted into a plain text document amounting to 277,374 words or tokens overall. With hindsight, I would advise to annotate similar corpora for meta-data, including speaker, date of the debate, and parliamentary chamber when compiling the corpus, in order to avoid having to go back to Hansard later to verify the origin of particular examples (see Chapter 7, this volume, for best practices in doing corpus-assisted discourse analysis).

Parliamentary language is very rich, so it was necessary to further sharpen the focus of what aspect of it I would investigate. Anecdotal evidence suggested that next to emotion lexis and intensification, metaphors of restraint and its opposite, freedom, were prevalent in the language use of MPs and lords, so I decided to focus on how such metaphors were realised and what scenarios they bring about. As my data comprised more than a quarter of a million words, a fully manual analysis was not feasible and I had to consider how to use corpus analysis software to identify metaphor. Given that there is no computer program to date that can reliably extract metaphors from a text in a fully automated fashion, the choice was between two possible semi-automated approaches. The first of those is a purely lexical method that involves drawing up lists of words and other lexical items (e.g. phrasal verbs) that denote the source domain, search the corpus for those items, and analyse their occurrences to see if the items are used metaphorically. While this method has been

88   *Veronika Koller*

used successfully before (e.g. Koller, 2004b), it only helps to find predetermined lexis and risks missing out on other realisations of a particular metaphor. A broader lexical approach is to search for predefined words related to the target domain and analyse concordance lines to see what metaphoric expressions have been used to conceptualise and talk or write about the target domain. However, this method, while potentially capturing more metaphoric expressions, is laborious and time-consuming, and only works for metaphoric expressions that feature target domain lexis (Stefanowitsch, 2008). I therefore chose a third semi-automated approach that combines word searches with semantic annotation (see Demmen et al., 2015, for more detail).

This lexico-semantic method works with the software suite Wmatrix (Rayson, 2008), which includes tools to analyse word frequencies and tag corpora for parts of speech and, importantly, semantic domains. The semantic annotation tool embedded within Wmatrix, called USAS, is based on a manually compiled lexicon in combination with 21 discourse domains, sub-divided into a total of 453 semantic categories. When a new corpus is uploaded and tagged, each lexical unit in that corpus is allocated one or more alpha-numerical semantic tags. For example, the word 'restraint' is classified first as A1.7+ (constraint) and second as E1–/E3+ (unemotional/violence, anger), with the second tag already indicating a metaphoric use of the word, as in 'restraining one's anger'. Once the corpus is fully tagged the analyst can either search for the tag to find all words with that tag or search for a word to see what semantic domain(s) it falls into. All tags and words can also be *concordanced* and compared to a general or purpose-built reference corpus (see Chapter 7, this volume).

To analyse the Brexit debate corpus, I started with anecdotally established words that MPs and peers used to talk about the EU–UK relationship (e.g. 'trapped', 'shackles'). I then established what semantic domains these words belonged to and searched for other words with the same tags. For some domains, the word lists were very long, in which case I selected those words that were most likely to be used as realisations of the conceptual metaphor AFFILIATION WITH THE EU IS RESTRAINT (Figure 5.2).

This step of the analysis resulted in 43-word stems (e.g. *b*nd* comprising 'binding', 'binds', 'bond(s)', 'bondage', 'bound', and 'unbound') across five domains (constraint, lack of constraint, law and order, obligation and necessity, hindering). Figure 5.3 shows the concordance for the word 'trapped', derived from the word stem *trap*.

Concordancing the words related to the word stems showed that some lexical items were not realised in the corpus, some were realised only literally, and some were realised as metaphoric expressions with different target domains, mostly in relation to conflict in parliament or between parliament and government. All told, 15-word stems were used metaphorically in the debates to talk about the relationship between the UK and the EU, totalling 83 instances. Table 5.1 details the results.

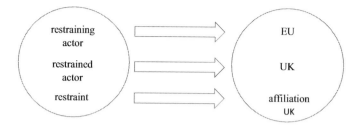

Figure 5.2 The conceptual metaphor AFFILIATION WITH THE EU IS RESTRAINT

15 occurrences.			Extend context
this withdrawal agreement , which seems to be totally	trapped	in negativity and in terms of finding any real solution	1 More | Full
e core concern of colleagues was that we should not be	trapped	indefinitely in the backstop . The Attorney General has	2 More | Full
e would be no risk that this country would find itself	trapped	in the backstop or that we would lose our ? democratic	3 More | Full
ternoon that there is a minimal legal risk of us being	trapped	in the prison of the backstop , because it is now more	4 More | Full
ly , we should care about the real-world risk of being	trapped	in the backstop , but that has been discussed very litt	5 More | Full
y little . What are the actual chances that we will be	trapped	in the backstop , not from a legal point of view but fr	6 More | Full
though we are certain to get into it and certain to be	trapped	. My right hon. Friend is making such a powerful case .	7 More | Full
ould weigh the minuscule risk , as I see it , of being	trapped	in the backstop against the far greater risk of not agr	8 More | Full
oretical , highly unlikely possibility that we will be	trapped	in the backstop really enough to risk Brexit altogether	9 More | Full
l of risks , and against the minimal risk of our being	trapped	in the backstop , which I believe to be minimal because	10 More | Full
r greater risk than the fairly small risk of our being	trapped	in the backstop forever . I appeal to my fellow Brexite	11 More | Full
mocratic threat posed by no Brexit . The fear of being	trapped	in the backstop and of the EU using its leverage in neg	12 More | Full
hip ; otherwise , we will spend the foreseeable future	trapped	in the agony of this interminable debate , which is cor	13 More | Full
nothing , which is nonsense again , or that we remain	trapped	, et cetera . Others have talked idiotically about pena	14 More | Full
on . Secondly , in an attempt to meet your wishes , we	trapped	ourselves in a set of red lines , which rendered our as	15 More | Full

Figure 5.3 Concordance for 'trapped' in the Brexit debate corpus

But how can we decide without a doubt that something is a metaphoric expression? The most systematic and accepted approach to date has been proposed by a group of metaphor scholars calling themselves the Pragglejaz Group (after the first letters of the members' names) and is referred to as the *metaphor identification procedure* (MIP). In a nutshell, the Pragglejaz Group propose the following steps (2007; see Steen et al., 2010, for a further development):

1. Read the whole text
2. Ascertain the lexical units
3. For each lexical unit:

    a. What is its meaning in context?
    b. Does it have a more basic contemporary meaning? ('Basic' can mean either more concrete, related to bodily action, precise, or historically older.)
    c. Does the more basic meaning contrast with the meaning in the text and if so, can the meaning in the text be understood in relation to the more basic meaning?

4. If the answer to b and c is yes, mark as a metaphor. Consult a corpus-based dictionary for ambiguous cases (e.g. the Oxford English Dictionary or the Macmillan English Dictionary).

Table 5.1 The RESTRAINT metaphor in the Brexit debate corpus

word stem	word(s)	example	occurrences
b*nd*	binding, binds, bondage, bonds (noun), bound	[The withdrawal agreement] is a fully binding treaty with no exit clause.	10
block*	block (verb), blocking	It is unthinkable that the EU could impose laws on us … without our having some means of blocking it.	2
escape	escape (noun, verb)	The withdrawal agreement has no escape clause either.	2
free*	free, freedom, freedoms, freely, freer	How do we embrace the opportunities that freedom from the EU will give us?	19
hamstrings	hamstrings (verb)	The backstop … hamstrings negotiations on a trade deal.	1
limit	limit (verb)	[T]he Prime Minister will be involved in negotiations about … any terms that might be sought by the European Council to limit the extent to which we might be able to act in accordance with the result of the referendum.	1
lock*	lock (verb), locked, locking, locks (verb)	[T]his is a bad deal that could lock the UK indefinitely in a backstop for a very long time.	10
prison	imprisonment, prison	[T]here is a minimal legal risk of us being trapped in the prison of the backstop.	4
restrains	restrains	[T]he UK observes single market rules and customs duties and restrains our right to compete for a period of three years.	1
restrictions	restrictions	[T]here would be restrictions on the UK's ability to participate in some EU tools.	1
shackles	shackles (noun)	The people's vision … was that of a strong United Kingdom, holding its head high, free from the shackles of the European Union.	1
stuck	stuck	[W]e can have open and seamless trade without being stuck within the European orbit as a form of satellite state.	2
tangle	disentangle, entangled, entanglement	Once free from our EU entanglement, we will be able to move forward.	3
tie*	ties (verb), tied	[T]he backstop … ties our hands for the future and sets us on a path to a subordinate relationship with the EU.	3
trap	entrapment, trap (verb), trapped	The idea that the EU wishes to trap us in the backstop is simply a wrong analysis.	22

This may seem like a cumbersome method to establish the metaphoricity or otherwise of a lexical item, but regular practice speeds up the process considerably and for an experienced analyst, it is usually only necessary to check ambiguous cases. This is what I did with the concordance lines derived from the word searches.

Going back to Table 5.1, the results show three main trends in the data: first, the RESTRAINT metaphor is mostly used to construct a scenario in which the EU restricts the UK's freedom. This is closely linked to a perceived lack of power for the UK, as illustrated in metaphoric expressions such as 'satellite state' and 'vassalage', which can be found next to non-metaphoric lexis such as 'subjugation' or 'subordinate'. This scenario is inherently negative and avoiding it is therefore seen as desirable. Reversed scenarios consequently either involve the UK as a self-confident actor ('head held high') who can 'move forward' and has 'opportunities', or cast the UK as restricting the EU:

(6) It is unthinkable that the EU could impose laws on us ... without our having some means of blocking it.

Second, this dominant scenario is only occasionally questioned by an alternative one in which the UK 'break[ing] bonds with our nearest neighbours' is seen as undesirable, as it would mean that the country denies itself access to perceived benefits of EU membership ('restrictions on the UK's ability to participate in some EU tools'). The third trend involves quoting metaphoric expressions from the dominant scenario and explicitly criticising them:

(7) [F]rom certain MPs ... who should know better come statements that the withdrawal agreement <u>binds</u> us permanently into subjugation.

However, quoting a certain use of language to criticise it runs the risk of reinforcing what one wishes to counter and can therefore defeat the speaker's purpose. In the ideological struggle conveyed in parliamentary Brexit debates, the better option may be to introduce a different metaphor altogether. One way to reframe the Brexit process would be to talk about it as a productive project, e.g. growing a plant or creating a work of art.

The case study in this section has illustrated how corpus linguistic methods can be employed in combination with manual analysis of text extracts to make empirically founded claims about the variation, scope, and function of metaphor in discourse. The remainder of this chapter will comment on how to present the findings of such an analysis and close by pointing out some problems with analysing metaphor in discourse.

Presenting findings and results

You will have noticed that throughout this chapter, I have employed certain typographic conventions. These are specific to linguistic work on metaphor and involve underlining or italicising metaphoric expressions (e.g. 'the journey ... will be complex and perilous') and using small capitals for conceptual domains (e.g. JOURNEY) and metaphors (e.g. LEAVING THE EU IS A JOURNEY). In addition, the corpus linguistic methods used in the case study call for features such as asterisks to indicate wildcards in word stems (e.g. tie*) and quotation marks for lexical items (e.g. 'tied'). More generally, it is advisable to quote sufficient co-text along with a metaphoric expression, to show that the lexical item is indeed used metaphorically and because metaphoric expressions from the same or conceptually different source domains often form clusters, as in the following example from the case study:

(8) Once free from our EU entanglement, we will be able to move forward.

Finally, while metaphor scenarios are perhaps best described in prose, mappings of semantic features from source to target, and conceptual links between metaphors, are often represented in abstract diagrams to aid explanation (such as Figure 5.2). Another way of showing results is with the help of tables, which make it possible to organise metaphoric expressions by word stem or word (as in Table 5.1) and conceptual metaphors by source and/or target domain. Wherever quantitative findings are given, these can be in absolute numbers as long as they refer to only one corpus or text, but where two data sets of different sizes are compared, numbers need to be either expressed as a percentage or be normalised per e.g. 1000 words.

Issues and limitations

As can be expected in a chapter on analysing metaphor in discourse, I have mostly focused on metaphoric expressions in text, i.e. on linguistic metaphor. However, the assumption is that metaphor in text is an expression of metaphor at the cognitive level and can ultimately be related back to it. Yet there is currently no agreed method for how to systematically derive conceptual metaphor, although suggestions have been put forward (Steen, 1999). As a result, there is a real risk for the analyst to rely too much on intuition and over- or under-interpret metaphoric expressions. Attributing particular source domains to lexical items therefore needs to be argued for and supported by textual evidenced. Likewise, caution should be taken not to over-interpret the entailments of metaphors: they may be there for analysts looking for them but are not necessarily there for lay readers (see O'Halloran, 2005:

Analysing metaphor in discourse 93

347). Lastly, metaphoric expressions can become conventionalised to the point where the source domain is unlikely to be activated in the reader or hearer who encounters them. In relation to the case study presented above, for example, the words 'leave', 'remain', and 'backstop' in Brexit discourse may no longer be perceived nor processed as metaphors, although they are figurative ways of referring to complex political processes. To put it metaphorically, those metaphoric expressions may not be dead yet, but they are certainly moribund (Alm-Arvius, 2006).

One other issue is analysing metaphor in languages other than the ever-dominant English. While there is no shortage of individual studies of metaphor in other languages, these are often comparisons with findings from English. It is only recently that the identification of linguistic metaphor in other languages has attracted scholarly attention (Nacey et al., 2019), but practical problems remain: how, for example, can metaphoricity be checked in ambiguous cases when there is no corpus-based dictionary for a language? In addition, if the analyst chooses the lexico-semantic corpus approach presented in this chapter they will find that many languages do not come with semantic annotation software. Clearly, it is imperative that more tools and resources are developed to assist metaphor researchers.

However, such issues and limitations should and indeed do not curb the analysis of metaphor in discourse. Critical metaphor analysis applying conceptual metaphor theory is a powerful way of understanding the realisation of metaphor in language and uncovering ideology in discourse, especially when aided by corpus linguistic methods to show how pervasive a metaphor is in discourse or when supported by experimental methods (see Chapter 10, this volume; Hart, 2018), which can help demonstrate empirically the ideological and persuasive power of metaphor.

Further reading

Seminal works inaugurating critical metaphor analysis include Charteris-Black (2004), Koller (2004b) and Musolff (2004). An overview of recent developments in corpus approaches to metaphor analysis can be found in Semino (2017). Lynne Cameron and colleagues developed an approach to analysing what they called systematic metaphor in dialogic spoken discourse. One good source to become familiar with their framework is Cameron et al. (2009). Throughout this chapter, I could only touch on visual and multimodal metaphor, the analysis of which comes with its own difficulties: for example, there are no automatic methods available, and researchers rely on a higher degree of subjectivity in establishing metaphoricity and in assigning particular source domains. Forceville

94 Veronika Koller

(2009) provides an overview of this area. More on this can also be found in Chapter 8, this volume.

Notes

1 'Transfer' is a direct translation into Latin of the Greek μεταφέρειν.
2 It should not come as a surprise that metaphor as a phenomenon is conceptualised differently in other languages. For example, the Arabic term إستعارة (isti'āra) means 'borrowing', with Al-Jurjani, an eleventh-century writer of the classical period, defining metaphor as 'claiming the meaning of a name [for another]' (Al-Jurjani, n.d: 335). Meanwhile, the Chinese characters making up the word for metaphor, 隐喻 (yǐnyù), mean 'hidden' and 'illustrate', indicating that metaphor is seen as bringing otherwise covert meanings to the fore.
3 Another frequently quoted example from Lakoff and Johnson (1980), LOVE IS A JOURNEY, is in fact a misnomer, because their examples concern intimate relationships rather than love as an emotion.
4 Examples taken from https://bothsidesofthetable.com/my-commencement-speech-life-at-your-crossroads-f30cb8ca2663 and https://ageuk.org.uk/information-advice/health-wellbeing/relationships-family/end-of-life-issues/, respectively.
5 It should be noted that forward movement as typical and circular movement as less than ideal – note the negative associations of 'going round in circles' – is very much a Western idea. Cultures that include a belief in reincarnation may conceive of life as a cyclical journey.
6 https://ikea.com/gb/en/ikea-family/
7 As a theory, primary metaphor was anticipated as early as 1920, in the psychophysical parallelism posited as a central element of gestalt psychology (Wertheimer, 1920).
8 Of course, the marriage scenario is subject to considerable cultural and historic variation: just like the number and gender of actors can vary, the idea of marriage as involving a romantic relationship rather than being a sexual, economic, and sometimes dynastic contract is relatively recent. In terms of metaphor, it should also be noted that MARRIAGE can feature both as a target domain structured by, for example, a JOURNEY source domain and as a source domain itself structuring, for example, international relations.
9 https://economist.com/leaders/2016/10/08/the-road-to-brexit
10 https://hansard.parliament.uk/

References

Al-Jurjani, A. (n.d.): البلاغة الاسرار (The Secrets of Eloquence). Available at https://dl.wdl.org/12946/service/12946.pdf, accessed 31 July 2019.
Alm-Arvius, C. (2006). Live, moribund, and dead metaphors. Nordic Journal of English Studies, 5(1), 7–14.
Ansah, G.N. (2011). Culture in embodiment: Evidence from conceptual metaphors/metonymies of ANGER in Akan and English. International Journal of Cognitive Linguistics, 2 (1), 62–82.
Aristotle (ca. 350 BC a). Poetics. Translated by S. H. Butcher. Available at http://classics.mit.edu/Aristotle/poetics.html, accessed 31 July 2019.
Aristotle (ca. 350 BC b). Rhetoric. Book III. Translated by W. Rhys Roberts. Available at http://classics.mit.edu/Aristotle/rhetoric.html, accessed 31 July 2019.
Cameron, L. (2003). Metaphor in educational discourse. London: Continuum.

Cameron, L., Maslen, R., Todd, Z., Maule, J., Stratton, P. and Stanley, N. (2009). The discourse dynamics approach to metaphor and metaphor-led discourse analysis. *Metaphor and Symbol, 24*(2), 63–89.

Charteris-Black, J. (2004). *Corpus approaches to critical metaphor analysis.* Basingstoke: Palgrave.

Chilton, P.A. (1996). *Security metaphors: Cold war discourse from containment to common house.* Bern: Peter Lang.

Deignan, A., Littlemore, J. and Semino, E. (2013). *Figurative language, genre and register.* Cambridge: Cambridge University Press.

Demmen, J., Semino, E., Demjén, Z., Koller, V., Hardie, A., Rayson, P. and Payne, S. (2015). A computer-assisted study of the use of violence metaphors for cancer and end of life by patients, family carers and health professionals. *International Journal of Corpus Linguistics, 20*(2), 205–231.

Fairclough, N. (1995). *Media discourse.* London: Bloomsbury.

Fauconnier, G. and Turner, M. (2002). *The way we think: Conceptual blending and the mind's hidden complexities.* New York: Basic Books.

Forceville, C. (2009). Non-verbal and multimodal metaphor in a cognitivist framework: Agendas for research. In C. Forceville and E. Urios-Aparisi (Eds.), *Multimodal metaphor.* (pp. 19–42). Berlin: de Gruyter.

Gibbs, R.W. (Ed.) (2008). *The Cambridge handbook of metaphor and thought.* New York: Cambridge University Press.

Grady, J. (1997). *Foundations of meaning: Primary metaphors and primary scenes.* PhD thesis, University of California Berkeley. Available at https://escholarship.org/uc/item/3g9427m2, accessed 4 August 2019.

Handl, S. and Schmid, H-J. (Eds.) (2011). *Windows to the mind: Metaphor, metonymy and conceptual blending.* Berlin: de Gruyter.

Hart, C. (2018). 'Riots engulfed the city': An experimental study investigating the legitimating effects of fire metaphors in discourses of disorder. *Discourse & Society, 29*(3), 279–298.

Jäkel, O. (2002). Hypotheses revisited: The cognitive theory of metaphor applied to religious texts. *Metaphorik.de, 2,* 20–42.

Koller, V. (2003). *Metaphor clusters in business media discourse: A social cognition approach.* PhD thesis, University of Vienna. Available at http://citeseerx.ist.psu.edu/viewdoc/download?doi=10.1.1.86.8386&rep=rep1&type=pdf, accessed 2 August 2019.

Koller, V. (2004a). Businesswomen and war metaphors: 'Possessive, jealous and pugnacious'? *Journal of Sociolinguistics, 8*(1), 3–22.

Koller, V. (2004b). *Metaphor and gender in business media discourse: A critical cognitive study.* Basingstoke: Palgrave.

Koller, V. (2014). Cognitive linguistics and ideology. In J. Littlemore and J.R. Taylor (Eds.), *The Bloomsbury companion to cognitive linguistics.* (pp. 234–252). London: Bloomsbury.

Koller, V. and Ryan, J. (2019). 'A nation divided': Metaphors and scenarios in the media coverage of the 2016 British EU referendum. In C. Hart (Ed.), *Cognitive linguistic approaches to text and discourse: From poetics to politics.* (pp. 131–156). Edinburgh: Edinburgh University Press.

Kövecses, Z. (2000). *Metaphor and emotion: Language, culture, and body in human feeling.* Cambridge: Cambridge University Press.

Kövecses, Z. (2017). Levels of metaphor. *Cognitive Linguistics, 28*(2), 321–347.

96 *Veronika Koller*

Lakoff, G. and Johnson, M. (1980). *Metaphors we live by*. Chicago: University of Chicago Press.

Musolff, A. (2004). *Metaphor and political discourse: Analogical reasoning in debates about Europe*. Basingstoke: Palgrave.

Nacey, S., Dorst, A.G., Krennmayr, T. and Reijnierse, W.G. (2019). *Metaphor identification in multiple languages: MIPVU around the world*. Amsterdam: John Benjamins.

O'Halloran, K. (2005). Causal cognition and socio-cognition in critical discourse analysis: A reply to Rick Iedema. *Linguistics and Education, 16*(3), 338–348.

Pragglejaz Group (2007). MIP: A method for identifying metaphorically used words in discourse. *Metaphor and Symbol, 22*(1), 1–39.

Rayson, P. (2008). From key words to key semantic domains. *International Journal of Corpus Linguistics, 13*(4), 519–549.

Ritchie, D. (2013). *Metaphor*. Cambridge: Cambridge University Press.

Semino, E. (2017). Corpus linguistics and metaphor. In B. Dancygier (Ed.), *The Cambridge handbook of cognitive linguistics*. (pp. 463–476). Cambridge: Cambridge University Press.

Semino, E. and Z. Demjén (Eds.) (2016). *The Routledge handbook of metaphor and language*. London: Routledge.

Semino, E., Demjén, Z. and Demmen, J. (2016). An integrated approach to metaphor and framing in cognition, discourse, and practice, with an application to metaphors for cancer. *Applied Linguistics, 39*(5), 625–645.

Steen, G. (1999). From linguistic to conceptual metaphor in five steps. In R.W. Gibbs and G. Steen (Eds.), *Metaphor in cognitive linguistics*. (pp. 57–77). Amsterdam: John Benjamins.

Steen, G.J., Dorst, A.G., Hermann, B.J., Kaal, A.A., Krennmayr, and Pasma, T. (2010). *A method for linguistic metaphor identification*. Amsterdam: John Benjamins.

Stefanowitsch, A. (2008). Words and their metaphors: A corpus-based approach. In A. Stefanowitsch and S. Th. Gries (Eds.), *Corpus-based approaches to metaphor and metonymy*. (pp. 63–105). Berlin: de Gruyter.

Wertheimer, M. (1920). *Über schlussprozesse im produktiven denken*. Berlin: de Gruyter.

Yu, N. (1995). Metaphorical expressions of anger and happiness in English and Chinese. *Metaphor and Symbol, 10*(2), 59–92.

6 Cognitive linguistic critical discourse analysis

Christopher Hart

Introduction

This chapter introduces a form of discourse analysis based in cognitive linguistics. Cognitive linguistics emerged in the late twentieth century as a radical revision of linguistic theory placing meaning, usage, and experientialism at the heart of its analyses. Although it developed primarily to account for 'traditional' rank levels of linguistic structure (phonological, lexical, and morphosyntactic), the focus found in cognitive linguistics on meaning in usage events makes it a particularly congenial framework to work with in various areas of discourse analysis – from poetics to politics. The research referred to in this chapter deals with discourses that can be characterised as political rather than literary. The studies described also all adopt a *critical* stance toward the data being analysed. They thus fall within a sub-branch of critical discourse analysis (CDA) known as cognitive linguistic critical discourse analysis (CL-CDA) (for studies of more literary forms of discourse based in cognitive linguistics, which fall under the banner of cognitive poetics or cognitive stylistics, see Further reading, below).

In many approaches to discourse analysis, the primary object of analysis is the text itself – its linguistic make-up as well as the social, historical, or interactional contexts of which it is a part. In cognitive approaches, however, the focus shifts away from the linguistic structures of a text per se to the conceptual structures that a text evokes in the minds of readers to constitute their understanding and experience of the situations or events described within it. The aim of CL-CDA is then to interpret the potential ideological effects of the conceptualisations evoked in the course of discourse. Where CDA is sometimes criticised for not taking cognition or the reader into account, and for being too ad hoc in its analyses, a major motivation behind the development of CL-CDA has been to address the impact of language choices on reader's cognition in a way that is systematic and psychologically plausible, informed by a model of language based in general cognitive principles. In the following section, I describe the general aims and commitments of CL-CDA in more detail.

98 *Christopher Hart*

Outline of approach

CL-CDA inherits from cognitive linguistics a number of key epistemological commitments or theoretical assumptions about language (see Croft and Cruse, 2004). These include: (i) that language is not an autonomous cognitive faculty; (ii) that language is linked to experience; and (iii) that language is usage-based. These positions place cognitive linguistics at odds with other approaches to language which prevailed throughout the twentieth century. For example, to say that language is not an autonomous cognitive faculty runs counter to the claims of Chomsky's generative grammar. According to cognitive linguistics, there is no single module of the mind responsible for language. Rather, language is distributed in cognition, adhering to the same general principles and making use of the same cognitive processes that govern and function in other areas of cognition like memory, reason, and perception. To say that language is linked to experience similarly goes against generative grammar as well as truth-conditional and structuralist semantics. According to cognitive linguistics, language is linked to experience in two ways. First, language is *grounded* in experience with the meanings attached to words, phrases, and grammatical structures being derived from the kinds of experiences we have of our bodies and our interaction with the physical environment as well as the kinds of experiences we have as members of a given culture. Second, language *encodes* experience. The meaning of a word or sentence cannot be reduced to a list of semantic features or truth conditions which must be satisfied in order for the linguistic formulation to correctly apply. Rather, the meaning of a word or sentence lies in the dynamic mental representation and encyclopaedic knowledge structures that it conjures. To say that language is usage-based is to say that conventional patterns of linguistic representation are not licensed by an abstract set of innately specified rules, as per generative grammar, but *emerge* to fulfil the communicative needs of speakers and then become stabilised within a given speech community.

These fundamental positions give rise to a number of important corollaries. For example, one upshot is that what constitutes linguistic knowledge is not particular to language. Linguistic knowledge and processes of meaning construction in discourse are not significantly different from, and can therefore be characterised in the same terms as, structures and processes in other areas of cognition like memory and perception. This means that linguistic knowledge is essentially conceptual structure and that meaning in discourse is achieved via processes of conceptualisation. It also means that cognitive linguistics makes frequent appeal to models in cognitive psychology, including models of memory, perception, attention, and categorisation, to help shed light on the mechanisms involved in language and discourse.

Another upshot is that there is no real basis on which to distinguish between different types of linguistic knowledge. Words and grammatical structures, for example, are both stored as discrete units coupled with abstract conceptual knowledge structures. They are distinguished only by the degree of abstractness in the conceptual structures they index. From this perspective, grammatical forms are in and of themselves meaningful by virtue of the conceptual structures they conventionally evoke. Similarly, the distinction between literal and figurative language breaks down as metaphorical expressions also index abstract conceptual knowledge structures in the form of conceptual metaphors.

At this point, you may be asking what does all this have to do with discourse analysis. Well, a third and crucial upshot for purposes of CDA is that the linguistic choices presented by a text encode a particular *construal* of the target scene.[1] Language, in other words, enables alternative conceptions of the same (type of) social situation or event to be promoted. From a critical standpoint, particular conceptions may be seen as motivated by and as serving to maintain specific ideologies or worldviews which, in turn, legitimate social actions that may be discriminatory or otherwise difficult to justify. The aim of CL-CDA is then to delineate the conceptual parameters along which ideology and the legitimation of social action are enacted in particular discursive contexts. Here, a number of *construal operations* are identified as relevant. These are presented in Table 6.1 in relation to the discursive strategies they realise on the one hand and the general cognitive systems on which they rely on the other.[2] Any project in CL-CDA will typically investigate one or more of these discursive strategies in discourse data relating to a particular social topic, group or event.

In *structural configuration* strategies, the basic structural properties of a situation or event are defined. This strategy is realised through the construal operation of *schematisation*, whereby a particular *image schema* is selected as a model representing the target scene. Image schemas are abstract conceptual structures which represent recurrent patterns of embodied experience. They develop pre-linguistically but come to form the meaningful basis of linguistic units. When indexed by linguistic units in discourse, including grammatical units, image schemas constitute our most basic understanding of the situation or event being described. Since image schemas represent complex scenes as holistic patterns of experience, this construal operation is treated as a manifestation of Gestalt principles of psychology. In CL-CDA, structural configuration strategies are examined in Hart's (2011a) study of force-dynamic representations in immigration discourse and in Hart's (2013a, 2013b) studies analysing conceptualisations of violence in press reports of political protests.

100 *Christopher Hart*

Table 6.1 Construal operations

Strategy \ System		Gestalt	Comparison	Attention	Perspective
Structural Configuration		Schematisation			
Framing			Categorisation		
			Metaphor		
Identification				Figure/Ground	
				Windowing	
				Metonymy	
Positioning					Point of View
					Deixis

In *framing* strategies, the basic conceptualisation defined through structural configuration is fleshed out with richer, more specific information derived from *frames*. Frames are encyclopaedic knowledge structures representing areas of cultural experience. In discourse, they are accessed by lexical items to further shape our understanding of the target scene. Frames provide a structured lens through which the target situation or event is seen and evaluated. Framing is realised through construal operations of *categorisation* and *metaphor*, both of which are examples of a more general cognitive ability to compare areas of experience. In CL-CDA, framing has been looked at most extensively in relation to metaphor. Indeed, cognitive research into metaphor as part of CDA has proved so revealing and been so widely taken up that it is generally treated as a form of CDA in its own right under the title of critical metaphor analysis (see Chapter 5, this volume). Here, framing, as performed by metaphor, has been explored in a plethora of contexts, including discourses of immigration (Charteris-Black, 2006; Hart, 2010; Santa Ana, 2002), national and supranational identity (Chilton and Ilyin, 1993; Musolff, 2004, 2010), war and national security (Chilton, 1996), domestic social and economic policy (Hart, 2014), business mergers and acquisitions (Koller, 2005), and industrial disputes (Hart, 2017).

Identification strategies concern which aspects of a given situation or event are selected for conceptual representation and to what degree of salience those aspects are represented relative to one another. Identification strategies thus have to do with inclusion/exclusion and foregrounding/ backgrounding. They are realised by a group of construal operations which reflect a general ability to distribute attention over a scene in different ways. These include *figure/ground segregation* and *windowing*. Identification

Cognitive linguistic CDA   101

has not been the main focus of any study but is addressed in the context of immigration discourse and discourse on political protests by Hart (2011b) and Hart (2013b), respectively.

Finally, *positioning* strategies exploit our ability to assume a different perspective on any given scene. Realised in the construal operations of *viewpoint* and *deixis*, positioning strategies concern where we situate ourselves in terms of space, time, and evaluation, and where we locate the actors, actions, and events referred to in a text relative to that position. Positioning strategies have been described in most detail in studies of discourses seeking justification for military intervention (Cap, 2006, 2008; Chilton, 2004).

We will return to Table 6.1 below, where we will see how to go about analysing discourse data within a cognitive linguistics framework.

Identifying research questions

In CDA, cognitive linguistics provides a kind of explanatory framework (Jeffries, 2010: 128) where the questions it answers are typically of the 'how' and 'what' kind. For example, at a superordinate level, CL-CDA helps to address questions such as 'how does language exert ideological influence?' or 'what are the cognitive mechanisms by which textual influence occurs?' Any project in CL-CDA will contribute something to the general picture being built in response to these questions. However, these are not at a level that can be directly addressed in a single piece of research. Research questions for a particular project need to be more targeted, focused on a particular feature of language or conceptualisation in a specific discursive context. The first question you should be asking yourself, then, is 'what am I analysing?' Again, this is not a research question. But addressing it will help to define the topic and scope of your project. The starting point here should always be some observed phenomenon in attested discourse practice. This might be, for example, the over-use or new coinage of a particular word, as in Lederer's (2013) study of the term 'anchor baby' in US anti-immigration discourse, the use of a particular set of metaphors, as in Koller's (2005) analysis of metaphors of evolutionary struggle in business media discourse on mergers and acquisitions, or the preference for a particular type of grammatical construction, as in Hart's (2013b) study of transitive versus reciprocal verbs in press reports of violence at political protests.

The precise topic and scope of your project may be determined by something you yourself have noticed in the discourses surrounding you which you consider worth probing further or it may be determined by a previous study whose findings point to a particular linguistic formulation as a salient feature of a given discourse but which does not analyse that formulation within a cognitive linguistics framework. In either case, some evidence should be supplied, in the form of examples and/or results from

102 *Christopher Hart*

quantitative distributional studies (see Chapter 7, this volume), that the linguistic phenomenon whose conceptual reflexes you are investigating is a real and notable feature of the discourse(s) in question.

Once you have defined the topic and scope of your project, you are ready to set out your research questions proper. Your research questions should be guided by the overarching aims of CL-CDA and asked in relation to the specific linguistic or conceptual feature you have selected for analysis. Your primary research questions will therefore look something like the following:

1. How is X construed in discourse Y?
   where X is a social group, situation or event-type and Y is a topic or genre of discourse and
2. What are the ideological implications of the construals involved?

In order to address questions (1) and (2) you may want to pose slightly more refined sub-questions, such as:

1a. What are the conceptual structures and processes associated with the linguistic form(s) Z?
2a. What are the potential ideological and legitimating functions of the conceptualisations evoked by linguistic form(s) Z in discourse Y?

Often the subjective construal encoded by a linguistic formulation only becomes apparent when contrasted with an alternative formulation. CL-CDA therefore lends itself especially well to comparative analysis, which may be qualitative or quantitative. Comparative analyses can be conducted over alternative attested practices in different data sets. An example of this is found in Hart (2013b) who looked at competing conceptualisations of violence at political protests as articulated by *The Guardian* compared to *The Telegraph*. Hart found that *The Telegraph* preferred to describe violent interactions between police and protesters using a transitive verb (e.g. *attack*) with protesters as the sole agent while *The Guardian* preferred to describe the same encounters using a reciprocal verb (e.g. *clash with*). The two competing formulations encode a one-sided versus a two-sided conceptualisation of the violence respectively and thus serve to distribute blame and responsibility in different ways. This is probably the most prototypical form of comparative analysis. In some cases, however, a linguistic formulation may be so conventionalised that you do not find alternative examples. In this case, you might want to compare your attested formulations with alternative *available* formulations which are not realised anywhere. This approach is often taken in studies of metaphor where analysts highlight differences in the conceptualisations evoked by dominant metaphors compared to other possible but suppressed metaphors. A good example of this is found in Koller (2005) who discusses the merits of dance and conversation metaphors as alternative models to metaphors of evolutionary struggle in conceptualising business mergers and acquisitions.

When comparative analysis is conducted over real-life instances of discourse, it can be along different dimensions. For example, you might compare *across* text-producers, as in Hart's (2013b) study mentioned above, where the aim is to highlight the ideological worldviews promoted by different text-producers. Or, alternatively, you might compare *within* text-producers and *across* some other dimension such as time. A particularly neat example of this is seen in Cap's (2006) study of 'proximisation' in official discourses of the US administration seeking justification for military intervention in Iraq. Cap compared texts produced before and after it was discovered that Saddam Hussein was not in possession of weapons of mass destruction (WMD). He found that the initial premises for intervention in Iraq relied on a deictic construal in which a physical threat (i.e. that resulting from the deployment of WMD) moves toward and impacts on the conceptualiser's location in space. Following the failure of weapons inspectors to find any evidence of WMD, however, legitimation efforts shifted to rely on a deictic construal involving an abstract ideological 'threat' to the belief and value systems of the conceptualiser.

Any comparative dimension that features in your analysis should also be built into your research questions. Thus, secondary research questions might look something like:

3. What alternative conceptualisations of X are evoked in different dis-courses Y?
4. How do conceptualisations of X vary according to dimension U?

The research questions addressed in the case study for this chapter are:

1. How is motion construed in media discourses of migration?
2. What are the ideological implications of different construals?

Data collection and ethics

Unlike some other forms of discourse analysis, such as those based in ethnography or corpus linguistics (see Chapters 2 and 7, this volume, respectively), CL-CDA is not associated with any particular type of data or method of data collection. It is fair to say, however, that CL-CDA has tended to work with texts that at least present themselves as monologic rather than texts which are manifestly dialogic produced in more interactional communicative settings. This includes texts such as newspaper reports, political speeches, legal and policy documents, mission statements, blog posts, and websites.

104 *Christopher Hart*

In most cases, textual material is gathered from online sources. In the case of news reports, for example, this may come from newspapers' own digital archives or from online databases such as Nexis (www.nexis.com). Nexis gathers the contents of major national newspapers as well as some local publications in one place and is updated daily. It has an interface that allows researchers to easily locate and download articles containing certain search words or phrases, published by particular newspapers within a specified time period. Nexis requires an institutional subscription but most universities will hold one of these. Likewise, access to newspapers' own online content is often limited if not completely paywalled. Again, though, most universities have some kind of access deal with those major national newspapers who paywall their content. In the case of party-political discourse, major political speeches, press releases, and election manifestos are often available via parties' own websites.[3] Alternatively, online databases compiling speeches from across political parties can be found. For example, British Political Speech (www.britishpoliticalspeech. org) holds texts of speeches given by Conservative, Labour, and Liberal/ Liberal Democrat Party leaders dating back to 1895.

In some cases, it may not be possible to obtain the desired data from online sources. For example, Nexis holds English language news only as far back as 1988 with content becoming increasingly patchy the further back you go.[4]

Depending on your data collection method, as well as the research goals of your project, you may choose to work with smaller or larger numbers of texts and analyse them qualitatively and/or quantitatively (perhaps with the assistance of corpus linguistic techniques if analysing particularly large numbers of texts). What you must remember, here, is that decisions about data size go hand in hand with the scope of your project. For example, Hart (2013b) analysed just four texts, comparing two produced by *The Guardian* with two, reporting on the same events, produced by *The Telegraph*. Such small amounts of data enable qualitative analyses across a range of linguistic and conceptual phenomena. Alternatively, however, you may want to work with a much larger collection of texts to explore in a quantitatively meaningful way the extent to which a particular pattern of representation is constitutive of, or how it is distributed within, a given discourse. This is the strategy pursued in some CL-CDA research into metaphor (e.g. Koller, 2004). Working with larger collections of texts will normally mean restricting your analyses to a single linguistic or conceptual phenomenon but it also means that you can investigate that particular phenomenon in a way that allows more reliable conclusions concerning its frequency and distribution. Another entirely different approach to data, which is often taken in CL-CDA, is to identify or collect yourself a reasonably large corpus of texts and treat this collection as a repository of examples which can be used to identify and illustrate the range of conceptual parameters along which ideology may be enacted in a given

Cognitive linguistic CDA 105

discourse. This is the strategy followed, for example, in Hart (2010) and which is followed in the case study for this chapter. The data for this chapter is gathered from four online news sources: *Mail Online*, *Telegraph. co.uk*, *Mirror.co.uk*, and *Express Online*. Nexis was used to retrieve all articles published by these newspapers that contained the words *immigrant(s)*, *migrant(s)*, *asylum seeker(s)*, or *refugee(s)* in the headline in a yearlong period leading up to the Brexit referendum on 23 June 2016. This search resulted in a bank of 8865 texts.

Whenever you conduct any kind of research project involving data, some consideration must be given to ethics if only to safely conclude that the ethics requirements of your university do not apply to your project. In CL-CDA, ethics is not normally a major issue. When collecting texts from public-facing organisations like newspapers, political parties, multinational corporations etc. most universities are unlikely to require any kind of ethics approval for your project. Examples when ethics requirements are more likely to apply include: working with discourse data that is produced by individuals who are not obviously considered public figures or which is not produced in an individual's capacity as a public figure; working with discourse data that is of a sensitive nature which has the potential to cause offence to yourself or others; working with discourse data that has the potential to place you in any difficult or dangerous situation; working with discourse data which to collect involves any kind of contact with other individuals or groups of people. For the case study presented in this chapter, there was no requirement to obtain ethics approval.

Analysing and interpreting data

Analysing and interpreting data in CL-CDA is at least a two-stage process addressing your two primary research questions. In the first stage, analysts look to establish the 'semantic base' of the linguistic formulation(s) under investigation. That is, analysts want to establish the conceptualisations evoked by specific language usages. At the second stage, analysts critically interpret the potential ideological or legitimating functions of those conceptualisations within their wider discursive context. Note that this distinctly sequential approach applies to the research process and not necessarily to the way you will present your analyses, which may integrate description and interpretation.

In the first stage, analysis is conducted with reference to particular frameworks in cognitive linguistics. Cognitive linguistics is not a single framework, then, but a paradigm made up of several frameworks addressing different aspects of language from a common perspective. Major frameworks include cognitive grammar (Langacker, 1987, 1991, 2002, 2008), conceptual semantics (Talmy, 2000), frame semantics (Fillmore, 1982, 1985) and conceptual metaphor theory (Lakoff and Johnson, 1980, 1999). Which framework you work with will depend on the linguistic and conceptual phenomena you have identified as interesting for the purposes of your study. And, of course, you may want to consult with more than one framework in the course of your analysis.

Depending on the goals of your project and the amount of data you have you may want to code and organise your data, as a form of preparatory analysis, according to the semantic distinctions made within your chosen framework. For example, if studying schematisation, you might want to code target situations for different types of image schema. In my study of British newspaper reports of political protests (Hart, 2013a), which used elements of both cognitive grammar and conceptual semantics to look at the way six national newspapers construed violent encounters between police and protesters at two major student demonstrations against rises in tuition fees, I identified, across 12 texts, all of the linguistic formulations that referred to a physical interaction between police and protesters. I then coded the resulting data according to whether the encounter was construed in terms of an action schema (e.g. *attacked*), a force schema (e.g. *held back*) or a motion schema (e.g. *moved in*). Different types of action, force, and motion schema were also coded for. Similarly, if studying metaphor, you may want to identify and code all the different source frames that are applied to a given target frame. Unfortunately, there are no automatic annotation programmes that can easily handle the type of semantic distinctions typically made in cognitive linguistics. If you are working with larger quantities of data that require coding, you will therefore need a manual annotation software such as ATLAS.ti (www.atlasti.com) or eMargin (www.emargin.bcu.ac.uk). Manually extracted data, as in the study just reported, can also be entered into an Excel document and coded there.

At the second stage, analysts rely on their own intuitions and critical thinking to evaluate the potential ideological and legitimating functions of the conceptualisations identified at stage one. To be critical here means to go beyond the standard 'scientific' task of describing and explaining data in as objective terms as possible to engaging with the data as a socially concerned citizen and consider, from a particular normative or ethical standpoint, its role in bringing about social injustices and inequalities. It is at this stage that construal operations are linked to ideological discursive strategies. Although this stage of analysis is necessarily subjective, reflective of a particular stance, it is important that the analysis remains evidence-based. One form of evidence for the analysis at stage two is that it follows logically and convincingly from an analysis at stage one that applies your chosen CL framework systematically and faithfully. Frameworks developed in linguistics to account for properties of language in general, outside of any particular context, carry with them a prior form of validity. Therefore, following a model of language, whether it is one based in systemic functional linguistics (see Chapter 4, this volume) or cognitive linguistics, in a way that is consistent and transparent, provides at the very least a solid basis for more interpretive claims arising from its application.

Above, we introduced a taxonomy of conceptual or 'construal' operations, presenting them in relation to the type of discursive strategy that they realise and the general cognitive systems on which they rely. Drawing on relevant frameworks in cognitive linguistics, then, studies in CL-CDA target one or more of these construal operations to account for different aspects or levels of meaning construction in response to texts. In the case study for this chapter, I focus on *structural configuration*, *identification*, and *positioning* strategies (see Chapter 5, this volume, for discussion of *framing strategies* realised in metaphor). Since immigration involves, most fundamentally, the movement of people from one place to another, an appropriate starting point for our analysis is the extensive body of typological work in cognitive linguistics describing the semantic domain of motion (e.g. Pourcel, 2010; Slobin, 2004; Talmy, 1985, 2000).[5]

Structural configuration

The default motion event in immigration discourse

For Talmy (1985, 2000), a motion event, as it is represented conceptually, is a pattern made up of at least four constituent elements: (i) a FIGURE, namely the entity or object that undergoes motion; (ii) MOTION[6] itself; (iii) a PATH along which the motion takes place, which is in turn divided into three elements or regions: SOURCE (initial), TRAJECTORY (medial), and GOAL (final); and (iv) a GROUND, i.e. a location or landmark, representing one of the three path elements, with respect to which the motion of the FIGURE is characterised.[7]

In addition to these 'core' or obligatory components, Talmy identifies two further elements that may receive representation: the MANNER and/or the CAUSE of the motion. These elements are *semantic* elements which get expressed in linguistic or 'surface' elements like nouns, verbs, prepositions, adverbs, and adverbial phrases. Importantly, this relationship is not one-to-one. A single surface element may express a combination of semantic elements or, conversely, a single semantic element may get expressed across a combination of surface elements. This can also differ across languages. For example, some languages, such as English, tend to express MOTION and MANNER together and PATH separately while other languages, such as Spanish, tend to express MOTION and PATH together and MANNER separately. One example in English where MOTION and PATH are conflated but MANNER is not specified is in the verb 'enter' as in (1).

(1) [Immigrants FIGURE] [have entered MOTION + PATH] [Europe GROUND]

The image schema evoked by (1) can be represented as in Figure 6.1. The FIGURE (F, immigrants) moves along a PATH (denoted by the arrow) to become located inside the GROUND (G, Europe). In this example, the PATH element selected as the GROUND is the GOAL.[8]

108 Christopher Hart

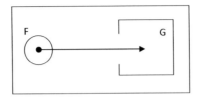

Figure 6.1 Default motion event in immigration discourse

In not expressing MANNER or CAUSE, the invented example in (1) may be said to represent the basic or default motion event in discourse on immigration. From a critical perspective, our task is to consider how the conceptualisations evoked by actual language usages differ from this basic model and what the ideological functions might be of alternative conceptualisations.

Manner of motion and configuration of the ground

One way in which real language usages depart from this model is through the inclusion of MANNER. Indeed, most English verbs of motion express MOTION and MANNER simultaneously while PATH gets expressed by a preposition. If we search our data for motion verbs referring to the process of immigration, we begin to see some patterns in the way that manner of motion is construed. For example, one group of verbs relates to the activity of walking. Verbs in this group include *walk* and *trek*. An example is given in (2):

(2) Incredible drone footage shows the moment [thousands of refugees $_{\text{FIGURE}}$] [trek $_{\text{MOTION + MANNER}}$] [across $_{\text{PATH}}$] [sprawling farmland $_{\text{GROUND}}$]. (M*irror.co.uk*, 26 October 2015)

Where the PATH element selected as GROUND is typically the TRAJECTORY, 'walking' verbs like *trek* point to the, often long and difficult, journey undertaken by migrants and thus articulate a more sympathetic discourse.[9] However, other walking verbs like *tramp* point to destructive effects of the motion event on the GROUND or, as in the case of *march*, enact a military metaphor.

Another group of verbs, also less favourable, present migrants as somehow devious or even dangerous. Verbs in this group include *sneak* and *slip* as in (3) and (4).

(3) Disguised as waiters [migrants $_{\text{FIGURE}}$] are [sneaking $_{\text{MOTION + MANNER}}$] [into $_{\text{PATH}}$] [Britain $_{\text{GROUND}}$] with the help of people smugglers charging them £6000 each, it has been revealed. (*Express Online*, 13 January 2016)

(4) The quiet ports where [illegal immigrants and terrorists ₍FIGURE₎] are [slip-ping ₍MOTION + MANNER₎] [into ₍PATH₎] [the UK ₍GROUND₎]. (*Express Online*, 30 May 2016)

These verbs also affect the conceptualisation of the GROUND, which in these examples represents the GOAL. While in (1) the GROUND is a bounded region, it is not completely 'sealed'. Rather, there is a designated 'opening' which allows the FIGURE to move freely into the GROUND. By contrast, the verbs in (3) and (4) construe the GROUND as supposedly sealed but with perforations which immigrants are able to exploit to enter the GROUND surreptitiously. The image schema evoked by these examples is modelled in Figure 6.2a. A further extension of this is found in verbs like *smash*, *storm*, and *breach*, which present migrants as entering the GROUND by physical force. In these cases, the sealed GROUND is construed as being broken or overcome in the course of the motion event. The image schema evoked is represented in Figure 6.2b where the stepped arrow denotes the resulting change of state to the GROUND. The ideological functions of examples (3)–(5), compared to (1), then, are to reinforce a discourse in which there is or should be restrictions to the free movement of people and, at the same time, to denigrate migrants by presenting them as devious or violent in not respecting these restrictions.

(5) [Masked migrant thugs ₍FIGURE₎] hurled rocks at Macedonian police today as they rushed the border in a violent bid to [smash their way ₍MOTION + MANNER₎] [into ₍PATH₎] [Europe ₍GROUND₎]. (*Express Online*, 10 April 2016)

A final set of verbs worth noting here is a set that express MANNER metaphorically and thus realise particular framing strategies as well as structural configuration strategies. These verbs fall into three types: verbs to do with war (*invade*, *march*), verbs to do with water (*flow*, *flood*, *stream*, *pour*) and verbs to do with animals (*flock*). Examples are given in (6)–(8).

(6) Between April and June 213,000 people claimed asylum in EU countries and [tens of thousands ₍FIGURE₎] are currently [marching ₍MOTION + MANNER₎] [across ₍PATH₎] [the continent ₍GROUND₎]. (*Mirror.co.uk*, 28 September 2015)
(7) [Thousands of people ₍FIGURE₎] are [flooding ₍MOTION + MANNER₎] [into ₍PATH₎] [Europe ₍GROUND₎] each day. (*Mail Online*, 4 November 2015)
(8) [A million migrants and refugees ₍FIGURE₎] [flocked ₍MOTION + MANNER₎] [to ₍PATH₎] [Europe ₍GROUND₎] last year, official figures reveal. (*Mirror.co.uk*, 22 December 2015)

The metaphorical construals established by these verbs, when used in reference to the migration of people, have already been extensively analysed elsewhere (Charteris-Black, 2006; Hart, 2010; Santa Ana, 2002) (see also Chapter 5, this volume, for a more detailed discussion of how to

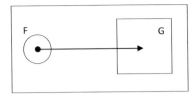

Figure 6.2a Inhibited motion

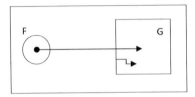

Figure 6.2b Impact on ground

analyse metaphor in discourse). Briefly, however, these verbs access different source frames (WAR, WATER, or ANIMAL) which then provide templates for understanding the target situation. In a cognitive account, metaphor involves: (i) establishing correspondences between elements in the source frame and elements in the target situation; (ii) attributing qualities associated with source frame elements to corresponding elements in the target situation; and (iii) making inferences about the target situation based on relations that hold inside the source frame. So, for example, in (7), *flood* activates the FLOOD frame establishing a connection between immigrants and moving water. The danger posed by flooding and its destructive power is then mapped across to the target situation so that immigration is similarly construed as dangerous and destructive. It then follows that, just as we would put barriers in place to prevent flooding, so we should put barriers in place to prevent immigration.

Number and plexity in the figure

Besides the addition of MANNER, another way in which actual language usages found in discourses of immigration depart from the default motion event is in the construal of the FIGURE. In (1), the number or extent of the FIGURE is not specified. However, a common way of conceptualising migrants is in terms of their, usually large, numbers (Gabrielatos and Baker, 2008). This can be achieved indirectly through verbs encoding

Cognitive linguistic CDA 111

manners of motion like *flood* and *flock*, which imply a FIGURE made up of large quantities, or directly through explicit quantifications of the FIGURE. Of course, these two strategies can co-occur as in examples (7) and (8) above.

Rather than a large number of individual entities, the FIGURE may alternatively be schematised as a single mass. Conceptually, this relates to a distinction Talmy makes between *uniplex* and *multiplex* structure. For example, in their plural form, count nouns like *migrants* encode multiplex structures, construing a group of individual entities as individuals, albeit lumped together under a single social category. By contrast, collective nouns encode uniplex structures, construing a group of individuals as a mass unit which behaves as though it were a single object or homogenous substance. The alternative schematisations are represented in Figure 6.3. In immigration discourse, a uniplex FIGURE is often evoked by collective nouns that are applied metaphorically as in *flock of migrants, army of asylum seekers*, or *column of refugees*:

(9) The extraordinary aerial photo of [a column of refugees and migrants FIGURE] [tramping MANNER + MOTION] [through PATH] [the fields of Slovenia GROUND] may come to symbolise the moment the EU began to fall apart. (*Telegraph.co.uk*, 27 October 2015)

Construing a group of people with a uniplex structure deindividuates them, occluding attention to their unique identities, histories, desires, and motives. It thus realises an identification strategy as well as a structural configuration strategy.

Rate and iteration of motion

Verbs expressing MANNER often provide information about the RATE or FORCE of motion. For example, *run* encodes a faster rate of motion than *walk*. Similarly, *flood* encodes a faster and more forceful motion than *flow*. Functionally, faster motion means that a motion event involving

Figure 6.3 Multiplex versus uniplex

112   *Christopher Hart*

larger FIGURE quantities can 'complete' in a shorter period of time. Thus, in examples expressing rapid rates of motion, we not only find quantification of the FIGURE but also an additional semantic element of TIME FRAME which, expressed by an adverbial phrase, is relatively compressed. Consider as an example (10):

(10)   Cameron's migrant pledge 'in tatters' as [336,000 FIGURE] [flood MOTION + MANNER] [into PATH] [UK GROUND] [in just 12 months TIME FRAME]. (*Express Online*, 26 November 2015)

When expressed by the verb, as in (10), RATE OF MOTION is imprecise, implied only to be fast, slow or somewhere in between. In immigration discourse, however, RATE OF MOTION is often specified, expressed through facts and figures in an adverbial phrase. Typically, such statistics present the rate of motion in a way that makes it easier to imagine and thus as more alarming.

(11)   [EU migrants FIGURE] [poured MOTION + MANNER] [into PATH] [Britain GROUND] [at the rate of one every 40 seconds RATE] [last year TIME FRAME], according to a bombshell report the Government tried to bury. (*Mail Online*, 12 May 2016)

Closely linked to RATE OF MOTION is ITERATION. Motion events can be construed as single events (semelfactive) or a series of events defined at given temporal intervals (iterative). Again, such intervals are typically shorter rather than longer (*days, weeks, months,* or *years* rather than *decades, centuries,* or *millennia*) making the scenario at the same time more tangible and more startling. At the surface level, ITERATION is typically expressed by an adverbial phrase as in (12).

(12)   [Since the New Year TIME FRAME] [1600 migrants FIGURE] have [arrived MOTION] [in PATH] [Europe GROUND] [every day ITERATION]. (*Express Online*, 20 January 2016)

Conceptually, ITERATION relates to *plexity*. A motion event construed as a one-off happening exhibits a uniplex structure while a motion event conceived as a series of repeated events is multiplex in structure. Ideologically, in discourses of immigration, motion events construed as iterative or with rapid rates of motion create a sense of unsustainability as the GROUND is faced with excessive quantities or forces within short periods of time. When a motion event configured this way is anchored in the present, the construal further creates a sense of urgency with the unmanageable situation requiring immediate interventionist action.

Identification

Windowing of attention

One construal operation realising an identification strategy that is related to the motion event itself is *windowing of attention*.[10] The complete motion event inherent in the process of immigration involves a FIGURE departing a SOURCE (the country of origin) and following a TRAJECTORY (the route taken) to eventually arrive at a GOAL (the destination country). However, when one or other PATH element is selected as the GROUND, our attention is focussed on this particular portion of the event. In respect to motion events, then, Talmy calls this *path windowing* and identifies three types: initial (focussed on the SOURCE), medial (focussed on the TRAJECTORY), and final (focussed on the GOAL). Of course, multiple GROUNDS may be specified and if all three PATH elements are expressed then our attention is directed over the entire event. This is illustrated in the invented example below.

(13) [Migrants FIGURE] have [travelled MOTION] [from PATH] their [home countries GROUND: SOURCE] [across PATH] [the Mediterranean GROUND: TRAJECTORY] [to PATH] [Europe GROUND: GOAL].

In practice, however, attested language usages tend to 'window' or select for particular attention different portions of this process. And different verbs are associated with different types of windowing. In immigration discourse, for example, a verb like *flee* is associated with initial windowing. By contrast, a verb like *arrive* is associated with final windowing, while a verb like *cross* is associated with medial windowing. The reflex of windowing is *gapping* which defocuses our attention on the unwindowed portion of the event so that, for example, final windowing concomitantly involves initial and medial gapping. Language usages involving these different types of windowing are exemplified in (14)–(16) and the conceptual representations evoked by them are modelled in Figure 6.4. Note that all three path elements are necessarily present in the conceptualisation of any motion event but those that receive linguistic representation are construed with greater saliency.

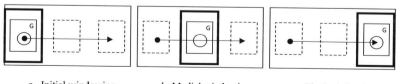

a. Initial windowing   b. Medial windowing   c. Final windowing

Figure 6.4 Windowing of attention

114 *Christopher Hart*

(15) [More than four million people FIGURE] have [fled MOTION + PATH] [Syria GROUND] [since the start of the civil war TIME FRAME]. (*Mirror.co.uk*, 23 December 2015)

(16) [More than 300,000 people FIGURE] have [crossed MOTION] [the Mediterranean GROUND] [so far this year TIME FRAME]. (*Telegraph.co.uk*, 29 August 2015)

(17) [One million migrants FIGURE] have [arrived MOTION] [in PATH] [Europe GROUND] [this year TIME FRAME]. (*Express Online*, 23 December 2015)

From a critical perspective, in immigration discourse, windowing of attention and its reflex in gapping can serve to highlight or ignore the causes and consequences of immigration, thus reflecting different discourses. For example, initial windowing can serve to highlight the difficult circumstances which lead people to migrate and may thus be said to instantiate a more humanitarian discourse.[11] By contrast, final windowing overlooks the impetus for migration and focuses only on its potential (usually negatively conceived) impact. Final windowing may therefore be associated with more hostile discourses.

Self-motion vs. caused motion

Closely related to windowing of attention and also realising an identification strategy is a distinction Talmy (1985, 2000)) makes between two types of motion: self-motion and caused-motion. In self-motion, the motion event is initiated by the FIGURE. All our examples so far have been of self-motion. In caused-motion, by contrast, the motion event is brought about by some other external factor. There are myriad ways to express caused motion but one way is through verbs like *forced to* in (18).

(18) [They FIGURE] have been forced to [leave MOTION + PATH] [their countries GROUND] due to the intolerable conditions. (*Mirror.co.uk*, 22 November 2015)

Conceptually, the distinction between self-motion and caused-motion has its basis in attention. In caused-motion, our attentional frame is expanded to take in a greater chain of events. Ideologically, in immigration discourse, construals of caused-motion function in a similar way to initial windowing by recognising the circumstances that lead people to migrate but also explicitly presenting migration as being borne of necessity rather than just desire or opportunity.

Cognitive linguistic CDA   115

Positioning

Spatial point of view and deixis

While structural configuration strategies are responsible for defining the properties of an event, positioning strategies determine the perspective from which an event is 'viewed' and the organisation of elements relative to that viewpoint. Talmy (2000) identifies four dimensions of *perspective*: location, mode, distance, and direction. In immigration discourse, it is *location* that most clearly functions ideologically. Location corresponds to what is traditionally called *deixis* and defines a *viewpoint* or 'deictic centre' from which the event is 'seen'. Two locations are available: interior and exterior to the GROUND. The two conceptualisations are modelled in Figure 6.5, where VP stands for viewpoint. Crucially, perspectival location is distinct from physical location. Thus, in (1), although the physical location of the speaker and intended hearer is presumed to be interior to the GROUND, the perspectival location is exterior. Anti-immigration discourses are made more arresting when perspectival location coincides with presumed physical location for this explicitly places the conceptualiser in the territory where the impact of immigration can be felt. It thus realises a positioning strategy that Cap (2013) calls *spatial proximisation*. An interior perspectival location is achieved via deictic verbs like *come* or deictic adverbs and noun phrases like *here* and *this country* in expressions of the GROUND.

(19) [More than 200,000 migrants FIGURE] are [coming MOTION] [to PATH] [Britain GROUND] [every year ITERATION]. (*Express Online*, 4 December 2015)
(20) [A total of 1,864 people FIGURE] [arrived MOTION] [in PATH] [this country GROUND] through the route in 2015. (*Express Online*, 20 April 2016)

Temporal grounding and telicity

The final two parameters that I will highlight are *temporal grounding* and *telicity*, which are expressed in *tense* and *aspect*, respectively. Temporal grounding refers to the fact that an event can be construed as taking place in the past, the present, or the future. Telicity refers to the fact that an event can be construed as either ongoing or complete (atelic versus telic). This is expressed in the *progressive* versus *perfect* aspect respectively. Conceptually, telicity reflects a perspectival location in time. Events construed as atelic assume a location interior to the time frame in which the event unfolds. Events construed as telic assume a location exterior to the time frame of the event. The distinction between a telic and an atelic construal is represented in Figure 6.6, where the arrow marked as T represents the unfolding of time.

In example (1), then, the present perfect *have entered* construes the event as complete having happened at some point in the recent past. However,

116 Christopher Hart

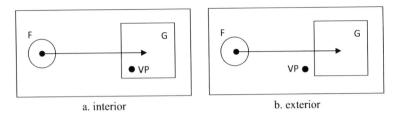

a. interior   b. exterior

Figure 6.5 Perspectival location

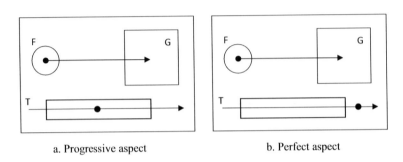

a. Progressive aspect   b. Perfect aspect

Figure 6.6 Aspect

media discourses on immigration often use the present progressive form, as in (21), to signal the current and ongoing nature of immigration. When immigration is conceived as a problem, construing the motion events involved as currently ongoing functions ideologically in two ways: (i) it conveys a sense of relevance or immediacy and (ii) it suggests that the situation will continue to occur into the future. It thus realises a positioning strategy of temporal proximisation which justifies the need for immediate interventionist action (Cap, 2013).

(21) [Hundreds of thousands of migrants FIGURE] are [flooding MOTION + MANNER] [into PATH] [Europe GROUND: GOAL] [from Syria and Africa GROUND: SOURCE], leaving a number of countries struggling to cope. (*Telegraph.co.uk*, 3 September 2015)

Presenting findings and results

As with many forms of discourse analysis, results emerge through your analysis rather than being something that is the subject of your analysis. As a consequence, findings and results are often presented only implicitly within your analysis. This is in contrast to the standard scientific method of reporting where results and analyses are presented separately. The principles, however, are the same as for all forms of research. Findings must be presented clearly, succinctly, and systematically. It is therefore a good idea, in your conclusion, to identify the main findings from your analysis and state explicitly how they address your research questions. Be clear, here, about the goals of your project. Did you set out to present a kind of typological study, highlighting the conceptual parameters along which ideology may be enacted in a given domain, as in the study presented above, or did you set out to scrutinise a particular set of texts for the frequencies, forms and functions of a given linguistic/conceptual phenomenon?

In discourse analyses based in cognitive linguistics, the first thing you are likely to have noticed is a fondness for diagrams. It is important to note that these diagrams are not just illustrations created to reflect the analyst's own impressions. Rather, they are born out of theoretical frameworks and follow particular conventions to represent meanings in a way that systematically captures certain semantic properties or distinctions. It is therefore important, in producing your own diagrams, that you follow these conventions, paying attention to details, and explaining what is signified by different diagrammatic features.

It is likely that, either in the course of your own analysis or based on previous research, patterns of representation or key semantic sites where ideology may be enacted will emerge. Such observations constitute part of your findings and should be reflected in the structure and organisation of your analysis. As in the analysis above, then, it is a good idea to group your analysis under sub-headings representing emergent themes.

Your findings will be both descriptive and interpretive or critical. You may choose to present your descriptive analysis upfront and then follow with more interpretive analyses. Alternatively, as in the study above, you may choose to interlace the two types of analysis. Either way, it is important to link form and function; to go beyond describing the conceptualisations evoked by language usages to consider also their implications for ideology and social action. At the same time, however, you should not privilege a critical analysis over a descriptive one. A major aim of using cognitive linguistics in CDA is to offer an account, based in a psychologically plausible model of language, of how textual choices might achieve ideological influence. A detailed, theoretically informed descriptive analysis is key to this endeavour.

More often than not, discourse analyses based in cognitive linguistics are qualitative rather than quantitative. That said, quantitative methods are clearly possible and there is now an ever-increasing body of work adopting mixed methods in cognitive linguistics-based CDA. This has proved most successful in the area of metaphor. If you are presenting quantitative analysis, there are a number of important things to remember. First how you obtained your results must be made apparent to your reader. For

118 *Christopher Hart*

example, in most cases, quantitative analysis will be based on the coding of your data. It is important that the reader has some access to this process. This involves giving a clear description of your coding protocol and, minimally, an example of its implementation. Where ethics permit, it is considered good research practice, for the sake of transparency, to make your coded data available for inspection by others. If you are working with a relatively small data set, it is a good idea to include your codings as an appendix. This may be a physical or electronic appendix depending on the size of your data. Clearly, if you are using auto-annotation methods to analyse very large data sets, it is not possible to present all of the coded data to your reader.

Second, be sure to make use of tables and graphs so that quantitative results are readily identified and easily digestible. If presenting your results in graphic form, however, note that pie charts are usually the least favourable format and are best avoided. Any quantitative results should be presented as 'raw' numbers but should also be normalised in some way, presented either as a percentage or as a number per N-words. For example, if comparing the use of transitive versus reciprocal verbs in right- and left-wing media reports of violence at political protests (as in Hart, 2013b), it is important to express the number of times that each verb-type occurs, within a given part of your data, as a percentage of the total number of references to violent interactions within that data region. This is because if, say, a transitive verb occurs more frequently in your right-wing data than in your left-wing data but your right-wing data happens to contain more references to violent interactions, then the higher number of transitive verbs does not represent a difference in *how* violent interactions are reported but only in *how often* they are reported. Quantitative analysis may be extended to include *inferential* as well as *descriptive* statistics. The aim of inferential statistics is to show whether any differences you find between different portions of your data are large enough to be meaningful – are *significant*. The statistical test you are most likely to come across or use yourself in this context is Pearson's chi-squared test or, for smaller sample sizes, Fisher's exact test (see Chapter 10, this volume, for discussion of which statistical test is most appropriate for different types of data). If you are presenting inferential statistics, it is important that you follow standard conventions for expressing them (see Field, 2013 or van Peer, Hakemulder, and Zyngier, 2007 for handy guides).

Of course, if you are not conducting a quantitative analysis, then it is important to avoid vague or unsubstantiated quantifications like 'a lot more often' or 'fairly frequent'. Similarly, if you are conducting a quantitative analysis but are not presenting inferential statistics, then you should avoid describing differences as 'significant'.

Issues and limitations

Cognitive linguistic approaches to discourse analysis account for the ideological influence of texts by showing the cognitive representations that different language usages evoke and the implications of those representations for ideology and social action. The status of 'cognitive' in a cognitive linguistic analysis, however, is subject to debate (see Fesmire, 1994 for discussion). Cognitive linguistics claims to be cognitive in so far as its analyses are motivated by and accord with what is already known from other disciplines like cognitive psychology about the mind and brain more generally. However, the extent to which the models proposed in cognitive linguistics genuinely reflect the way language works in the mind and brain has remained empirically unverified. This is important for CL-CDA because it concerns whether the representations ascribed to language usages are cognitively 'real' or not. Are the diagrams we are so fond of just a handy notational device or do they reflect genuine underlying cognitive processes? Fortunately, there is now growing evidence from multiple sources, including gesture studies, eye-tracking studies, and neuro-imaging studies, that points to the psychological reality of models in cognitive linguistics (see Gonzalez-Marquez et al., 2007 for an overview).

Similarly, although cognitive linguistics helps move CDA toward studies of text-reception, something that has for a long time been called for (Stubbs, 1997; Widdowson, 2004), it does not take us all of the way. Cognitive linguistic analyses theorise the ideological significance of different construals but do not themselves empirically demonstrate the ideological influence of competing construals in affecting, at the moment of interaction with the text or more long-term, audience's judgements, decisions, inferences, and emotions etc. In Chapter 10, this volume, we discuss the use of experimental methods in discourse analysis to investigate the ideological effects that arise from the conceptualisations evoked by textual choices.

A final issue for CL-CDA, which we have already touched upon, is that it does not readily extend to large-scale corpus-based studies where auto-annotation methods are required. Currently, there is no automatic semantic annotation software whose categories or underlying 'lexicons' reflect semantic distinctions of the kind made in cognitive linguistics. This hinders if not prevents the kind of 'up-scaling' we might want to do to check whether findings from a qualitative analysis or small-scale quantitative analysis are generalisable or not. At the time of writing, there is one exception on the horizon. FrameNet (https://framenet.icsi.berkeley.edu/fndrupal/) provides an index of semantic frames, including event-frames, and currently has people working to develop parsing tools that can automatically assign frame semantic tags to the lexical items in a text. This may help in analysing structural configuration and framing strategies. However automatic annotation of attentional and perspectival phenomena remains beyond current capabilities.

120 *Christopher Hart*

Further reading

Primary texts outlining particular frameworks in cognitive linguistics include Talmy (2000) and Langacker (2008). These are very advanced texts though. Langacker's *Cognitive Grammar: A Basic Introduction* is neither basic nor introductory! More accessible overviews of key concepts in cognitive linguistics are provided by Ungerer and Schmid (2006) and Dirven and Radden (2007). In CDA, Chilton (2004) and Hart (2014) both apply a range of Cognitive Linguistic frameworks to a variety of textual data and both are reasonably accessible. Recent edited collections that include cognitive linguistic analyses of political discourses are Hart (2019) and Filardo-Llamas, Hart, and Kaal (2016). For applications of cognitive linguistics to literary forms of discourse see Giovanelli and Harrison (2018), Harrison (2017), Harrison et al. (2014), and Stockwell (2002). For applications in a forensic context see Luchjenbroers and Aldridge (2007).

Notes

1 For Ronald Langacker, a key figure in cognitive linguistics, *construal* refers to 'our manifest ability to conceive and portray the same situation in alternate ways' (Langacker, 2008: 43).
2 Note that the discursive strategies in Table 6.1 are not mutually exclusive but operate simultaneously contributing different layers or dimensions of meaning in any language event. Note also that the table is not intended to be exhaustive or unmalleable. Other construal operations may be added to the basic framework and any one construal operation may realise more than one discursive strategy.
3 In 2013, the UK Conservative Party removed from their website a publicly searchable archive of political speeches made by its members.
4 When I wanted to investigate media coverage of the 1984–1985 British Miners' Strike (reported in Hart, 2017), I had to do it the old fashioned way visiting the Reading Rooms at the British Library and trawling through reels of microfilm to find relevant articles.
5 Also relevant are psycholinguistic studies empirically investigating the domain motion at the language-cognition interface (Gennari et al., 2002; Lindsay, Scheepers, and Kamide, 2013; Papafragou, Massey and Gleitman, 2002; Papafragou and Selimis, 2010).
6 Talmy treats both motion itself and the state of being located as MOTION events (MOVE vs BE$_{LOC}$ respectively).
7 Roughly equivalent terms to *figure* and *ground* in cognitive grammar are *trajector* and *landmark*.
8 This type of motion, whereby the location of the FIGURE changes over time, is known as translational and contrasts with other types of motion which the FIGURE may undergo such as rotation or oscillation.
9 MANNER is also expressed indirectly through a by-phrase as in the following example where 'by sea' suggests a manner otherwise explicitly encoded by 'sail' or 'swim': '[Over 1,000,000 people $_{FIGURE}$] [entered $_{MOTION + PATH}$] [Europe $_{GROUND}$] [by sea $_{MANNER}$] last year' (*Express Online*, 19 May 2016).
10 A roughly equivalent term to windowing of attention in Langacker's cognitive grammar is *profiling*.
11 Initial windowing may therefore be more likely to occur with the word *refugee* rather than *migrant* or *asylum seeker*.

References

Cap, P. (2006). *Legitimisation in political discourse*. Newcastle: Cambridge Scholars Publishing.

Cap, P. (2008). Towards a proximisation model of the analysis of legitimisation in political discourse. *Journal of Pragmatics, 40*(1), 17–41.

Cap, P. (2013). *Proximization: The pragmatics of symbolic distance crossing*. Amsterdam: John Benjamins.

Charteris-Black, J. (2006). Britain as a container: Immigration metaphors in the 2005 election campaign. *Discourse & Society, 17*(6), 563–582.

Chilton, P. (1996). *Security metaphors: Cold war discourse from containment to common house*. New York: Peter Lang.

Chilton, P. (2004). *Analysing political discourse: Theory and practice*. London: Routledge.

Chilton, P. and Ilyin, M. (1993). Metaphor in political discourse: The case of the 'Common European House'. *Discourse & Society, 4*(1), 7–31.

Croft, W. and Cruse, A. (2004). *Cognitive linguistics*. Cambridge: Cambridge University Press.

Dirven, R. and Radden, G. (2007). *Cognitive English grammar*. Amsterdam: John Benjamins.

Fesmire, S.A. (1994). What is 'cognitive' about cognitive linguistics? *Metaphor and Symbolic Activity, 9*(2), 149–154.

Field, A.P. (2013). *Discovering statistics using IBM SPSS Statistics*. (4th ed.). London: Sage.

Filardo-Llamas, L., Hart, C., and Kaal, B. (Eds.) (2016). *Space, time and evaluation in ideological discourse*. London: Routledge.

Fillmore, C. (1982). Frame semantics. In Linguistics Society of Korea (Ed.), *Linguistics in the morning calm*. (pp. 111–137). Seoul: Hanshin Publishing Co.

Fillmore, C. (1985). Frames and the semantics of understanding. *Quaderni di Semantica, 6*, 222–254.

Gabrielatos, C. and Baker, P. (2008). Fleeing, sneaking, flooding: A corpus analysis of discursive constructions of refugees and asylum seekers in the UK press 1996–2005. *Journal of English Linguistics, 36*(1), 5–38.

Gennari, S.P., Sloman, S.A., Malt, B.C. and Fitch, W.T. (2002). Motion events in language and cognition. *Cognition, 83*, 49–79.

Giovanelli, M. and Harrison, C. (2018). *Cognitive grammar in stylistics: A practical guide*. London: Bloomsbury.

Gonzalez-Marquez, M., Mittelberg, I., Coulson, S. and Spivey, M.J. (Eds.) (2007). *Methods in cognitive linguistics*. Amsterdam: John Benjamins.

Harrison, C. (2017). *Cognitive grammar in contemporary fiction*. Amsterdam: John Benjamins.

Harrison, C., Nuttall, L., Stockwell, P. and Yuan, W. (Eds.) (2014). *Cognitive grammar in literature*. New York: John Benjamins.

Hart, C. (2010). *Critical discourse analysis and cognitive science: New perspectives on immigration discourse*. Basingstoke: Palgrave.

Hart, C. (2011a). Force-interactive patterns in immigration discourse: A Cognitive Linguistic approach to CDA. *Discourse & Society, 22*(3), 269–286.

Hart, C. (2011b). Moving beyond metaphor in the cognitive linguistic approach to CDA: Construal operations in immigration discourse. In C. Hart (Ed.), *Critical discourse studies in context and cognition.* (pp. 171–192). Amsterdam: John Benjamins.

Hart, C. (2013a). Constructing contexts through grammar: Cognitive models and conceptualisation in British Newspaper reports of political protests. In J. Flowerdew (Ed.), *Discourse and contexts.* (pp. 159–184). London: Continuum.

Hart, C. (2013b). Event-construal in press reports of violence in political protests: A cognitive linguistic approach to CDA. *Journal of Language and Politics, 12*(3), 400–423.

Hart, C. (2014). *Discourse, grammar and ideology: Functional and cognitive perspectives.* London: Bloomsbury.

Hart, C. (2017). Metaphor and intertextuality in media framings of the (1984–85) British Miners' Strike: A multimodal analysis. *Discourse & Communication, 11*(1), 3–30.

Hart, C. (Ed.) (2019). *Cognitive linguistic approaches to text and discourse: From poetics to politics.* Edinburgh: Edinburgh University Press.

Jeffries, L. (2010). *Critical stylistics: The power of English.* Basingstoke: Palgrave.

Koller, V. (2004). *Metaphor and gender in business media discourse: A critical cognitive study.* Basingstoke: Palgrave.

Koller, V. (2005). Critical discourse analysis and social cognition: Evidence from business media discourse. *Discourse & Society, 16*(2), 199–224.

Lakoff, G. and Johnson, M. (1980). *Metaphors we live by.* Chicago, IL: University of Chicago Press.

Lakoff, G. and Johnson, M. (1999). *Philosophy in the flesh: The embodied mind and its challenge to Western thought.* New York: Basic Books.

Langacker, R.W. (1987). *Foundations of cognitive grammar, volume I: Theoretical prerequisites.* Stanford, CA: Stanford University Press.

Langacker, R.W. (1991). *Foundations of cognitive grammar, volume II: Descriptive application.* Stanford, CA: Stanford University Press.

Langacker, R.W. (2002). *Concept, image, and symbol: The cognitive basis of grammar.* (2nd ed.). Berlin: Mouton de Gruyter.

Langacker, R.W. (2008). *Cognitive grammar: A basic introduction.* Oxford: Oxford University Press.

Lederer, J. (2013). 'Anchor baby': A conceptual explanation for pejoration. *Journal of Pragmatics, 57,* 248–266.

Lindsay, S., Scheepers, C. and Kamide, Y. (2013). To dash or to dawdle: Verb-associated speed of motion influences eye movements during spoken sentence comprehension. *PLoS ONE, 8* (6): e67187. doi: 10.1371/journal.pone.0067187.

Luchjenbroers, J. and Aldridge, M. (2007). Conceptual manipulation by metaphors and frames: Dealing with rape victims in legal discourse. *Text & Talk, 27*(3), 339–359.

Musolff, A. (2004). *Metaphor and political discourse: Analogical reasoning in debates about Europe.* Basingstoke: Palgrave.

Musolff, A. (2010). *Metaphor, nation and the Holocaust: The concept of the body- politic.* London: Routledge.

Papafragou, A., Massey, C. and Gleitman, L. (2002). Shake, rattle 'n' roll: The representation of motion in language and cognition. *Cognition, 84,* 189–219.

Papafragou, A. and Selimis, S. (2010). Event categorisation and language: A cross-linguistic study of motion. *Language and Cognitive Processes, 25*(2), 224–260.

Pourcel, S. (2010). Motion: A conceptual typology. In V. Evans and P. Chilton (Eds.), *Language, cognition and space: The state of the art and new directions.* (pp. 419–450). London: Equinox.

Santa Ana, O. (2002). *Brown tide rising: Metaphors of Latinos in contemporary American public discourse.* Austin: University of Texas Press.

Slobin, D.I. (2004). The many ways to search for a frog: Linguistic typology and the expression of motion events. In S. Strömqvist and L. Verhoeven (Eds.), *Relating events in narrative, volume 2: Typological and contextual perspectives.* (pp. 219–257). Mahwah, NJ: Lawrence Erlbaum Associates.

Stockwell, P. (2002). *Cognitive poetics: An introduction.* London: Routledge.

Stubbs, M. (1997). Whorf's children: Critical comments on critical discourse analysis (CDA). In A. Ryan and A. Wray (Eds.), *Evolving models of language.* (pp. 100–116). Clevedon: British Association for Applied Linguistics.

Talmy, L. (1985). Lexicalization patterns semantic structure in lexical forms. In T. Shopen (Ed.), *Language typology and syntactic description, volume 3: Grammatical categories and the lexicon.* (pp. 36–149). Cambridge: Cambridge University Press.

Talmy, L. (2000). *Toward a cognitive semantics.* Cambridge, MA: MIT Press.

Ungerer, F. and Schmid, H-J. (2006). *An introduction to cognitive linguistics.* London: Longman.

van Peer, W., Hakemulder, J. and Zyngier, S. (2007). *Muses and measures: Empirical research methods for the humanities.* Newcastle: Cambridge Scholars Publishing.

Widdowson, H.G. (2004). *Text, context, pretext: Critical issues in discourse analysis.* Oxford: Blackwell.

7 Corpus-assisted discourse analysis

Paul Baker

Introduction

This chapter outlines an approach to analysing discourse which involves computer-aided analysis of large amounts of electronic data, collected to be representative of a particular text or register. Specialist software identifies frequent or salient linguistic patterns in the data and analysis is based around the concept of the incremental effect of discourse, with people being exposed to repeated pairings of the same concepts over time (discourse prosodies), showing how language influences perceptions.

The case study that forms the backbone of this chapter involves an analysis of the concept of the term *council estate* in newspaper articles in the British national press. Using keyword, collocational, and concordance analyses I show how council estates are generally constructed with a negative discourse prosody (e.g. co-occurring with adjectives like *bleak, tired, rough*, and *derelict*), while a concordance analysis indicates that social actors who live on council estates are described as tough and the articles often use a narrative of people who have grown up on council estates and now have successful lives away from them. Such people are also represented as exceptional, indicating a way in which expectations about people from council estates are subtly presented to readers.

Before presenting the case study, however, in the following section, I first describe some of the main principles of corpus-assisted discourse analysis

Outline of approach

Corpus-assisted discourse analysis is the name given to an approach towards discourse analysis which uses computer software to assist the analysis any collection (or body) of naturally occurring texts (known as a *corpus* – from the Latin word for 'body'). Such software can count linguistic patterns including single words, types of words (for example all the proper nouns in a corpus), sequences of words, or words that occur in the vicinity of other words (known as collocates) as well as implementing algorithms or statistical tests which help to identify words which are especially frequent in one corpus when compared against another (known as keywords). The software can also sort and present language data from a corpus visually so that human analysts can interpret complex linguistic patterns and relationships more easily. While software is fast and accurate at processing very large amounts of textual data, qualitative human analytical skills need to be employed at almost every stage of the research process, in terms of deciding how to build a corpus, which procedures to use, and how to interpret, explain, and critique the linguistic patterns found.

This is an approach which emerged from work by Stubbs and Gerbig (1993), Caldas-Coulthard (1993), and Hardt-Mautner (1995) with book-length treatments emerging in the following decades, e.g. Baker (2006) and Partington et al., (2013). The thinking behind the approach is to identify large-scale linguistic patterns which may not always be visible to the human eye but can indicate value judgements or stances which may sometimes be present without the text producer, or indeed the reader, being aware of them. For example, Stubbs (2001) shows that the verb *cause* tends to co-occur or *collocate* with a group of words which refer to negative phenomena (like *damage, death, disease, cancer, pain,* and *trouble*). Even though *cause* has no intrinsic negative meaning, it acquires a so-called negative *discourse prosody* through the words with which it collocates and could therefore be used to subtly signal negative author stance, even if paired with a seemingly neutral or positive word (Stubbs gives 'cause amusement' as an example).

An advantage of conducting research on large datasets is that doing so allows us to be more confident that our findings are representative of a particular type of text or author. This is important if we want to make convincing claims about bias. For example, we may develop a hypothesis that a particular social group is written about in negative ways in a certain newspaper and collect five articles where this is clearly the case, leading us to conclude that the newspaper is biased. However, researchers could be accused of 'cherry-picking' (Widdowson, 2000) those five articles to prove their point, while ignoring 500 other articles which are perhaps more positive. Additionally, if we draw our analysis from a large corpus, we are likely to find cases of the most frequently cited linguistic patterns but we also have the capacity to uncover instances that are much less frequent and may direct us towards minority positions in the dataset. Again, a much smaller dataset is far less likely to afford the range of possible perspectives around a particular topic or concept.

Identifying research questions

A corpus-assisted approach is often good at identifying representations of individuals as well as social or national identities. Examples include studies on representations of gay men (Baker, 2005), refugees and asylum seekers (Baker et al., 2008) and Muslims (Baker et al., 2013). Other research has

126   *Paul Baker*

focused on language use around more abstract concepts such as events or illnesses, e.g. representations of eating disorders (Hunt and Harvey, 2015), the environment (Bevitori, 2015) or the concepts embodied in the words *science* (Taylor, 2010) or *moral* (Marchi, 2010). Such topics would suggest research questions along the lines of 'How is language used to represent topic/group X in corpus A?'

Corpus-assisted approaches also lend themselves well to comparative analyses, for example, comparing the representation of two or more phenomena in the same corpus, such as Pearce's (2008) comparison of verbs and adjectives which collocate with the words *man* and *woman* in the British National Corpus or Hunt's (2015) study of body parts of boys and girls (focusing on words like *eye*, *hand*, *face*, and *arm*) in the Harry Potter book series. Other studies may compare how the same concept or group is constructed across different registers or time periods; an example is Partington's (2015) study of the term 'the Arab world' in news articles from 2010 and 2013 and in British and Middle Eastern news stories. These types of research questions would take the format 'What differences and/or similarities exist in the language around groups/topics X and Y in corpora A, B, and C?' Our research question may explicitly highlight the existence of either typical or infrequent patterns and depending on our framework we may want to claim that the language patterns we find are indicative of various attitudes, beliefs, stances, or indeed discourses.

Finally, we may want to include specific questions which attempt to provide explanations or critiques for the patterns found, even if some researchers in this field are cautious of aspects of critical discourse analysis (e.g. Partington, 2015: 222) and prefer that the findings 'speak for themselves' or allow readers to develop their own critiques. Hunt and Harvey's analysis of language around eating disorders (2015: 149–150) is a good example of how the corpus-assisted approach may not find discourses which maintain social inequalities but still have personal and political implications. This caution around critique is part of a current debate within corpus-assisted approaches to discourse about the extent to which the approach enables an objective perspective: after all, it could be argued that our personal and political beliefs influence the topic that we choose to study, and that even with computer software pointing out frequent patterns that we have to account for, we will still go on to select and interpret our findings from within the discourses that we align with.

The research question used for the case study in this chapter falls into the first category above, asking: how is language used to represent council estates in the British national press?

Data collection and ethics

In some cases the texts in a corpus can consist of millions or even billions of words, although it is also possible to carry out research on much smaller datasets. Researchers must decide whether to build their own corpus or use

Corpus-assisted discourse analysis 127

all or part of an existing one. The latter decision usually entails less preparatory work but means that we are then bound by the decisions of the original corpus builder, so the corpus may not be ideal for our needs. Many large reference corpora in a wide variety of languages are incorporated into free online corpus software platforms (see Table 7.1), so it is worth checking that the corpus you are intending to build does not already exist.

As a demonstration of corpus building, I turn now to the case study used in this chapter, which involves an examination of the ways that council estates are represented in the British press. In the UK, council estates are building complexes of public or social housing built by local municipalities, mostly constructed between 1918 and 1980. Council estates have traditionally housed working-class people as well as some of the neediest people in society. I chose this topic partly based on its personal relevance: I grew up on a council estate and currently live in what is sometimes called an 'ex-council estate', where around half of the homes are now privately owned. Having observed how people talk about council estates, I thought this would be an illuminating topic to consider how social class is represented in the British media. Social class is a concept that is central to issues of power and inequality and as such is relevant to critical discourse research.

I used an online database called Nexis UK (available via subscription from my university's library) to obtain the articles which comprised the corpus I examined. Nexis allows users to download articles which contain certain search words or phrases and can be restricted to specific newspapers or time periods. I chose nine British national newspapers (*The Express*, *The Guardian*, *The Independent*, *The Mail*, *The Mirror*, *The Star*, *The Sun*, *The Times*, and *The Telegraph*) and their Sunday equivalents, collecting data from a five-year period which covered 2013 to 2017 inclusive (although the last two months of 2017 were not available when

Table 7.1 Popular online corpora

Tool	Cost	Selection of Corpora included
CQPweb	Free	The British National Corpus, Times Online, Early English Books Online, The Brown Family, ukWaC, Longman Learners Corpus, International Corpus of Learner English
Corpus.byu.edu	Free	News on the Web, Hansard, Wikipedia, Corpus of Contemporary American English, Corpus of Historical American English, TIME Magazine Corpus, Corpus del Español
Sketch Engine	Free trial option	ukWaC, German Web 2013, French Web 2012, Italian Web 2011, Chinese Web 2011, New Corpus for Irish, Quran Annotated Corpus, Danish Web 2014

128   *Paul Baker*

the research was carried out). The search term for identifying appropriate articles was *council estate* and the search function automatically collected articles containing the plural form *council estates*, too. This resulted in 4899 articles totalling 6,473,834 words. The corpus contains 4945 occurrences of the term *council estate* and 1266 occurrences of the plural form.

When collecting newspaper articles using an online database, issues around copyright and ethics are relatively minimal. The online database gives permission (for a fee) to collect the articles for private use, so I would not be able to share this corpus with others. This is less than ideal but in providing the details of how I collected the data I can at least enable other researchers to build the same corpus. As newspaper articles are publicly available I do not normally need to consider ethical issues around confidentiality or anonymisation, although I might want to anonymise reference to some individuals (either journalists or subjects of articles) if I feel that it would be ethically compromising to mention them. If I had been collecting a corpus of spoken conversations or social media language (such as data from Twitter, online forum comments or blogs), then, assuming that we can resolve copyright issues, we still need to consider ethical ones. In such cases I would want to take care in terms of anonymising text snippets, perhaps even altering the wording of any text I quoted in order to ensure that the originals cannot be traced via online search tools. While ethical guidelines in the social sciences usually advise researchers to seek permission before using language data produced by someone else, with corpus linguistics studies this can be unfeasible as a corpus can consist of short texts produced by thousands of people, who may no longer be contactable. However, if we are collecting data from a smaller number of people (e.g. a community of people who blog about the same subject), then it would be good practice to seek permission to include their texts, even if such blogs are publicly viewable. People's personal uses of language which occur online and are not publicly available (e.g. a dating website which can only be seen by people who sign up for an account) should be handled with special care and ideally copyright clearance and permission should be sought from the site owner as well as the people who created the texts.

Corpus annotation

Before corpora are analysed it is sometimes helpful to create versions of them which contain additional information. This process is called annotation or *tagging* and involves the assignation of codes (or tags) to parts of the corpus which can help computer software to process it more efficiently. One type of annotation involves providing information about each text in the corpus such as its source, author, or date of publication (although we could incorporate some of this information into the file names of the corpus texts or through the folder structure the texts occur in). Some corpus analysis software (e.g. WordSmith Tools) allows us to carry out searches on files in a corpus that only contain certain tags so this can be a useful way to make targeted searches, e.g. if we only wanted to look at texts that had been tagged as being created by male authors as opposed to female ones.

Another form of tagging involves applying information to the language in the text. This could involve noting certain formatting choices such as the use of bold print or italics. Most corpus software requires text to be in plain text format so these formatting choices can be lost in the process of building the corpus. Additionally, we could assign codes to words in the corpus, which can give information about the grammatical function or meaning of a word. This could help us to distinguish between, say, the noun and verb uses of a word like *block*. Such tagging would be time-consuming if done manually so is often carried out with additional software which employs a pre-determined set of codes. Such software relies on rules about language to help it to assign codes, e.g. the word *the* is almost always an article and any word coming directly after the word *the* is likely to be an adjective or a noun. The automatic tagging process, while good, is not perfect and its outcome can depend on the extent to which the tagger is familiar with the sorts of language used in the texts in the corpus. Many large existing reference corpora are grammatically tagged, allowing analysts to refine their searches (e.g. we may want to find all the cases of proper nouns followed by verbs in a corpus), although the codes are usually made invisible as they would otherwise make reading the text in the corpus difficult. If you are building your own corpus you should bear in mind that tagging is optional and only needed if you would not be able to answer your research questions without it. A useful online tool for semantic and grammatical tagging is Wmatrix which offers a one-month free service as well as access to a range of pre-tagged reference corpora.[1]

Analysing and interpreting data

Corpora require specialist software in order to carry out analysis. In addition to the online tools which come with the pre-loaded corpora in Table 7.1, there are a number of other tools, also found online, which can be downloaded as standalone applications for use with your own corpora. Table 7.2 details three such tools.

AntConc is a good tool with a simple interface and as such probably best for people who are new to corpus linguistics. #LancsBox enables the creation of *collocational networks*, a visual representation which shows how multiple words repeatedly co-occur in the vicinity of one another, (see Baker and McEnery, 2015) while WordSmith Tools is one of the most well-established pieces of corpus analysis software and features a large suite of tools allowing users to create *frequency lists* of multiple corpora, work

130 Paul Baker

Table 7.2 Popular standalone corpus tools

Tool	Cost	Website
AntConc	Free	http://laurenceanthony.net/software/antconc/
#LancsBox	Free	http://corpora.lancs.ac.uk/lancsbox/
WordSmith Tools	£50 for full version	http://lexically.net/wordsmith/

with tagged data, generate *collocational profiles* and bring up *concordances* for further qualitative analysis. It also contains various text processing tools that can be helpful for corpus building e.g. for identifying and removing duplicate texts. However, for the purposes of our case study, we will use AntConc.

Having loaded our corpus into AntConc we now need to consider how to address our research question on the representation of council estates. There is no single analytical route through which we can carry out corpus-assisted discourse analysis, but we can employ a number of different procedures which can help us in our analysis. Some techniques may be more useful than others and some may provide overlapping findings, so an initial stage of analysis can involve considering what techniques the tool offers (and indeed if the tool is right for the task), and then deciding which ones to try, and in what order. The following sections describe some of the techniques available in AntConc, noting when they are most useful, as well as detailing what they produce when we use them with our corpus data.

Keywords

A *keyword* is a word which occurs exceptionally frequently in a particular corpus. It is not necessarily one of the most frequent words in the corpus in itself, but its frequency is higher than we would expect if we compared our corpus against a second corpus. Such a comparison corpus often acts as some sort of reference, telling us what the typical frequencies of words are in the way a particular language is used. In order to find the keywords in our corpus we need to compare the *word frequencies* in our corpus against the frequencies in such a standard reference. For the study at hand, I used the 90 million word written section of the British National Corpus. When I run the keywords procedure, AntConc obtains the frequencies of all of the words in both my corpus of news articles and the words in the written BNC and then compares them together using a statistical test called a *Log-Likelihood test*. For each word in the council estate corpus a keyness score is obtained via the Log-Likelihood test, and the higher the keyness number the higher the likelihood that a word is a keyword.

A keyword analysis is useful because it can reveal concepts in a corpus that are relatively frequent, and repeated usage is one way of signifying that a word is considered important to a text producer. We are often not able to accurately identify such keywords using qualitative techniques so they can provide a more objective way of helping us to narrow our research focus. The procedure can be used on any corpus, even on a relatively small one of a few thousand words in size (although in such cases we may want to privilege analysis of the higher frequency keywords). If our dataset is unfamiliar to us, then a keyword list can provide an overview of what some of the most salient concepts in the corpus are. If, on the other hand, we are already quite familiar with the texts in our corpus, the list might reveal some words that we had not considered as important.

The concept of keyness is based on one of gradience – some words are more key than others but there is no definite cut-off point where we can say with certainty 'this word is a keyword but the next word on the list is not'. (The same applies to other measures like collocation, discussed below.) The words in our corpus are ordered in terms of keyness and we then need to apply some sort of cut-off point in terms of deciding how many of them to consider for analysis. Practical considerations can delimit the number of keywords which are feasible to analyse, and I would advocate that a good analysis will cover a few keywords in-depth rather than produce a shallow, rushed analysis of lots of them. A possible approach could be to take a larger number than we intend to analyse to begin with (e.g. the top 20, 50, or 100 keywords) and categorise these words into groups based on theme or grammatical class or semantic field. We may then want to carry out a more in-depth analysis of a smaller number of keywords based on trying to cover a range of categories. It is usually not necessary to spend a lot of time on two keywords that are used in similar ways (e.g. if the words *red* and *crimson* were keywords and were used essentially as synonyms in the same contexts). Instead, we can take one as a case study and then quickly note the others that have similar functions. Other criteria for selecting a keyword could be that its analysis helps to answer our research question, and that its analysis reveals something that we did not already know or runs counter to expectations. Such keywords are likely to be of more relevance to our analysis.

In terms of the council estate corpus, the strongest 50 keywords are shown in Table 7.3, calculated for their Log-Likelihood keyness score using AntConc. All keywords had a keyness score of between 2767 and 7318, which indicate high keyness: a Log-Likelihood calculator gives a score of just 15.13 as being statistically significant at the 0.01% level[2] although if we had taken this score as the cut-off, it would have resulted in 11,113 keywords. The numbers in brackets give the frequency of each word in the corpus and I categorised the keywords into themes by hand.

132 Paul Baker

Table 7.3 Strongest 50 keywords, categorised into themes

Theme	Keywords
Council estates	block (2116), council (9625), estate (7318), estates (1957), homes (2363), housing (3587)
Grammatical words	am (5839), has (26,821), he (61,116), I (77,413), my (19,478), she (34,143), who (25,212),
Media	BBC (3736), film (2978), tv (2656), Twitter (1457)
People	kids (1984), family (5920), mum (2131), people (15,792),
Places	UK (5605)
Politics	Boris (1737), Brexit (2353), Cameron (3223), Conservative (2693), Corbyn (2241), Crabb (818), David (3855), EU (2851), Farage (866), Gove (1245), Jeremy (1448), Jo (1063), Johnson (2305), Khan (1639), Labour (7451), leader (2767), Miliband (798), MP (2989), MPs (1749), Osborne (1044), referendum (1835), Theresa (1136), Tory (3162), UKIP (1787), vote (2526)
Time	pm (6692), year (11,128)
Reporting	says (12,140)

When categorising words into themes, each keyword should ideally be examined via a *quick concordance* (see below) in order to gain an impression about its typical usage. For example, the word *block* could refer to the practice of blocking someone on social media or to a child's toy (e.g. a wooden block), but concordancing revealed that in the corpus it unsurprisingly almost always referred to a council block. Table 7.3 indicates that political words and concepts including names of political parties and leaders as well as reference to the referendum to leave the European Union (known as Brexit) were key in the corpus. To an extent this reflects the different time periods that the council estate corpus was collected in (2013–2017) as opposed to the texts in the reference corpus (the 1990s). However, other political keywords (*Labour, Conservative, vote*) are less period-specific and indicate that council estates are often referred to within the context of political news. Other keywords like *film* and *tv* also suggest other contexts within which council estates are discussed – as settings for forms of media entertainment. Finally, we should note that words comprising the original search term (*council, estate*) also appeared as keywords. This is, of course, unsurprising, although we should also note related words like *housing, block,* and *homes,* which were not part of the search term but suggest other ways of referring to the same concept and thus may be relevant for qualitative analysis. To take the analysis forward, I would prioritise analysing keywords from different categories such as *vote, film, council,* and *family* in more detail, although for this illustrative case study, the following sections focus on just the word *council*.

Collocates

In our corpus, the frequency of *council* is 9625, so it would be difficult to account for every usage in the corpus in great detail. In such cases it can be helpful to obtain a word's collocates, as they provide more focus and can enable the identification of patterns or prosodies around words. A *collocate* is a word which often occurs near or next to another word and suggests that the two words share an important relationship with one another. As with keywords there are different ways of measuring collocation but they all produce a list of words with a collocation score indicating either the strength of collocation such as *Mutual Information* (e.g. how attracted are two words to one another) or the certainty with which we can say they are collocates, such as Log-Likelihood. The same issues discussed above about deciding cut-off points for keywords apply to collocates as well, and we also need to make a few other decisions such as how many words either side of the search word we want to consider for collocates – the default is usually around three to five words but if our search or node word is not very frequent then we may want to make the collocational span larger to allow a wider range of words to be considered. However, if a word is infrequent (occurring less than 100 times, say), then a collocational approach is probably not the best in any case and it might make sense to skip to a concordance analysis of all the occurrences of the word (see below).

Table 7.4 shows the strongest 50 collocates of the word *council* in the corpus, using the Mutual Information (MI) score, a minimum frequency of ten and a span of five words either side of the search word. The collocates in the table all had an MI score of between 7 and 9. Durrant and Doherty (2010: 145) claim that for collocations to be 'psychologically real', e.g. for one word to trigger the thought of another, there needs to be an MI score of at least 6). As with keywords, I have categorised the collocates into themes and the number of times each word co-occurs with *council* is given in brackets.

Many of the top collocates relate to towns or localities in the UK where council estates are situated and thus refer to different news stories about council estates, showing the range of stories across the press. For our purposes, some of the other categories may be more interesting to analyse though and certainly any category which appears to indicate evaluation is worth examining closely. The negative words *rundown*, *impoverished*, *shabby*, and *scruffy* suggest that council estates are regularly described as being neglected, as the following examples from the corpus indicate:

[T]he thief told her to follow him into a rundown council estate
(*Daily Mail*, 5 October 2016)

He was brought up with two sisters, a brother and a number of step-siblings in a shabby terrace on a council estate
(*Daily Mail*, 30 January 2016)

134   *Paul Baker*

Table 7.4 Strongest 50 collocates of *council*

Theme	Collocates
Destruction	bulldozed (10), bulldozing (10), demolish (22)
Living	dwellings (10), estate (5059), estates (1299), hails (12), tenancies (30), tenancy (15)
Negative evaluation	impoverished (21), rundown (28), scruffy (13), shabby (10)
Places	Acton (27), Barnet (61), Bradford (45), Camden (53), Carlisle (22), Clifton (17), county (78), Galway (14), Gateshead (11), Gloucester (11), Guildford (19), Haringey (39), Hounslow (10), Huyton (10), Lambeth (47), Morpeth (12), Newham (34), parish (32), Peckham (53), Scunthorpe (12), Southwark (48), Stevenage (55), Stockport (11), Warrington (17), Watford (19), Wolverhampton (58), Wythenshawe (32)
Size	bordered (26), grew (786), sprawling (27)
Social actors	Claus (24), Coel (15), fools (23), Kathleen (11), Santa (16), scum (30), tenants (169)

> Anne-Marie Duff remembers where it all began – on a scruffy Manchester council estate
>
> (*Daily Mirror*, 25 October 2013)

Not all of these collocates directly modify *council* (*estate*): in the second example, *shabby* modifies *terrace* but as the terrace is described as being on a council estate, we could argue that the association still holds.

The examination of other categories of collocates reveals stories about council estates being demolished and replaced with private housing while other collocates like *sprawling* are indicative of large size but also suggest something rather ungainly and disordered, as in this example:

> In the middle of a sprawling inner-city council estate, community elders hunch over pool tables and PlayStations
>
> (*Daily Mirror*, 30 April 2017)

The general impression, then, from the collocates of *council*, is that council estates are large and neglected and that there is a move to demolish them. They do not seem to be associated with positive concepts.

However, collocates and keywords can only hint at representations in the corpus and must be supplemented with concordance analyses which consider context in more detail.

Concordances

A *concordance* is a list of all of the occurrences of a word, phrase, or sequence of word/tag combinations (if our corpus is tagged) in a corpus with each one occurring with a few words of co-text. Figure 7.1 shows a screenshot of a concordance of the phrase *council estate* from AntConc.

With 4945 occurrences of the term, only lines 25–38 are shown here and we would need to scroll up or down to see the others. We often also need to scroll sideways to see more co-text – at present the co-text (search window size) has been set to 80 characters but it is often useful to expand this number to around 150 characters to enable more co-text to be seen. Concordances can also be sorted alphabetically on any number of words to the left or right of the search term, which can help us to spot linguistic patterns. For example, if I sort the concordance in Figure 7.1 by one word to the left of the search term, I can scroll down the concordance and easily notice that the phrase *rough council estate* appears 26 times in the corpus. I also notice other frequently repeated words at the L1 (one place to the left) position like:

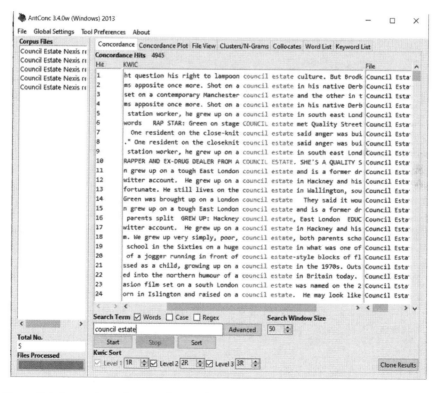

Figure 7.1 Screenshot of concordance of council estate using AntConc

136 *Paul Baker*

bleak (2 cases), crappy (1), crime-ridden (5), damp (1), dark (1), depressed (1), deprived (13), dismal (2), dodgy (1), dreary (1), empty (6), forgotten (1), gloomy (2), godforsaken (2), grey (1), grim (1), grimy (6), gritty (9), grotty (5), hapless (1), humble (1), impoverished (3), neglected (2), notorious (6), poor (4), rat-infested (1), rubbish (1), rundown (12), squalid (1), tough (38), troubled (1).

These words (158 in total or 3.19% of all cases) used to modify *council estate* indicate an explicit negative prosody linked to poverty, crime and neglect, building on the smaller set of negative evaluative collocates found above. While 3.19 is quite a small percentage, the concordance analysis yielded only two positive adjectives – *lovely* and *marvellous* – with only one occurrence each, accounting for a negligible 0.04% of all cases. Concordance analysis indicates that such cases are marked as exceptional, as in the following example:

> I wondered about the basic premise of The Estate We're In, which purports to show how a lovely council estate (see how difficult it is to cope with that oxymoron) is being attacked by the usual combination of complacent local government officials and big bad business
> *(i-Independent*, 12 March 2016)

Other concordance lines also suggest negative evaluations, albeit slightly more subtle ones:

> Kenny Doughty oozes council estate charisma as a jack-the-lad
> *(Daily Mail*, 28 February 2014)

Here, while the phrase *council estate charisma* suggests a positive evaluation, the verb *oozes* calls this into question. It can be useful to consult a larger reference corpus in order to obtain an impression of the kinds of prosodies that particular words are imbued with. In this case I examined the word *ooze* and related forms like *oozing* in the full 100-million-word British National Corpus, finding that it strongly collocates with liquid materials like *blood* (20 cases) and *mud* (6 cases) as well as less frequent instances *like pus, poison,* and *slime*. In other words, things that ooze are not usually good and to ooze council estate charisma is therefore not necessarily a fully positive evaluation.

However, the analysis needs to go beyond simple evaluation in order to obtain an impression of the reasons for the evaluation and the contexts in which it occurs. This involves a close reading of concordance lines and grouping lines together which are similar. If we have a large number of concordance lines we may want to take random samples (e.g. of 100 lines) and note patterns there – adding further sets of samples if patterns are inconclusive or complex. For example, one pattern found when reading the concordance lines involved references to people who were featured in news stories and were described as having grown up on council estates.

Corpus-assisted discourse analysis   137

A self-made man who grew up on a council estate but made
£610 million in business

(*Daily Mail*, 1 February 2013)

I'm now an ambassador for the Prince's Trust. I grew up on a council
estate in Watford. It's not the best place to start out.

(*Daily Star*, 29 August 2013)

Does admit that his success is a huge deal to him: a boy from a council
estate in East London who got bullied at school due to the colour of
his skin

(*The Sun*, 29 June 2013)

A genuine televisual first – a sitcom about intellectuals from a council
estate

(*The Guardian*, 24 December 2013)

Most of the examples above describe successful people who have come
from council estates, and so we may want to conclude that the media
actually sometimes engages in positive representations of people from
council estates. However, the examples indicate some of the assumptions
about council estates which are articulated in implicatures. In the first
example, a man is described as having grown up on a council estate but
having made £610 million. The word *but* is a case of negating expectations,
suggesting that such a man would not normally be expected to have made
so much money. In the second example, someone describes themselves as
being an ambassador for the Prince's Trust, a respectable position in
a charity sponsored by the Royal Family. However, the person speaking
describes himself as being from a council estate which is 'not the best place
to start out'. The third line also pairs success with coming from a council
estate – although the success is described as a 'big deal', again presumably
gained in spite of the boy's background. In the final example, a sitcom
about intellectuals from a council estate is described as a 'televisual first',
implying that such people are unusual – in other words, intellectuals are
not normally from council estates.

There are a number of messages we can take away from this part of the
analysis then. First, the media do occasionally (but not often) represent
people from council estates as being successful. However, such people are
implied to be exceptional and their success is actually part of the narrative
of a news story – it is seen as newsworthy that someone who grew up on
a council estate should be successful in later life. In terms of Galtung and
Holmboe Ruge (1965) news values, the success is newsworthy because it is
unexpected. The implicature then, is that council estates do not normally
breed success stories.

138 *Paul Baker*

A second interpretation we could derive from the analysis is that the people who are described as successful are constructed as coming from or being brought up on a council estate as opposed to currently living on one. This suggests that either their success is viewed as linked to them leaving the council estate, or that once they became successful they decided to live elsewhere. In other words, again, council estates are not viewed as places where successful people choose to live. Other examples in the corpus confirm this sense, with concordance lines detailing people who have left council estates (note the word *escape* below) and describe their memories of them:

> Sarah Callaghan is garnering plaudits for her first fringe hour, which is about her struggle to escape council estate life in Uxbridge, west London
>
> (*The Guardian*, 19 August 2015)

> When I was a kid I couldn't wait to get out on the grass on our council estate and take part in the 15-a-side games we used to have every night
>
> (*The Sun*, 14 December 2014)

> I went back recently to my old council estate in South Oxhey, where all these poky tin houses were identical
>
> (*The Guardian*, 8 February 2013)

Due to space limitations this can only be a partial analysis but at this point we might want to consider the ways that these repeated representations of council estates could impact on different types of readers. A range of negative associations involving shame, fear, disgust, and anger could be evoked upon encountering these types of articles. Generally, council estates are not portrayed as places that successful people usually come from or live on, and the higher proportion of negative to positive portrayals may make people feel that they are places to be avoided, along with the sorts of people who come from them. The articles frequently focus on the worst aspects of council estates and thus could contribute towards an ideological stance that social housing is a wrong-headed policy. On the other hand, it could make readers feel that successive governments have failed people who live in social housing, generating sympathy for them. More analysis would need to be done in order to identify the sorts of underlying messages in the articles and the various 'readings' that they afford, perhaps focusing on some of the political keywords found earlier.

Presenting findings and results

It is good practice to try to be as clear as possible about the settings and procedures that were used to obtain the results, so that they can be verified by someone else who is given the same corpus and research question(s).

For example, if identifying collocates, we should be clear regarding the statistical algorithm that was used, what the minimum frequency for collocation had to be and what collocational span was chosen. We should also be specific in terms of presenting findings, e.g. how many times the pairs of words co-occurred. If a random set of concordance lines was examined, then that should be made clear, and large amounts of information about dozens or hundreds of words might be better off placed in a summary table (such as Tables 7.3 and 7.4 above). Analysts should also try to provide information about frequencies of patterns in their corpus, along with collocational and keyword scores where appropriate. Specific quantification is generally preferable to using vaguer wording like 'there are some cases of'.

When comparing frequencies across two or more corpora of different sizes, then it is sensible to carry out standardisation, e.g. by also presenting the frequencies not only in absolute terms but also in terms of the number of occurrences per million words in each corpus. This allows a more meaningful comparison of the two rates of occurrence. Some corpus tools (such as CQPweb) provide this figure, but otherwise it will need to be calculated by the analyst.

Figures and bar charts can be useful in order to present patterns, particularly if we are comparing multiple corpora or frequencies of related words. However, such graphics should be used sparingly and are at their best when they help readers to identify a more complex pattern, such as comparing the change in frequency over time of two or more words. It is also a good idea to illustrate patterns with around two to four typical examples from the corpus data, along with brief details about the text source. However, cited examples should be as brief as possible in order to focus on the analytical point(s) being made, and ethical considerations should also be taken into account when citing examples, especially if working with social media or other forms of personal language use.

Issues and limitations

Obtaining access to appropriate corpora and learning to get the most out of corpus tools can present hurdles to new researchers. With a range of different procedures to hand, it can also be difficult to know which ones to use and in which order. Beginning analysts may stick with the default settings of a tool or focus too much on reporting frequencies that may not reveal very much of interest as opposed to carrying out more detailed concordance analyses. It is important to bear in mind that a keyword or collocational analysis only represents the start, a 'way in' to the corpus and should always be supplemented with qualitative analyses. Additionally, analysis should ideally go beyond the texts. The corpus can only represent its own contents and to fully interpret and explain our findings we usually need to draw on other forms of contextual analysis, in keeping with other forms of critical research (such as conditions of production and reception). As a result, analysts may feel overwhelmed at the wide array of skills required in order to carry out and combine the different quantitative and qualitative aspects of the research. Additionally, analysts who are not linguists may tend towards producing a content analysis of the corpus which may not provide insights into how language is used to maintain or contest representations or discourses.

Corpus linguistics is a developing field and the application of the most appropriate statistical tests and algorithms to language data is still subject to debate among practitioners. The Log-Likelihood test, which was once the staple of keyword calculations, now exists alongside newer algorithms like log-ratio[3], %Diff (Gabrielatos and Marchi, 2012), and text dispersion keyword analysis (Egbert and Biber, 2019). Corpus analysis software can be slow to implement newer procedures and it can be difficult to know which ones will become standard. Additionally, more work needs to be done in order to pair up theories about language use with cognitive experiments which indicate, for example, what happens in people's minds when they encounter collocations or keywords in a text.

Corpus linguistics is a field which is relatively young but shows increasing potential to make a significant contribution towards our understanding of how discourses are formed. However, it is important to note that the computer tools are there to assist rather than replace the human analyst. They cannot make analytical decisions or provide interpretations, explanations or critiques. The role of the critical discourse analyst remains safe, just with an additional set of tools under her belt.

Further reading

Baker (2006) is a good place to start in terms of finding a way into the field, and Baker (2014) acts as a companion book, which while focused on gender, and provides updated information on methods. Partington et al., (2013) gives an excellent overview of the corpus-assisted discourse studies approach while Baker et al., (2013) operates as a detailed case study using corpus approaches to examine Islam in the news from a critical perspective.

References

Baker, P. (2005). *Public discourses of gay men.* London: Routledge.
Baker, P. (2006). *Using corpora for discourse analysis.* London: Continuum.
Baker, P. (2014). *Using corpora to analyse gender.* London: Bloomsbury.
Baker, P., Gabrielatos, C., Khosravinik, M., Krzyzanowski, M., McEnery, T. and Wodak, R. (2008). A useful methodological synergy? Combining critical discourse analysis and corpus linguistics to examine discourses of refugees and asylum seekers in the UK press. *Discourse & Society, 19*(3), 273–306.

Baker, P., Gabrielatos, C. and McEnery, T. (2013). *Discourse analysis and media attitudes*. Cambridge: Cambridge University Press.

Baker, P. and McEnery, T. (2015). Who benefits when discourse gets democratised? Analysing a Twitter corpus around the British Benefits Street debate. In P. Baker and T. McEnery (Eds.), *Corpora and discourse studies: Integrating discourse and corpora*. (pp. 244–265.). Basingstoke: Palgrave MacMillan.

Bevitori, C. (2015). Discursive constructions of the environment in presidential speeches 1960–2013: A diachronic corpus-assisted study. In P. Baker and T. McEnery (Eds.), *Corpora and discourse studies: Integrating discourse and corpora*. (pp. 110–133). Basingstoke: Palgrave MacMillan.

Caldas-Coulthard, C.R. (1993). From discourse analysis to critical discourse analysis: The differential representation of women and men speaking in written news. In J. M. Sinclair, M. Hoey and G. Fox (Eds.), *Techniques of description*. (pp. 196–208). London: Routledge.

Durrant, P. and Doherty, A. (2010). Are high frequency collocations psychologically real? Investigating the thesis of collocational priming. *Corpus Linguistics and Linguistic Theory*, 6(2), 125–155.

Egbert, J. and Biber, D. (2019). Incorporating text dispersion into keyword analyses. *Corpora*, 14(1), 77–104.

Gabrielatos, C. and Marchi, A. (2012). Keyness: Appropriate metrics and practical issues. CADS International Conference 2012. Corpus-assisted Discourse Studies: More than the sum of Discourse Analysis and computing? 13–14 September, University of Bologna, Italy.

Galtung, J. and Holmboe Ruge, M. (1965). The structure of foreign news.: The presentation of the Congo, Cuba and Cyprus crises in four Norwegian newspapers. *Journal of Peace Research*, 2, 64–91.

Hardt-Mautner, G. (1995). 'Only connect': Critical discourse analysis and corpus linguistics. *UCREL Technical Paper* 6. Lancaster University.

Hunt, D. and Harvey, K. (2015). Health communication and corpus linguistics: Using corpus tools to analyse eating disorder discourse online. In P. Baker and T. McEnery (Eds.), *Corpora and discourse studies: Integrating discourse and corpora*. (pp. 134–154). Basingstoke: Palgrave MacMillan.

Hunt, S. (2015). Representations of gender and agency in the Harry Potter series. In P. Baker and T. McEnery (Eds.), *Corpora and discourse studies: Integrating discourse and corpora*. (pp. 266–284). Basingstoke: Palgrave MacMillan.

Marchi, A. (2010). 'The moral in the story': A diachronic investigation of lexicalised morality in the UK press. *Corpora*, 5(2), 161–190.

Partington, A. (2015). Corpus-assisted comparative case studies of representations of the Arab world. In P. Baker and T. McEnery (Eds.), *Corpora and discourse studies: Integrating discourse and corpora*. (pp. 220–243). Basingstoke: Palgrave MacMillan.

Partington, A., Duguid, A. and Taylor, C. (2013). *Patterns and meanings in discourse: Theory and practice in corpus-assisted discourse studies* (CADS). Amsterdam: John Benjamins.

Pearce, M. (2008). Investigating the collocational behaviour of Man and Woman in the BNC using Sketch Engine. *Corpora*, 3(1), 1–29.

Stubbs, M. (2001). *Words and phrases. Corpus studies of lexical semantics*. Oxford: Blackwell.

Stubbs, M. and Gerbig, A. (1993). Human and inhuman geography: On the computer-assisted analysis of long texts. In M. Hoey (Ed.), *Data, description, discourse*.

142   *Paul Baker*

Papers on the English language in honour of John McH Sinclair on his sixtieth birthday. (pp. 64–85). London: Harper Collins.

Taylor, C. (2010). Science in the news: A diachronic perspective. *Corpora*, 5(2), 221–250.

Widdowson, H.G. (2000). On the limitations of linguistics applied. *Applied Linguistics*, 21(1), 3–25.

8 Multimodal discourse analysis

Christopher Hart

Introduction

This chapter introduces the field of multimodality. Multimodality does not represent an approach to discourse analysis but, rather, a commitment to studying the range of modes, besides language, that are drawn upon to convey meaning in any act of communication. The term 'mode' refers to a set of representational resources, existing in different channels or modalities, which carry conventionalised meanings within a given community. Besides language, examples of modes include gesture and prosody in spoken face-to-face interaction and typography and page layout in written discourse. Relatively late in the twentieth century there was a 'multimodal turn' within discourse analysis as researchers begun to recognise the increasingly multimodal nature of texts and discourses. Accordingly, researchers in critical discourse analysis have sought to understand the role that non-linguistic modes of communication play in constructing social identities and relations. To a large extent, this has involved the application of analytical models developed originally in linguistics to modes other than language and especially to modes that exist within the visual modality.[1] This chapter illustrates how you might go about conducting a multimodal critical discourse analysis from the perspectives of systemic functional linguistics and, to a lesser extent, conceptual metaphor theory. The data analysed by way of a case study is taken from online news coverage of civil disorder.

Outline of approach

Multimodality does not describe a specific approach to discourse analysis. Rather, multimodality represents a commitment to studying the multiplicity of modes that contribute meaning in any communicative encounter. Although texts and discourse have always been inherently multimodal, non-linguistic modes have come to occupy an increasingly significant space in the semiotic landscape. This is most evident, for example, if you compare an early printed newspaper article of, say, 1878 (see Figure 8.1) with the online news articles of today (see Figures 8.14, 8.15, and 8.16 for examples). Although the text in

Figure 8.1 contains multimodal features in the form of page layout and typography, it is markedly different in its multimodality compared to contemporary news texts, especially online news texts. The meanings communicated by any modern text, partly due to what is understood to count as 'a text', are communicated through a great variety of semiotic modes. Multimodality is concerned to explore the role that these modes play, including as they interact with language, in the creation of meaning. Crucially, multimodality does not privilege language and see non-linguistic

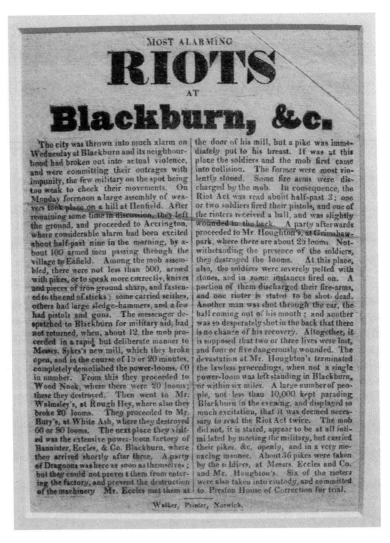

Figure 8.1 Reports of riots in Blackburn, 1878

Multimodal discourse analysis 145

modes as playing secondary or merely supporting roles. Rather, texts are seen as *multimodal ensembles* with different modes contributing different kinds of meanings, all of which are equally responsible for the overall message that a text conveys.

As a field of application, multimodality is explored in different academic disciplines from a variety of theoretical perspectives. In discourse analysis, multimodality could, in principle, be approached within any of the frameworks covered in this book. Broadly, however, multimodal discourse analysis falls into two categories. *Multimodal interaction analysis* (e.g. Norris, 2004) focuses on the different modes that interlocutors exploit to make meanings and manage social relationships in situated, face-to-face interactions. It has its roots in conversation analysis (Hutchby and Woofitt, 1998), interactional sociology (Goffman, 1981) and interactional sociolinguistics (Gumperz, 1982). In line with these frameworks, multimodal interaction analysis views communicative interactions, whether in 'everyday' or institutionalised settings, as constitutive of the social order of things. Modes studied include gesture, gaze, facial expression, body posture, head movement, proxemics and the prosodic features of speech. Norris (2004) calls these *embodied* modes in contrast to *disembodied* modes, such as pictures on a wall or the layout of a room, which also contribute to and constrain meaning in any interaction. *Multimodal social semiotics* focuses on the different modes present in 'texts' rather than face-to-face interactions. The two most influential approaches here are based in extensions of *systemic functional linguistics* (e.g. Kress and van Leeuwen, [1996] 2006) and *conceptual metaphor theory* (e.g. Forceville, 1998). Similar to multimodal interaction analysis, multimodal social semiotics views texts, including seemingly banal texts, as constitutive of social experience and social organisation. Think, for example, about the signs on most toilet doors designating 'male' and 'female' thus serving to reinforce binary gender identities. Modes studied in multimodal social semiotics include typography and page layout but also (moving) images and materiality. Many of the modes observed in situated interaction are also studied in multimodal social semiotics as they get represented in images.[2] Multimodal social semiotics has been applied to texts produced in a variety of contexts ranging from art and architecture (O'Toole, 1994) to science (Lemke, 1998) and mathematics (O'Halloran, 2005). This work is largely descriptive. Some researchers, however, adopt an explicitly *critical* position from which they are concerned to expose, with a view to challenging and ultimately resisting, the ideologies and power relations encoded in and enacted through the multimodal features of texts. Research from this perspective is said to fall within *multimodal critical discourse analysis* (Machin, 2007: Machin and Mayr, 2012) where the kinds of texts analysed have included: advertisements (Lazar, 2009); lifestyle and business magazines (Koller, 2005, 2008); editorial cartoons (Bounegru and Forceville, 2011; El Refaie, 2003); news articles (Bednarek and Caple, 2012; Hart, 2017); war memorials

146 *Christopher Hart*

(Abousnnouga and Machin, 2013); and computer games (Machin and Suleiman, 2006). In this chapter, I focus on multimodal social semiotics assuming a critical perspective. Illustrative data is taken from a single genre – online news articles – reporting instances of civil disorder in the form of riots and protests.

A mode is understood to be any set of resources which is systematically exploited to communicate meaning. In other words, a mode is any system of tacitly or institutionally agreed upon *signs*. From an SFL perspective, the semiotic resources presented by any mode have different *meaning-potentials* (Halliday, 1978), which have been shaped by the social, historical and cultural contexts in which those resources have previously been used. The plural in 'meaning-potentials' here is important, for just as in language, where the same word can have multiple meanings, the resources in other modes are similarly polysemous so that the same resource can signify different things in different contexts. The meaning-making potential of any semiotic resource is *realised* by its instantiation in texts but *actualised* only in readers' uptake and interpretation of texts. It is important to note that the focus of multimodal social semiotics has not been on readers' reception of texts. When we speak about the 'meanings' of a text, therefore, we are not talking about what the text necessarily means for every reader, everywhere, on every occasion. Rather, we are talking about the meanings which, from a particular theoretical perspective, a text appears to promote (Björkvall, 2017: 179).

Kress and van Leeuwen ([1996] 2006: 2) point out that meanings belong to culture rather than to any specific mode. Some meanings are therefore capable of being realised across multiple modes so that, for example, what can be said verbally can, in some instances, also be 'said' visually. However, meanings cannot be directly translated between modes any more than they can between languages. Different modes present different resources and the means of realisation will affect the message. Different modes also have different *constraints* and *affordances* with respect to the meanings they accommodate. Speech and writing, for example, both involve language. However, speech also involves the mode of sound, or prosody, which has semiotic resources that are not available in writing, including in rhythm, tempo, pitch, volume, etc. Although the modes involved in writing, such as typography, have some equivalent resources, e.g. in the use of bold or italics, writing is more restricted in its ability to communicate the kinds of meanings afforded to speech by sound. Similarly, when compared to speech or writing, the resources that contribute meanings to images, such as colour, size, or shape, allow for much finer gradations of meaning. For example, the word 'red', whether in speech or writing, denotes only a class of colour whereas the red in any image is always an instantiation of something more particular – a red of a specific shade and luminosity. In other words, then, different modes provide different sets of meaning-potentials, so that what is readily communicated in one mode is not necessarily so easily communicated in another. Hence, communicators rely on multiple modes in order to convey the full complexity of their intended message.

The task for researchers in multimodal social semiotics is to map out the resources presented by different modes and consider the meaning-potentials they realise in different contexts. In approaches to multimodality based in SFL, this takes the form of a 'grammar', conceived as systems of semiotic choices open to the communicator. Thus, in their seminal work, Kress and van Leeuwen ([1996] 2006) describe a 'grammar of visual design'.

In line with SFL, the grammar of any mode is seen as having been shaped to meet the communicative demands of its users. Modes can therefore differ across cultures or communities of practice. Gestural modes, for example, are elaborated differently in different cultures. Gestures are typically larger in Mediterranean cultures than they are in northern European cultures (Cavicchio and Kita, 2013). And organisations like the military have developed their own institution-specific gestural codes. At the broadest level, Halliday (1978) argues that any communicational system has evolved to simultaneously fulfil three *metafunctions*: in the *ideational* metafunction, communicators construct representations of the world; in the *interpersonal* metafunction, communicators manage and maintain social identities and relations; and in the *textual* metafunction, communicators organise meanings into coherent assemblages (texts) that enable and enact the other two metafunctions. Although in practice all three metafunctions are necessarily served by any communicative act, in multimodal social semiotics they are often isolated to help structure analyses.

The semiotic choices made in fulfilment of these metafunctions are what makes it possible for power and ideology to be constructed through the multimodal features of texts. In any mode, the selection of one semiotic resource over another reflects a particular worldview or societal arrangement which is presented to the 'reader' of a text as factual or somehow natural. For example, news photographs are usually assumed to provide objective, documentary evidence of events as they happen in the world. However, choices in content, composition and co-textual embedding mean that photographs do not just document social realities but construct and evaluate them, standing as symbolic representations which have emotional appeal (Bednarek and Caple, 2012: 112). In other words, there is a distinction between the literal meaning of the text (its denotation) and the values carried by elements within it (its connotation) (Barthes, 1973). It should be noted that the 'choices' presented by a text may be a function of institutional norms and practices as much as the personal perspectives or communicative goals of the text-producer. However, this does not subtract from the imprint that a text bears of power and ideology. Thus, from a critical perspective, as Abousnnouga and Machin (2011: 327) argue,

148 *Christopher Hart*

just as we can study the lexical and grammatical resources of language to reveal underlying discourses, so we can study the semiotic choices made within other modes to show how these can serve to persuade, position and legitimise.

It has been suggested above that modes work together to give meaning to a text. Part of multimodal social semiotics is therefore to go beyond describing the meanings contributed by different modes independently of one another and consider the different kinds of meaning relation that modes can enter into in a multimodal text. For example, there is a whole field, with its history in the work of Roland Barthes (1977), dedicated to exploring intermodal relations between language and image (see Bateman, 2014 for an overview). Barthes distinguished between *anchorage* and *relay* relations. Starting from the position that all images are polysemous, language provides an anchorage function in so far as it 'directs the reader through the signifieds of the image, causing him to avoid some and receive others' (p. 40). For Barthes, anchorage is the most frequent function of language accompanying images. It is characteristic, for example, of the relationship between press photographs and their captions (ibid.). In relay, language and image stand in a complementary relationship, cohering with one another as a function of the larger story to which they are each contributing (p. 41). For Barthes, relay relations are comparatively rare but are seen particularly in cartoons, comic strips and film (ibid.).

Several other frameworks modelling language–image relations have been proposed which are based in various aspects of SFL. Kress and van Leeuwen ([1996] 2006: 63–78) argue that the model of clause transitivity described in SFL (see Chapter 4, this volume) extends to images so that visual representations can be analysed as configurations of participants, processes, and circumstances. Royce (1998, 2007) takes this as a basis for comparing abstract representations in each mode and then considering the *cohesive relations* that exist between them. In SFL, cohesion is what gives 'texture' to texts (Halliday and Hasan, 1976). In Royce's model, the cohesive ties that establish texture in multimodal artefacts are modelled in terms of *intersemiotic sense relations*, which include repetition, synonymy, antonymy, hyponymy, meronymy, and collocation. In another framework, Martinec and Salway (2005) account for language-image relations by extending the clause-combining relationships described in SFL as *logico-semantic relations*. This part of grammar is concerned with the way clauses are joined together to create larger 'clause complexes' (Halliday and Matthiessen, 2004: 373–378). Logico-semantic relations are divided into two broad categories: projection and expansion. In language, projection is associated with reported speech and thought. In multimodal texts, such as cartoons or comic strips, projection is established through things like speech bubbles and thought clouds. Expansion accounts for the different ways that information in one clause or mode can add to information expressed in another clause or mode. It is divided into three sub-types: elaboration, extension, and enhancement. Distinguishing

Multimodal discourse analysis   149

types of expansion in practice, however, is not always easy, especially in the case of intersemiotic expansion. Finally, Liu and O'Halloran (2009) model language-image relations in terms of *discourse-conjunctive relations* as originally set out by Martin (1992). Martin's focus was on discourse–semantic relations that seem to operate independently of grammatical realisations. Based on Martin's classification, four principle types of intersemiotic relation are identified: additive, comparative, consequential and temporal.

While SFL-based approaches to multimodal social semiotics have been the most prominent, other theories of language have also been successfully extended to account for meaning in multimodal discourse. Another notably influential approach is based in conceptual metaphor theory (Lakoff and Johnson, 1980). For Lakoff and Johnson, metaphorical expressions in language reflect metaphorical ways of thinking at a more abstract, conceptual level. In other words, metaphors in texts instantiate a conceptual system that is organised, largely, metaphorically. Indeed, in common with Kress and van Leeuwen ([1996] 2006), who view meanings as independent of modes, for Lakoff and Johnson, metaphor is primarily a matter of thought and action and only derivatively a matter of language (Lakoff and Johnson, 1980: 153). In a series of works, Forceville (1998, 2002, 2006, 2008) has therefore argued that we should expect to find conceptual metaphors, which involve a comparison between a 'source' and a 'target', realised non-verbally and multimodally as well as verbally. Specifically, Forceville investigates the role of visual modes in realising underlying conceptual metaphors. He distinguishes between *pictorial metaphors*, where the metaphor is expressed through visual elements of the text alone, and *multimodal metaphors*, where the metaphor is dependent for its recognition on an interaction between verbal and visual elements.

Many conceptual metaphors emerge through connections in embodied experience (Lakoff and Johnson, 1999) but many are based in discourse where they constitute an entrenched view of social actions, identities, and relations. From a critical perspective, metaphors in text, as they occur both cross- and inter-modally, therefore play a key part in the discursive construction of power and ideology and in the legitimation of social practice.

Identifying research questions

Research questions in multimodal critical discourse analysis can take many different forms depending on the nature of the data you are analysing and the size and scope of the project you are undertaking. However, research questions are typically exploratory rather than confirmatory. That is, they ask 'how', 'why', and 'what' rather than 'whether'. In line with critical discourse analysis more generally, research questions often start from a desire to investigate a particular social phenomenon. So, you might ask, for example:

1. What are the multimodal semiotic resources exploited in the discursive representation of X in text or discourse Y?

150   *Christopher Hart*

where X is a particular topic, social group, action, or event-type and Y is a particular text or text genre. This question involves a largely descriptive answer and so an additional *critical* question would be:

2. What are the social and ideological implications of different patterns of multimodal representation in texts relating to X?

For example, Abousnnouga and Machin (2011) investigated size, shape, and surface texture in representations of male soldiers and 'women at home' in British war monuments. They found that, through choices made with respect to these semiotic resources, war monuments celebrated and glorified the efforts of male soldiers while masking the harsh realities of physical combat and denying the active role of women in wartime.

Questions of the form given in 1 and 2 are broad questions which in order to address require in-depth qualitative analyses of texts 'as a whole'. That is, in response to these questions, your aim would be to fully account for the meanings contributed by different modes in a select number of texts. Typically, this will be a relatively small number of texts since such an analysis is incredibly labour intensive. In the case of music or film, you may analyse just a single text or part of a text and consider in detail the various layers of meaning contributed by different semiotic modes and their interaction. As an example, Mano (2019) offers an exquisitely fine-grained multimodal analysis of a short online video released by Manchester United Football Club (MUFC) announcing the signing of a new player. He shows how the semiotic resources selected in language, image and sound constructed MUFC in the 'manifest image' of sport (Walsh and Guilianotti, 2007) while simultaneously adhering to and feeding its 'sports-as-business' model. Analyses of this kind are often structured in terms of Halliday's three metafunctions of communication, in which case you may ask a series of sub-questions which together help to address your primary research questions (see Jones, 2012: 123, for specific examples of questions relating to each metafunction):

1a. What ideational resources are relied on in the discursive representation of X?
1b. What interpersonal resources are relied on in the discursive representation of X?
1c. What textual arrangements are relied on in the discursive representation of X?

Question 1a is to ask who or what is presented in the text and how, while question 1b is to ask how the text positions the reader in relation to its subject matter and how realistic the proposition presented is. Question 1c is to ask how the message is organised. Of all of these sub-questions we can ask: what do different patterns of representation reveal about underlying discourses?

Alternatively, you may be interested in further exploring a particular semiotic mode or feature and so pose a more specific research question along the following lines:

3. What role does Z play in the multimodal discursive construction of X in discourse Y?

where Z might be a semiotic mode, like language, image or body posture, or a semiotic feature like metaphor. Such a question recognises the multimodal nature of texts but homes in on a particular parameter to provide a detailed exposition. For example, Ostermeyer and Sittler (2019) consider body movement as a semiotic mode involved in the discursive construction of rioting. They analysed stills taken from live television broadcasts and showed how rioters draw, interdiscursively, on a repertoire of body moves sourced from mediatised popular culture activities like American football and breakdance.

A more specific question centred around a particular mode or feature may be inspired by the literature or may be data-driven, where as you collect and begin to explore a larger data set, one mode or feature emerges as especially important and your research questions become more refined in light of this. For example, in my own work, when I began researching UK media coverage of the British Miners' Strike (Hart, 2017, 2019a), I did not set out to conduct a multimodal analysis or to focus exclusively on metaphor. However, having collected a corpus of data, sifting through it I found a particular metaphor (STRIKE IS WAR) to be a recurring motif and, moreover, that this metaphor was being articulated across modes as well as intermodally.

Analyses of this kind, centred on a specific semiotic mode or feature, may be qualitative, quantitative, or mixed. Regardless, it is often revealing to introduce a comparative dimension to your analysis. So, for example, you might want to investigate how newspapers differ in their multimodal representation of a given social phenomenon. In which case, you may formulate a further research question along the lines:

4. How does Z vary in multimodal representations of X in discourses Y according to dimension U?

where U is an additional variable like time, political stance or geographical region.

Although the majority of research in multimodal social semiotics is exploratory, confirmatory research questions are also possible. This is especially the case if you want to investigate a specific hypothesis concerning intersemiotic relations. For example, you might want to test a hypothesis that representations of X in two different modes will tend to have

152 Christopher Hart

a convergent structure – 'intersemiotic repetition' in Royce's (2007) terms. Such questions would most likely need to be addressed quantitatively.

Data collection and ethics

Multimodal social semiotics tends to work with texts that exist already (as opposed to multimodal interaction analysis which creates texts in the recording of face-to-face interactions). Collecting data in multimodal social semiotics is therefore comparatively more straightforward. Data, in the form of newspaper or magazine articles, advertisements, webpages, online videos or video footage, for example, is readily available.

Depending on your research questions, you will want to collect smaller or larger amounts of data. You may be analysing just a single text or a number of texts. Regardless, which text(s) to sample represents an important issue and the choices you make must be transparent and justified. Questions to ask yourself include: is your data representative or has it been sampled on some other basis? For example, are the text(s) you are analysing characteristic of texts produced in a particular context or genre? Perhaps they have been selected because they are culturally salient or widely disseminated, or because they hold some other form of social or political significance? Or perhaps they have been selected on the basis that they are semiotically rich or because they serve as examples illustrating the use of particular modes and resources?

If your research questions require you to analyse multiple texts, you may choose to collect a corpus by defining a fixed set of criteria in advance and gathering all the texts that meet it. For example, in researching media representations of the British Miners' Strike, I identified, based on historical contextual knowledge rather than linguistic factors, six salient moments in the yearlong strike. I then gathered a targeted set of news articles covering these events. Eight national newspapers were sampled with all articles that were published in the first editions the following day or two days later in cases where the story continued to run being included. Alternatively, you may pursue a more open and continuous approach to data collection. For instance, by mining the internet for data pertinent to your research questions. The issue you then face is how much data do you need or when should you stop? Qualitative researchers tend to speak of stopping at the point of *saturation* (Miles and Huberman, 1994). That is, when adding to the sample no longer provides any substantive new insight.

Regardless of how you collect your data, if it involves multiple texts, it is important to keep an organised log of it that includes as much relevant *meta-data* as possible. For example, where and when was an image published, what is it an image of, how can it be accessed again, and who owns the copyright? (See below.) You might also include notes as to why you included an item in your sample. It ought to go without saying but, of course, you must also be sure to save that data itself so that you can continue to access it in case it becomes otherwise unavailable. It is important to save data like images or screenshots as the highest quality files possible. This is especially the case if you think you might publish parts of your project.

Although collecting data in multimodal social semiotics is ethically relatively straightforward, at least compared to collecting data in multimodal interaction analysis, this does not mean that ethics is unimportant for projects in this area. On the contrary, ethics is a significant factor for any project that involves data of any kind and careful consideration must be given to relevant ethics issues before any decisions on data collection are taken. Perhaps the first thing to consider is whether the data you intend to collect should be treated as 'public' or 'private'. Newspaper or magazine articles, editorial cartoons, campaign leaflets, or websites of political parties etc. are all clearly intended for public consumption and therefore the issue of consent does not apply. Things are considerably more complicated, however, when it comes to multimodal data sourced from social media platforms (see Chapter 9, this volume, for a discussion). Other issues that do apply to data in the public domain include, for example, risks to the researcher themselves. Multimodal data might be extremely sensitive, unpleasant, graphic, or offensive. Think about analysing images of war or poverty or videos produced by gangs or terrorist organisations, for example. It is important to consider the effects that searching for and being exposed to such data may have on one's personal safety and wellbeing. There is also the issue of copyright. Researchers publishing their work are required to obtain permission, usually for a fee, from copyright holders to reproduce their content. This goes for material, such as images in newspaper articles, that is often erroneously assumed to fall under the 'fair use: criticism and review' exception in copyright law. Although it is not normally considered problematic to reproduce copyright material in student research projects, it is worth checking ethics policies in your own institution if you think you might publish your analysis yourself or, for example, if your university keeps an online publically accessible repository of student research papers.

Analysing and interpreting data

How you analyse your data will depend on whether you are taking a more theory-driven or more data-driven approach. In a theory-driven approach (sometimes called *deductive*), you start with a set of pre-defined analytical categories and use these to probe your data. Categories are sourced from prior research. They may be based on a particular theory or classification system. So, for example, you may set out to analyse your data in terms of van Leeuwen's (1996) system for classifying representations of social actors or Halliday's (1978) transitivity system as instantiated in the multimodal features of texts. In a data-driven approach (sometimes called *inductive*), you start from your data and formulate your analytical categories in response to it. An inductive approach involves immersing yourself in the data and allowing patterns and themes to emerge. The analytical categories you use may still have a basis in previously developed frameworks but they are not chosen in advance and they may bring together aspects of several different frameworks as dictated by the data. Inductive approaches are therefore often more eclectic. So, for example, you might end up analysing your data in terms of visual transitivity, multimodal metaphor, and 'image acts'. In practice, most research in multimodal social semiotics involves some combination of deductive and inductive approaches.

In multimodal social semiotics, especially when coming from a critical perspective, it is important that your analysis goes beyond describing the data to consider the social functions that semiotic resources are performing in the specific context of the text. For example, a close-up shot in an image may, in one context, connote threat or intimidation but in another connote intimacy or familiarity. By context it is meant both co-text, i.e. the meanings co-present in the text by virtue of semiotic choices in other modes, and the wider social and cultural contexts in which the text is embedded.

Analyses in multimodal critical discourse analysis, then, are necessarily context-informed and involve some degree of interpretation on the part of the researcher. However, they should always start from a solid descriptive base where the analytical categories of your framework are applied systematically and consistently. Whether you are analysing a single text or multiple texts, this will normally involve the annotation or *coding* of your data. At this point in time, there are no software programmes that allow the automatic annotation of multimodal data as there are for purely linguistic data (see Chapter 7, this volume). There are, however, several programmes available for the manual coding of multimodal data which allow both qualitative and quantitative analysis. A fairly universal programme for data coding and management, which many universities have a subscription to, is ATLAS.ti (www.atlasti.com). ATLAS.ti allows you to define your own analytical categories and code your data accordingly. It then allows you to search and perform basic operations over your data to discover recurrent themes and patterns contained within it. An example of the ATLAS.ti interface is given in Figure 8.2. A similar tool is NVivo (www.qsrinterna tional.com). Another software programme, which is free to download, is the UAM Image Tool (www.wagsoft.com/ImageTool). The UAM Image Tool is particularly useful when working with coding schemes inspired by SFL, such as those based in Halliday's (1978) transitivity system, Martin and White's (2005) appraisal system or van Leeuwen's (1996) classification system for the representation of social actors. For quantitative research, the UAM Image Tool has the added advantage of having an in-built statistical analysis module. Another data annotation and management tool which is free to download is ELAN (https://tla.mpi.nl/tools/tla-tools/elan/).

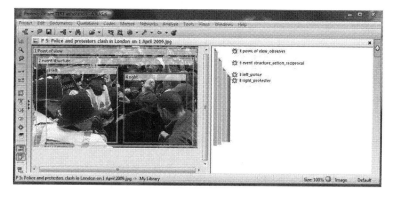

Figure 8.2 Semantic annotation in ATLAS.ti

ELAN has been developed specifically to handle 'dynamic' rather than 'static' data and is therefore the most appropriate choice when analysing videos or audio recordings.

In what follows, I provide an illustrative, qualitative multimodal analysis structured around Halliday's three metafunctions, intersemiotic relations, and metaphor. The idea is to show the kinds of analysis you might perform in a multimodal discourse analysis project.

Ideational metafunction

Recall from earlier that texts, in fulfilling the ideational metafunction of communication, represent aspects of the world. Texts represent objects or entities in the world and the processes and relations they enter into. However, representations in texts do not correspond, truth-conditionally, with the world around us. Semiotic modes offer choices in the representation of objects, entities, processes, and relations. These choices are instantiated in texts where they reflect or construct a particular experience of the world. In multimodal social semiotics, researchers have extended the notion of *transitivity* in SFL to account for choices made in fulfilment of the ideational metafunction within visual modes of communication. Transitivity describes the system of choices responsible for the realisation in the clause of an underlying semantic configuration made up of three elements: a process, participant(s) and, optionally, circumstance(s) (see Chapter 4, this volume). In language, these semantic elements are typically realised in verbal, nominal, and adverbial groups, respectively (Halliday and Matthiessen, 2006: 55).

In the case of images, processes in 'narrative' patterns are realised by *vectors* (Kress and van Leeuwen, [1996] 2006) which connect participants – the objects

156 *Christopher Hart*

or entities depicted.[3] Vectors depart from participants, formed by elements that create oblique lines within the image, such as outstretched limbs, direction of gaze, or instruments used 'in action' (p. 59). Circumstances are typically realised in what constitutes the background of the image.

Ideologically, in any text, social actors can be represented as participants in different types of process and as playing different role-types within a given process, which can be presented as happening in different circumstances. Six process types are identified in SFL: material, mental, verbal, behavioural, existential, and relational. In his study of photographs of US and allied forces' occupation of Iraq, beginning in 2003, Machin (2007) showed that US and allied soldiers were typically depicted as engaged in behavioural processes of observing or searching. Material processes of combat action were not found. Such choices in visual transitivity, Machin suggests, served to reinforce the discourse that the mission of American and allied forces in Iraq was one of peacekeeping rather than military occupation. Moreover, the circumstances in which these processes were depicted were non-descript and decontextualised, removed from cityscapes, thus serving to disassociate US and allied forces from the destructive impact of military action on civilisation. In discourses of political protest, protesters can be depicted as 'actors' in material processes of violence, as in Figure 8.3a, or 'sayers' in verbal processes, as in Figure 8.3b. In Figure 8.3b, the placards represent a visual form of projection (associated in SFL with reported speech). The image as a whole tells us what the protesters had to 'say'. The choice between material and verbal process in this context serves to construct very different versions of events which are perhaps reflective of competing discourses of civil disorder more generally. Depicting protesters as actors in a material process, for example, focusses on the destructive nature of the protest while depicting protesters as sayers in a verbal process highlights the cause or message behind the protest. Thus, the image in Figure 8.3a conforms to a standard discourse of deviance, known in media studies as the 'protest paradigm' (Chan and Lee, 1984; Lee, 2014; McLeod, 2007), whereby the press habitually disparage, depoliticise and criminalise protesters. By contrast, the image in Figure 8.3b articulates a counter-discourse in which protest is seen as a legitimate form of political expression.

Other ideological dimensions of transitivity can also be seen. The image in Figure 8.3a involves an inanimate 'goal' in the form of a glass window while the image in Figure 8.3b is non-transactional. When there are two human (or otherwise animate) participants in a transactional process, there is a choice as to who is represented as the actor in the process (the *doer*) and who is represented as the goal (the one *done to*). Consider the contrast between images in Figures 8.4a and 8.4b. In Figure 8.4a, the actor is a protester and the goal is a police officer. Conversely, in Figure 8.4b, it is a police officer who is the actor in the process and a protester who is the goal. In comparison to

a. Material process (© Getty)

b. Verbal process (© Shutterstock)

Figure 8.3 Process types

a. Protester as Actor (© Unknown)

b. Protester as Goal (© Reuters)

Figure 8.4 Participant roles

Figure 8.4a, in which a police officer is depicted as the victim of a violent attack, the image in Figure 8.4b may be read as suggesting excessive use of state power in response to the protest. This is perhaps further reinforced by the 'collectivisation' (Van Leeuwen, 1996: see also Chapter 4, this volume) of police officers in this image.

Of course, it is not necessary for two (sets of) participants to be explicitly represented in an image as in Figure 8.5. This might be considered the visual analogue of the agentless passive voice (Kress and van Leeuwen, [1996] 2006: 64) serving to conceal responsibility for violent actions.

Some transactional structures, as Kress and van Leeuwen ([1996] 2006: 66) point out, are bidirectional with each participant simultaneously or successively playing the roles of actor and goal (in the case of material processes). This is the case for the images in Figures 8.6a and 8.6b, which serve to assign more or less equal degrees of agency in the interaction. I say *more or less* because the two images are not identical but differ in respect of the viewpoints they present, which is something we turn to in the following section.

Interpersonal metafunction

In the section above, we were concerned with interactions and relations depicted between participants in an image (*represented participants*). In this section, we are concerned with the interactions and relations established between represented participants and participants in the communicative event itself (*interactive participants*). Texts do more than express

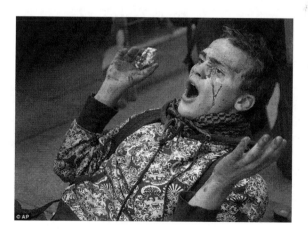

Figure 8.5 Agent-deletion
(© La Presse)

Figure 8.6a Bidirectional transaction 1
(© PA)

Figure 8.6b Bidirectional transaction 2
(© Shutterstock)

Multimodal discourse analysis 161

propositional content. Through the interpersonal metafunction, text-producers are able to express attitudes toward the content of their message and engage with audiences in different ways. In language, resources for this are to be found, for example, in the systems of mood, modality, polarity, and appraisal (Halliday and Matthiessen, 2004; Martin and White, 2005). In images, resources for this are provided by modes including gesture, gaze, and body posture, as well as the point of view presented by the image (taking in horizontal and vertical angle as well as distance of the shot).

A major distinction is between images that constitute an act of 'offer' versus those that constitute an act of 'demand' (following Halliday, 1985). An image is said to constitute an 'offer' when participants are presented to the viewer impersonally as 'items of information, objects of contemplation' (Kress and van Leeuwen, [1996] 2006: 119). An image is said to constitute a 'demand' when it directly addresses the viewer and explicitly asks that they enter into some relationship with one or other of the represented participants. This is achieved through gaze as represented participants look directly 'out of' the image toward the viewer. Exactly what kind of relation the viewer is being invited into is signalled by other semiotic means, including facial expression, body language, gesture, and point of view, as well as cultural codes like dress, which may serve as 'connotators' (Barthes, 1973; see also Machin, 2007: 21–43) of social identities, statuses, and stereotypes. For example, the image in Figure 8.7 constitutes a demand as the subject's gaze is fixed firmly on the viewer. The image shows a participant in the London Riots and was published on the front page of several national newspapers on 9 August 2011, including *The Daily Star, The Daily Express, The Daily Mail, The Financial Times,* and *The i.* The relationship established is one of deviance and antagonism. The covered hands and face, as well as body posture, connote threat, aggression, and potentially criminality too, while the tracksuit and trainers worn may be read as connotators of low social class and possibly gang-related activities.

Offer images also invite the viewer into different kinds of relationship with represented participants. One of the ways they do this is through perspective or point of view where, as Kress and van Leeuwen ([1996] 2006: 146) state, 'the addition of perspective adds nothing to the representational meaning of [images]; but it does add attitudinal meanings'. A key parameter is the extent to which the viewer is 'involved' with participants represented in the image. Here, an oblique angle suggests detachment while a frontal angle suggests involvement. Thus, the images in Figures 8.6a and 8.6b present the interaction to the viewer as something to be observed, as though they were a neutral witness to the scene. By contrast, the frontal angle presented by images in Figures 8.8a and 8.8b involves the viewer in the interaction so that they see it from the perspective of a particular participant. In this context, the frontal angle is asking viewers to 'take sides'.[4] In Figures 8.8a and 8.8b we see the same

Figure 8.7 Demand image
(© Shutterstock)

type of interaction but in 8.8a it is presented to us from the perspective of protesters in confrontation with the police while in 8.8b it is presented from the perspective of the police.[5] From the perspective in 8.8a, then, we see the police as forming a line of attack while from the perspective in 8.8b we see them as forming a line of defence (see Hart, 2014: 85–91, for further discussion of these images).

Compared to images in Figures 8.8a and 8.8b, then, the images in Figures 8.6a and 8.6b present a more neutral perspective. However, they are not entirely neutral. This is because the alternative viewpoints presented by these images result in different spatial arrangements relative to

a. Perspective of protesters (© Getty)

b. Perspective of police (© Getty)

Figure 8.8 Perspective

164   *Christopher Hart*

the viewer – in Figure 8.6a, the protesters are on the left and the police are on the right, while the opposite is the case in Figure 8.6b – and researchers in multimodality argue that spatial values left and right carry symbolic meaning. There is disagreement, however, in precisely how to interpret their symbolic functions. We will see in the next section that Kress and van Leeuwen ([1996] 2006) interpret left and right as signifying 'known' and 'not subject to question' versus 'unknown' and 'contestable', respectively. This is based on a mapping between the sequence and status of information structures in the written clause ('Given' versus 'New') and spatial organisation in the image. From this perspective, the image in Figure 8.6a problematises the role of the police, contesting their 'right to be there', while the image in Figure 8.6b construes police presence as common sense and calls into question the right to protest. Other researchers, though, interpret the symbolism of left and right differently with left said to signify bad, immoral, or sinful and right said to signify good, moral or virtuous (McManus, 2002; Needham, 1973).[6] The likelihood is that both accounts are to some extent correct and the evaluative functions of left and right will vary according to context.

Besides horizontal angle, choices are also available in vertical angle. This can be seen in Figure 8.8, for example, where there is also a clear contrast in vertical angle between images 8.8a and 8.8b. The image in Figure 8.8a presents a lower angle which, in this context, suggests subjugation in the face of state power. Conversely, the image in 8.8b presents a high angle placing the viewer in a shared (with the police) position of power.

One final dimension to discuss here is distance. Participants can be seen from afar or up-close and 'the choice of distance can suggest different relations between represented participants and viewers' (Kress and van Leeuwen, [1996] 2006: 124). Like the oblique versus frontal angle, distance encodes degrees of involvement. The more distal the point of view, the more detached is the viewer. One type of shot which combines maximal distance with maximal vertical angle is the 'aerial shot' as seen in Figure 8.9. The viewer is entirely removed from the scene depicted so that details of participants and the interactions between them are not discernible. In this sense, the aerial shot can be thought of as the visual analogue of nominalisation. Distance can also invite affective responses. Derived from the proxemics of face-to-face interaction, a close-up shot from 'on the ground' can suggest familiarity or intimacy in one context but in another, as in Figures 8.4a, 8.4b and 8.8a, creates a sense of threat and aggression.[7]

Textual metafunction

The textual metafunction concerns the organisation of the message into something that is both *cohesive* (fits together as a text) and *coherent* (fits with situational context and world knowledge) (Halliday and Hasan, 1976). It is through the textual metafunction that speakers create a sense of continuity or

Figure 8.9 Aerial shot
(© ABC News)

texture in texts. In language, resources that serve the textual metafunction belong to five categories of cohesive device: reference, substitution, ellipsis, conjunction and lexical cohesion. The textual metafunction is also seen to operate in two types of structure: thematic structure and information structure. Thematic structure concerns the position of elements in the clause and is made up of *theme* (the departure point of the clause which serves to locate and orient it within its context) and *rheme* (everything else). Information structure concerns the status of information within the clause and distinguishes between *given* and *new* information. Given information points to something the hearer can already be expected to 'know' as part of context or background knowledge while new information provides something as yet unknown.[8] Typically, though not always, given information is presented in the theme while new information is presented in the rheme. Resources which serve the textual metafunction in the visual modality have to do with composition and layout. For example, Kress and van Leeuwen ([1996] 2006: 175–201) argue that the various 'zones' of an image carry different informational values.[9] When texts or images are structured along the vertical axis, for instance, top and bottom are associated with *ideal* and *real* respectively. Information presented in the upper region is presented as something promised or to be aspired to while information presented in the lower region represents the reality of things. When texts or images are organised along the horizontal axis, then following information structure in a typical written clause of English, information on the left side is presented as given while information on the right side is presented as new. By way of example, consider the pair of abutted images given in Figure 8.10, which

Figure 8.10 Given and New information
(© Unkown)

occurred as a single 'image complex' in the multimodal text given as Figure 8.14. The left image functions as theme and contains given information while the right image functions as rheme providing new information. The left image, in other words, identifies what the story is about (the protest), while the right image provides the story itself, telling us something about the protest, namely that it turned violent.[10]

Intersemiotic relations

So far in this chapter, we have looked at meanings communicated in a non-linguistic mode, images. However, images (of this kind at least) normally occur in multimodal texts where they are accompanied by language. Part of the task for researchers in multimodal social semiotics is not just to consider the affordances of different modes but to consider the interaction between modes in multimodal texts. As we mentioned earlier, different ways of modelling intersemiotic relations have been proposed (Liu and O'Halloran, 2009; Martinec and Salway, 2005; Royce, 1998, 2007). Here I focus on just one: Royce's model of *intersemiotic complementarity*.[11] Royce outlines the different types of relation that language and image can enter into within the three metafunctions of communication. In the ideational metafunction, for example, this is based on transitivity with intersemiotic texture provided by cohesive relations existing between the transitivity frames presented in each mode. As intersemiotic cohesive relations, Royce proposes the same set of lexical cohesive devices identified by Halliday and Hasan (1976) for verbal cohesion, namely: repetition, synonymy, antonymy, meronymy, hyponymy, and collocation. To exemplify this, consider the image in Figure 8.11 which was accompanied by the caption: 'Israeli soldiers across the border from the Gaza Strip watched the protesters'.

The transitivity structure realised by clause elements in the caption is comprised of a participant (*Israeli soldiers*) in the role of Senser, a mental process (*watched*), a second participant (*the protesters*) in the role of

Figure 8.11 'Israeli soldiers across the border from the Gaza Strip watched the protesters'
(*New York Times*, 14 May 2018) (© Getty)

phenomenon, and a circumstance of location (*across the border from the Gaza Strip*). This can be represented as in Figure 8.12 (following Bateman, 2014: 168). The same transitivity structure is realised by *visual message elements* in the image. Thus, the cohesive relation between linguistic and visual material is one of intersemiotic repetition. This is illustrated as in Figure 8.13 (again following Bateman, 2014: 168–169). Intersemiotic repetition creates textual convergence (Liu and O'Halloran, 2009: 374). Rhetorically, in the genre of news reporting, intersemiotic repetition serves to corroborate the version of events presented in each mode.

Such parallel structures are not restricted to transitivity structures. In the interpersonal metafunction, forms of address (offer versus demand) may be repeated across modes. Similarly, the attitudes and evaluations expressed in language and image may be congruent or dissonant (see Swain, 2012 for detailed method of analysing interpersonal meanings in multimodal texts). In the textual metafunction, information structures may be repeated in multiple modes. For example, the abutted images in Figure 8.10 occurred as part of the multimodal news text shown in Figure 8.14 where the given/new structure of the conjoined images is repeated in the headline. Convergence here reinforces what is tellable about the story.

168 *Christopher Hart*

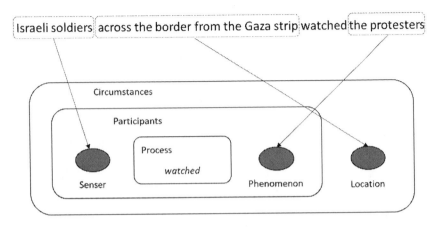

Figure 8.12 Transitivity configuration for caption 'Israeli soldiers across the border from the Gaza Strip watched the protesters'

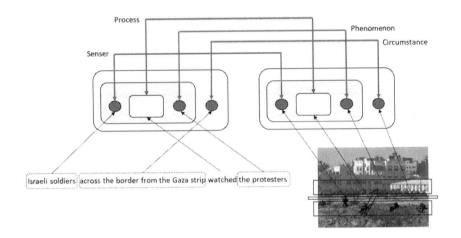

Figure 8.13 Intersemiotic repetition between language and image

Multimodal metaphor

Another way in which language and image can be seen to interact is in instances of multimodal metaphor. Within a cognitive linguistics framework (Lakoff and Johnson, 1989), metaphorical expressions in discourse are treated as surface-level realisations of underlying conceptual metaphors, which involve a mapping between a source

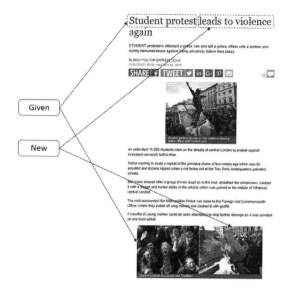

Figure 8.14 Information structure repeated across language and image
(*Express.co.uk*, 24 November 2010) (© Express/Getty)

domain and a target domain with consequences for thoughts, feelings and actions within or toward the target domain (see Chapter 5, this volume). Based on Lakoff and Johnson's (Lakoff and Johnson, 1980: 153) claim that metaphor is primarily a matter of thought and action and only derivatively a matter of language, then, Forceville (2006: 381) argues that metaphors should be expected to occur non-verbally and multimodally, as well as verbally. And indeed, researchers in multimodal critical discourse analysis have found that metaphors identified in language as constitutive of particular discourses are reproduced in visual and multimodal articulations of those same discourses (El Refaie, 2003; Fridolfsson, 2008; Hart, 2017; Koller, 2005, 2009). For example, El Refaie (2003) shows how the metaphors NATION IS A BUILDING and IMMIGRATION IS MOVING WATER, characteristic of right-wing discourses of immigration (Charteris-Black, 2006), are realised cross-modally in editorial cartoons. In relation to civil disorder, a frequent metaphor is CIVIL DISORDER IS WAR. The metaphor is realised linguistically in descriptions of protesters as 'militant' and, in the reporting of violence, in vocabulary associated with warfare, such as 'battles', 'skirmishes', 'armies', and 'invasions' (Davies and Nophakhun, 2019; Hart, 2014). Visually, the metaphor may be realised by photographs which make reference to war aesthetics, such as people

170   *Christopher Hart*

hunching down in the streets or frightened faces seeking protection in smoky environments (Fridolfsson, 2008). In which case, there is an interdiscursive link with the genre of war reporting. Alternatively, it may be realised by images (photographs and cartoons) which make intertextual references to other iconic images associated with specific wars (Hart, 2017, 2019a). In a multimodal text, of course, the same metaphor may be realised in more than one mode, each reinforcing the metaphorical reading in the other. Metaphors repeated cross-modally, then, are another way that texts display intersemiotic cohesion. Ideologically, metaphors repeated cross-modally present a consistent framing which is more likely to receive uptake by readers. An example where the metaphoricity of the image is a function of interdiscursivity is found in the text in Figure 8.15, which is reporting on the London riots of 2011. The war metaphor is realised in the headline by the description of Croydon as a 'war zone'. It is repeated in the image as the scenes of fire and rising plumes of smoke are associated with the aesthetics of war. The point of view, from afar and above, is particularly characteristic of television footage of aerial warfare such as found in news coverage of the bombardment of Iraq (Chouliaraki, 2006: 268).[12]

An example where the metaphoricity of the image is a function of intertextuality is found in the text in Figure 8.16, which reports on the *gilets jaunes* (yellow vests) protests in Paris in 2018. Unlike the text in Figure 8.15, the text in Figure 8.16 does not reference a genre of discourse but a specific text. As in the text in Figure 8.15, the war metaphor is repeated cross-modally. It is strung throughout the verbal portions of text, realised by repeated descriptions of Paris as a 'war zone' as well as the description of police 'battling' protesters. In the visual modality, the metaphor is realised by the intertextual reference that the image makes to Victor Hugo's *Les Misérables* and, specifically, to depictions of the famous 'barricades' scene such as found in promotional literature for the 2012 screen adaptation of the novel.[13] The image, in turn, also makes an intertextual reference to a famous painting, namely Eugène Delacroix's *Liberty Leading the People*, which was produced to commemorate the July Revolution of 1830 and shows Marianne, a national symbol of the French Republic, personifying the Goddess of Liberty (see Figure 8.17).[14]

Of course, the metaphorical interpretation of the images in Figures 8.15 and 8.16 is not necessarily there for every reader. Much depends on the reader having the cultural capital to recognise the interdiscursive or intertextual reference points that support a metaphorical reading (Werner, 2004). In such cases, however, metaphors in accompanying language serve an anchorage function and help guide the reader toward a metaphorical interpretation.

Multimodal discourse analysis 171

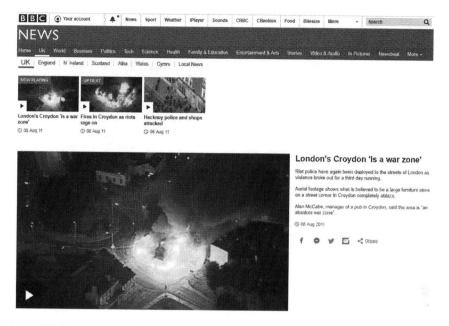

Figure 8.15 Metaphor and interdiscursivity
(BBC.co.uk, 8 April 2011) www.bbc.co.uk/news/av/uk-14453264/london-riots-croydon-is-a-war-zone (© BBC)

Presenting findings and results

How you present your findings and results will depend on your research questions and design and whether or not you have taken a quantitative approach in analysing your data. If you have taken a purely qualitative approach, then, as with most forms of discourse analysis, your findings and results will be communicated through your analyses rather than necessarily presented in a separate discussion or analysis section. However, in the course of your research, you will discover different patterns, themes, and distributions in your data and these can serve as a basis on which to organise the write-up of your analysis. You may wish to highlight particularly significant or salient findings in a summary of your analysis.

Your analysis may be both descriptive and interpretive (or 'critical'). Again, depending on your research questions and design and whether or not you are using quantitative methods, you may choose to present your descriptive results upfront followed by your more interpretive findings or you may choose to interlace these two dimensions of analysis.

If you are analysing your data quantitatively, then the usual rules apply (see Chapters 7 and 10, this volume, for a fuller discussion). Frequencies should be given as both raw numbers and as percentages or otherwise

172 Christopher Hart

Figure 8.16 Metaphor and intertextuality
(*The Sunday Times*, 2 December 2018) www.thetimes.co.uk/article/paris-becomes-a-war-zone-as-police-clash-with-protesters-l6s92jvsj (© The Times/Getty)

normalised values, and claims to significance should be avoided without the appropriate statistical backing. And the coding on which your results are based, or at least a sample of it, should be made available to your reader.

Whether you have taken a qualitative or quantitative approach, the general principles for presenting findings and results remain the same. They must be communicated clearly, succinctly and systematically. And they must be interpreted and commented on in a way that links directly back to your research questions.

Issues and limitations

Perhaps the most fundamental issue facing multimodal social semiotics concerns the use of analytical frameworks based in or inspired by linguistics. While, as Machin (2013: 348) points out, such an approach allows a deeper and more systematic level of description, there are also problems in imposing concepts from linguistics onto non-linguistic modes of communication (Bateman, Delin, and Henschel, 2004; Machin, 2013;

Multimodal discourse analysis 173

Figure 8.17 Eugène Delacroix's *Liberty Leading the People*

Stöckl, 2004). For example, relying on models developed in linguistics may cause us to miss crucial aspects of visual communication which those models are not designed or equipped to provide a handle on. As Stöckl (2004: 18) states:

> The danger in contrasting two modes ... is that we tend to somehow look at one mode in terms of another. So, mostly, due to language's dominance, we seem to be asking which linguistic properties images have. Thus we run the risk of overlooking some important design features of image which are outside of the linguistic perspective.

Other models, developed outside of linguistics and with non-linguistic modes in mind, might be better placed to analyse multimodal data. There is also the danger that linguists turning their trade to multimodality are simply reinventing the wheel – 'discovering' things that have long been known to researchers in areas such as media and film studies, game studies, or journalism studies, which have evolved specifically in relation to

174   *Christopher Hart*

multimodality, and applying unnecessarily complex terminologies which yield little or no extra insight (Machin, 2013).

Other potential limitations, which beset many approaches to critical discourse analysis, fall around the issue of subjectivity. Much of multimodal social semiotics and multimodal critical discourse analysis in particular involves ascribing ideological meanings to the multimodal properties of texts. But on what basis are such ascriptions made? In relation to information value, for example, Kress and van Leeuwen ([1996] 2006: 218) themselves concede that:

> The major challenge to our approach is the epistemological status of our claim … [H]ow can we know that left and right, and top and bottom, have the values we attribute to them, or more fundamentally have any value at all?

One possible source of evidence actually comes from conceptual metaphor theory where the conceptual metaphors gleaned from patterns of lexical realisation may help establish an experiential basis for the associations claimed between spatial and ideological values (Feng, 2011; Feng and Espindola, 2013).

A similar limitation concerns the role of the audience, which is not generally taken into account in multimodal social semiotics. How do we know that the meanings we as analysts ascribe to texts actually form part of how readers respond to texts on particular encounters? As Holsanova (2014: 286) states:

> although the composition of multimodal documents and its potential for meaning–making have been discussed in the social semiotic tradition (Kress & Van Leeuwen, 1996) … the actual reception of the messages by actual users in a particular context of use has not been studied empirically.

To address the issue of audience reception, researchers in multimodality have at their disposal a range of empirical methods. For example, Holsanova, Rahm, and Holmqvist (2006) used eye-tracking methods to investigate predictions which emerge from multimodal social semiotics concerning reading path and attention phenomena in encounters with printed newspaper pages. Questions they asked included: What do we choose from a newspaper spread? Which items and areas of the spread do we attend to in most detail? Are reading paths influenced by layout? Other researchers have used 'offline' experimental methods to investigate the ideological effects of particular semiotic features in multimodal texts (Arpan et al., 2006; Hart, 2019b; Powell et al., 2015). For example, Hart (2019b) gave subjects pictures of violent interactions between police and protesters where the only variable was point of view. He found that subjects were more likely to assign blame equally for images presented with an oblique angle compared to those presented with a frontal angle. He also found that in oblique angle images, the protester was perceived as more aggressive when they occurred in the left of the image while in frontal angle images, they were perceived as more aggressive when they occurred in the back, ego-opposed position. (see Chapter 10, this volume, for discussion of experimental methods which could easily be extended to investigations of non-linguistic and multimodal discourse).

Further reading

Kress and van Leeuwen ([1996] 2006) is the landmark text in multimodal social semiotics. Machin (2007) provides an accessible introduction to many of the same concepts covered in Kress and van Leeuwen ([1996] 2006) applied in a series of more critical case studies. Forceville (1996) offers an early account of visual and multimodal metaphor. Bateman (2014) provides the most comprehensive overview of text-image relations theory there is.

Notes

1 For explorations into the social semiotics of sound see van Leeuwen (1999), Machin (2010, 2014), Way and McKerrell (2017) and Mano (2019).
2 It is important to recognise that what counts as a mode is the subject of some debate. For example, some authors treat writing as a mode while others see writing as itself multimodal. The same goes for speech and image.
3 Narrative patterns present participants in relations of *doing*. They serve in the representation of unfolding actions and events, processes of change, and transitory spatial arrangements. This is in contrast to 'conceptual' patterns which represent participants in terms of their class, structure or definition (see Kress and van Leeuwen, [1996] 2006: 59–106)
4 In other contexts, of course, a frontal angle may perform a different function. The same goes for vertical angle and distance values.
5 It should be noted that oblique versus frontal angle is not an absolute distinction but is, naturally, a matter of degree. The image in Figure 8.8a is treated as presenting a frontal angle because its main vanishing point falls within the boundaries of the image and because if you imagine a line running from the left-most police officer to the right-most police officer, this would run parallel to the frontal plane of the photographer (see Kress and van Leeuwen, [1996] 2006: 135–137)
6 The English word *sinister* is derived from Latin *sinestra*, which originally meant 'left hand'. The word *left* in English is derived from Old English *lyft*, which meant 'weak'.
7 What function a close-up shot has depends on other semiotic features in the text, such as facial expression and body-posture, as well as background knowledge and prior attitudes of the viewer.
8 Of course, what the hearer can be expected to know will change as discourse unfolds so that new information becomes given. Similar labels are *topic* and *comment*.
9 Besides information value, composition and layout also have affordances in salience and framing (Kress and van Leeuwen, [1996] 2006: 177).

176 *Christopher Hart*

10 The conjoined images may also be read as representing different 'acts' in the story as the protest went from being peaceful in the first act to violent in the second. In that sense, the left-right axis can represent a kind of timeline.
11 It is called intersemiotic complementarity not because language and image necessarily covey the same meanings but because they function alongside one another in contributing to the overall meaning of the text.
12 The image is in fact a moving image which, like coverage of the bombardment of Iraq (Chouliaraki, 2006: 268), tracks and zooms to capture the 'explosion' of shapes and colours illuminating an otherwise still and dark cityscape. The effect is a somewhat mesmerising sense of awe and spectacle.
13 Published in 1862, *Les Misérables* covers the time between Napoleon's defeat at Waterloo (1815) and the 1832 June Rebellion in Paris in which the barricades scene was set.
14 The character Gavroche in *Les Misérables* is said to have been inspired by the figure of the pistol-wielding boy in Eugène Delacroix's painting.

References

Abousnnouga, G. and Machin, D. (2011). Visual discourses of the role of women in war commemoration: A Multimodal analysis of British war memorials. *Journal of Language and Politics*, 10(3), 322–346.
Abousnnouga, G. and Machin, D. (2013). *The language of war monuments*. London: Bloomsbury.
Arpan, L.M., Baker, K., Youngwon, L., Taejin, J., Lorusso, L., and Smith, J. (2006). News coverage of social protests and the effects of photographs on prior attitudes. *Mass Communication & Society*, 9(1), 1–20.
Barthes, R. (1973). *Mythologies*. New York: Noonsday Press.
Barthes, R. (1977). *Image music text*. London: Fontana Press.
Bateman, J.A. (2014). *Text and image: A critical introduction to the visual/verbal divide*. London: Routledge.
Bateman, J.A., Delin, J. and Henschel, R. (2004). Multimodality and empiricism: Preparing for a corpus-based approach to the study of multimodal meaning-making. In E. Ventola, C. Cassily, and K. Kaltenbacher (Eds.), *Perspectives on multimodality*. (pp. 65–87). Amsterdam: John Benjamins.
Bednarek, M. and Caple, H. (2012). *News discourse*. London: Continuum.
Björkvall, A. (2017). Multimodal discourse analysis. In K. Boréus and G. Bergström (Eds.), *Analyzing text and discourse: Eight approaches for the social sciences*. (pp. 174–207). London: Sage.
Bounegru, L. and Forceville, C. (2011). Metaphors in editorial cartoons representing the global financial crisis. *Visual Communication*, 10(2), 209–229.
Cavicchio, F., and Kita, S. (2013). English/Italian bilinguals switch gesture parameters when they switch Languages. *Proceedings of TiGeR 2013*. 305–309.
Chan, J.M. and Lee, C.C. (1984). Journalistic paradigms on civil protests: A case study of Hong Kong. In A. Arno and W. Dissanayake (Eds.), *The news media in national and international conflict*. (pp. 183-202). Boulder, CO: Westview Press.
Charteris-Black, C. (2006). Britain as a container: Immigration metaphors in the 2005 election campaign. *Discourse & Society*, 17(5), 563–581.
Chouliaraki, L. (2006). The aestheticization of suffering on television. *Visual Communication*, 5(3), 261–285.

Davies, M. and Nophakhun, R. (2019). Media 'militant' tendencies: How strike action in the news press is discursively constructed as inherently violent. In C. Hart and D. Kelsey (Eds.), *Discourses of disorder: Riots, strikes and protests in the media*. (pp. 109–132). Edinburgh: Edinburgh University Press.

El Refaie, E. (2003). Understanding visual metaphor: The example of newspaper cartoons. *Visual Communication*, 2(1), 75–96.

Feng, D. (2011). Visual space and ideology: A critical cognitive analysis of spatial orientations in advertising. In K.L. O'Halloran and B.A. Smith (Eds.), *Multimodal studies: Exploring issues and domains*. (pp. 55–75). London: Routledge.

Feng, D. and Espindola, E. (2013). Integrating functional and cognitive approaches to multimodal discourse analysis. *Ilha do Desterro*, 64, 85–110.

Forceville, C. (1998). *Pictorial metaphor in advertising*. London: Routledge.

Forceville, C. (2002). The identification of target and source in pictorial metaphors. *Journal of Pragmatics*, 34(1), 1–14.

Forceville, C. (2006). Non-verbal and multimodal metaphor in a cognitivist framework: Agendas for research. In G. Kristiansen, M. Achard, R. Dirven, and F.J. Ruiz (Eds.), *Cognitive linguistics: Current applications and future perspectives*. (pp. 372–402). Berlin: Mouton de Gruyter.

Forceville, C. (2008). Metaphor in pictures and multimodal representations. In R.W. Gibbs, Jr (Ed.), *The Cambridge handbook of metaphor and thought*. (pp. 462–482). Cambridge: Cambridge University Press.

Fridolfsson, C. (2008). Political protest and metaphor. In T. Carve and J. Pikalo (Eds.), *Political language and metaphor: Interpreting and changing the world*. (pp. 132–148). London: Routledge.

Goffman, E. (1981). *Forms of talk*. Oxford: Blackwell.

Gumperz, J. (1982). *Discourse strategies*. Cambridge: Cambridge University Press.

Halliday, M.A.K. (1978). *Language as social semiotic*. London: Edward Arnold.

Halliday, M.A.K. (1985). *An introduction to functional grammar*. London: Edward Arnold.

Halliday, M.A.K. and Hasan, R. (1976). *Cohesion in English*. London: Longman.

Halliday, M.A.K. and Matthiessen, C.M.I.M. (2004). *An introduction to functional grammar*. (3rd ed.). London: Edward Arnold.

Halliday, M.A.K. and Matthiessen, C.M.I.M. (2006). *Construing experience through meaning: A language-based approach to cognition*. London: Continuum.

Hart, C. (2014). *Discourse, grammar and ideology: Functional and cognitive perspectives*. London: Bloomsbury.

Hart, C. (2017). Metaphor and intertextuality in media framings of the (1984–85) British Miners' Strike: A multimodal analysis. *Discourse & Communication*, 11(1), 3–30.

Hart, C. (2019a). Metaphor and the (1984–85) Miners' Strike: A multimodal analysis. In C. Hart and D. Kelsey (Eds.), *Discourses of disorder: Riots, strikes and protests in the Media*. (pp. 133–153). Edinburgh: Edinburgh University Press.

Hart, C. (2019b). Spatial properties of ACTION verb semantics: Experimental evidence for image schema orientation in transitive versus reciprocal verbs and its implications for ideology. In C. Hart (Ed.), *Cognitive linguistic approaches to text and discourse: From poetics to politics*. (pp. 181–204). Edinburgh: Edinburgh University Press.

Holsanova, J. (2014). Reception of multimodality: Applying eye tracking methodology in multimodal research. In C. Jewitt (Ed.), *Routledge handbook of multimodal analysis*. (2nd ed., pp. 285–296). London: Routledge.

Holsanova, J., Rahm, H. and Holmqvist, K. (2006). Entry points and reading paths on newspaper spreads: Comparing a semiotic analysis with eye-tracking measurements. *Visual Communication, 5*(1), 65–93.

Hutchby, I. and Wooffitt, R. (1998). *Conversation analysis: Principles, practices and applications.* Oxford: Polity Press.

Jones, R.H. (2012). *Discourse analysis: A resource book for students.* London: Routledge.

Koller, V. (2005). Designing cognition: Visual metaphor as a design feature in business magazines. *Information Design Journal, 13*(2), 136–150.

Koller, V. (2008). 'Not just a colour': Pink as a gender and sexuality marker in visual communication. *Visual Communication, 7*(4), 395–423.

Koller, V. (2009). Brand images: multimodal metaphor in corporate branding messages. In C. Forceville and E. Urios-Aparisi (Eds.), *Multimodal metaphor.* (pp. 45–71). Berlin: De Gruyter.

Kress, G. and van Leeuwen, T. ([1996] 2006). *Reading images: A grammar of visual design.* (2nd ed.). London: Routledge.

Lakoff, G. and Johnson, M. (1980). *Metaphors we live by.* Chicago: University of Chicago Press.

Lakoff, G. and Johnson, M. (1999). *Philosophy in the flesh: The embodied mind and its challenge to Western thought.* New York: Basic Books.

Lazar, M. (2009). Gender, war and body politics: A critical multimodal analysis of metaphor in advertising. In K. Ahrens (Ed.), *Politics, gender and conceptual metaphors.* (pp. 209–234). Basingstoke: Palgrave.

Lee, F.L.F. (2014). Triggering the protest paradigm: Examining factors affecting news coverage of protests. *International Journal of Communication, 8*, 2725–2746.

Lemke, J.L. (1998). Multiplying meaning: Visual and verbal semiotics in scientific text. In J. Martin and R. Veel (Eds.), *Reading science: Critical and functional perspectives on discourses of science.* (pp. 87–113). London: Routledge.

Liu, Y. and O'Halloran, K. (2009). Intersemiotic texture: Analysing cohesive devices between language and images. *Social Semiotics, 19*(4), 367–388.

Machin, D. (2007). *Introduction to multimodal discourse analysis.* London: Bloomsbury.

Machin, D. (2010). *Analysing popular music: Image, sound, text.* London: Sage.

Machin, D. (2013). What is multimodal critical discourse studies? *Critical Discourse Studies, 10*(4), 347–355.

Machin, D. (2014). Sound and discourse: A multimodal approach to war. In C. Hart and P. Cap (Eds.), *Contemporary critical discourse studies.* (pp. 281–296). London: Bloomsbury.

Machin, D. and Mayr, A. (2012). *How to do critical discourse analysis: A multimodal introduction.* London: Sage.

Machin, D. and Suleiman, U. (2006). Arab and American computer war games: The influence of a global technology on discourse. *Critical Discourse Studies, 3*(1), 1–22.

Mano, P. (2019). Synthesizing support: analyzing Manchester United's aestheticization of solidarity from an MCDS perspective. *Critical Discourse Studies.* doi: 10.1080/17405904.2019.1692047

Martin, J.R. (1992). *English text: Systems and structure.* Amsterdam: John Benjamins.

Martin, J.R. and White, P.R.R. (2005). *The language of evaluation: Appraisal in English.* Basingstoke: Palgrave.

Martinec, R. and Salway, A. (2005). A system for image-text relations in new (and old) media. *Visual Communication, 4*(3), 337–371.

McLeod, D.M. (2007). News coverage and social protest: How the media's protest paradigm exacerbates social conflict. *Journal of Dispute Resolution, 2007*(1), 185–194.

McManus, C. (2002). *Right hand, left hand: The origins of asymmetry in brains, bodies, atoms and cultures*. London: Phoenix.

Miles, M.B. and Huberman, A.M. (1994). *Qualitative data analysis: An expanded sourcebook*. (2nd ed.). Thousand Oaks, CA: Sage.

Needham, R. (1973). *Right and left: Essays on dual symbolic lassification*. Chicago: University of Chicago Press.

Norris, S. (2004). *Analysing multimodal interaction: A methodological framework*. London: Routledge.

O'Halloran, K. (2005). *Mathematical discourse: Language, symbolism and visual images*. London: Continuum.

O'Toole, M. (1994). *The language of displayed art*. London: Leicester University.

Ostermeyer, S. and D. Sittler (2019). Rioting and disorderly behaviour as political media practice: Body postures on the streets of L.A. during the Riots of 1992. In C. Hart and D. Kelsey (Eds.), *Discourses of disorder: Riots, strikes and protests in the media*. (pp. 194–210). Edinburgh: Edinburgh University Press.

Powell, T.E., Boomgaarden, H.G., DeSwert, K., and de Vreese, C.H. (2015). A clearer picture: The contribution of visuals and text to framing effects. *Journal of Communication, 65*(6), 997–1017.

Royce, T.D. (1998). Synergy on the page: Exploring intersemiotic complementarity in page-based multimodal text. *Japan Association for Systemic Functional Linguistics Occasional Papers, 1*(1), 25–49.

Royce, T.D. (2007). Intersemiotic complementarity: A framework for multimodal discourse analysis. In T.D. Royce and W.L. Bowcher (Eds.), *New directions in the analysis of multimodal discourse*. (pp. 63–110). London: Lawrence Erlbaum Associates.

Stöckl, H. (2004). In between modes: Language and image in printed media. In E. Ventola, C. Charles and M. Kaltenbacher (Eds.), *Perspectives on multimodality*. (pp. 9–30). Amsterdam: John Benjamins.

Swain, E. (2012). Analysing evaluation in political cartoons. *Discourse, Context & Media, 1*(2–3), 82–94.

van Leeuwen, T. (1996). The representation of social actors. In C. Caldas-Coulthard and M. Coulthard (Eds.), *Texts and practices: Readings in critical discourse analysis*. (pp. 32–70). London: Routledge.

van Leeuwen, T. (1999). *Speech, music, sound*. Basingstoke: Palgrave.

Walsh, A. and Guilianotti, R. (2007). *Ethics, money and sport: This sporting mammon*. London: Routledge.

Way, L. and S. McKerrell (Eds.) (2017). *Music as multimodal discourse: Semiotics, power and protest*. London: Bloomsbury.

Werner, W. (2004). On political cartoons and social studies textbooks: Visual analogies, intertextuality and cultural memory. *Canadian Social Studies, 38*(2). www.educ.ualberta.ca/css/Css_38_2/ARpolitical_cartoons_ss_textbooks.htm.

9 Digitally mediated discourse analysis

Johann W. Unger

Introduction

This chapter will begin by considering what is unique about digitally mediated discourse, but will also outline some of the continuities with other forms of discourse. It will present the basic tenets of three main frameworks (which also overlap to a considerable extent): computer-mediated discourse analysis (based on the work of Herring, e.g. 2004), discourse-centred online ethnography (based on Androutsopoulos, 2008) and digitally mediated discourse studies (DMDS) (based on KhosraviNik and Unger, 2016, also called social media critical discourse studies in KhosraviNik's more recent work, e.g. 2017). It will then go on to suggest how elements of each can be adopted to form a coherent methodology in investigations in digital media contexts. The ethical issues specific to digital media research will be discussed in some detail, with reference to examples of different approaches to e.g. anonymisation, inclusion of usernames/identities, and inclusion of verbatim data. Towards the end of the chapter, a case study of the US politician Alexandra Ocasio-Cortez's tweets will illustrate how to carry out an achievable investigation into digitally mediated discourse that nevertheless draws on the latest theoretical and methodological insights in more advanced scholarly work, followed by some suggestions on presenting the findings arising from studies of digitally mediated data.

Outline of approach

At one level, there is nothing special about digitally mediated language. Huge sections of the internet are formal written documents such as government reports, newspaper articles, and company mission statements. Other than being viewed on a screen rather than on paper, these can be said to be almost identical to their printed counterparts. A key notion here is *affordances*, defined by Gibson (1977) as the action possibilities of objects (or technologies). For example, a large computer screen allows viewers to see a whole page, or perhaps two side-by-side. This is similar to paper on

Digitally mediated discourse analysis **181**

a desk, which can be laid out side-by-side. Paper texts do not allow readers to click on hypertexts, or search for particular words by typing them into a search box. On the other hand, pieces of paper can be used to make paper aeroplanes. These two technologies (computer screens versus paper) thus have different affordances.

On social media platforms, there is a lot of informal written language which has some similarities with older, pre-digital texts. For instance, Gillen (2013) argues that posts on Twitter have many similarities with Edwardian postcards. Increasingly social media posts incorporate images, audio, and video elements, which again have some similarities to pre-digital texts. Some vlogs, for example, are not unlike home movies that people used to create using video cameras. Herring (2013) identifies three different kinds of genres (text types)/genre features in social media texts:

- *Familiar*: genres that do not differ substantially from their pre-digital counterparts, such as the government reports mentioned above. Familiar genre features include the use of emoticons or non-standard spelling in texts, which have existed in various forms for centuries.
- *Reconfigured*: genres that have been repurposed or reshaped in line with digital affordances, for instance, status updates. These do exist in other forms (for instance, the signs some university staff put on their doors saying whether they are available or in a meeting), but social media status updates have considerably extended and changed the function of such texts.
- *Emergent*: genres that are not found in pre-digital or pre-social media contexts, and include examples such as collaborative knowledge-sharing platforms like Wikipedia, which allow multiple users to write and edit text.

There are some fairly well-established features and affordances of digitally mediated communication that may differ somewhat from non-digital communication, and this should be borne in mind when undertaking a project (for further detail, see Page et al., 2014, or Herring, 2007 on medium and situation factors). For instance, digitally mediated communication can:

- often be faster than written, but slower than spoken exchanges
- have multiple participants (e.g. in a WhatsApp group) and involve different relationships of addresser to addressee, for instance, one-to-many (Twitter posts); many-to-one (online petition sites)
- be addressed to an unseen audience, but increasingly is personalised via algorithms, allowing social media platforms and advertisers to target people based on specific identity characteristics, habits, and behaviours
- be a 'narrower' channel than face-to-face communication, which involves not only verbal but also visual, auditory, and gestural information, but increasingly the use of video and other multimodal

182 Johann W. Unger

features mean digital communication is becoming more similar to face-to-face interactions

Still, there are more continuities and similarities between non-digital communication and digital communication than there are differences. With the above points in mind, which may lead to some adaptations, the other approaches outlined in this book can therefore be applied to digitally mediated communication.

There is no single correct or best way to research digitally mediated communication. Which specific frameworks and tools researchers use for a particular project depends very much on the context, the kind of data available, the particular questions being asked (see next section), and finally, but importantly, the specific interests and capabilities of the researcher. While digital communication today is ubiquitous, and it is scarcely possible to imagine that a person below retirement age does not use any kind of digital communication in their daily life, this was not always the case. A number of linguists, primarily in the US initially, started analysing how people use digital technology to communicate from the very early era of digital computing in the 1970s onwards. The focus was primarily on verbal text, which was typed into a device (usually a terminal and later a PC) using a keyboard and then appeared on a screen (usually monochrome, in the early days) on the recipient's device. This incorporated research into so-called bulletin board systems (akin to today's online discussion forums and platforms like Reddit) and email lists (still in existence today). This early work used the label *computer-mediated communication* (CMC) to describe its main object of analysis. The particular focus was on how the medium (typing, electronic devices) affects the message. There was a belief that CMC was generally 'between' speech and writing, with some spoken and some written features – although this belief does rest on particular assumptions about writing being generally formal and planned, and speech being informal and spontaneous, whereas it is easy to find counter-examples. CMC research often was largely descriptive, giving accounts of linguistic behaviours, and focussed particularly on differences to other written (or spoken) genres, such as the use of emoticons (☺ 'smiley face') or abbreviations (*CU L8R* 'see you later') (see Barton and Lee, 2013 for an overview of these).

More recently (from the 1990s onwards) researchers, in particular, Herring, started to develop a framework for *computer-mediated discourse analysis* (CMDA), which focussed on language as an online social behaviour. Later still (from the mid-2000s onwards), researchers started to take an interest in what was then an emerging group of digital platforms which can loosely be grouped under the label 'social media'. There are different understandings of what social media includes, ranging from only 'classic' social networking sites such as Facebook or Twitter, perhaps with the addition of peer-to-peer instant messaging platforms, to a much broader understanding that would also incorporate, platforms such as online review and advice sites, newspaper discussion pages, Wikipedia, and even email (see Page et al., 2014: 5 for further discussion). During this period, Androutsopoulos (e.g. 2008) developed the *discourse-centred online ethnography* (DCOE) approach, in which he emphasised that observation of digitally mediated behaviours should be accompanied with direct contact and interviews with the people producing and consuming these texts. Towards the middle of the 2010s, a number of critical discourse researchers started to take a greater interest in digital and social media, and started to consider how the traditional theories and frameworks of critical discourse studies could be applied or reframed for digitally mediated contexts. While this research is still very much in development, and different labels are used for it, I will here refer to it as *digitally mediated discourse studies* (DMDS). The three more recent approaches mentioned above (CMDA, DCOE, DMDS) are discussed in more detail in the remainder of this section.

Computer-mediated discourse analysis (CMDA)

Herring (2001: 612) describes CMDA as concerned with 'language and language use in computer-networked environments'. Importantly, like discourse studies, CMDA is an eclectic approach with no single unified methodology or theoretical assumptions. Instead, Herring (2004: 342) argues that 'CMDA as an approach to researching online behaviour provides a methodological toolkit and a set of theoretical lenses through which to make observations and interpret the results of empirical analysis'. While CMDA emerged as a sub-field of CMC in the 1990s, it eventually developed its own identity, and a particular focus on the first four categories set out in Table 9.1, below: *structure*; *meaning*; *interaction*; and *social behaviour*. The table lists the main issues that researchers concerned themselves with (e.g. formality, what is communicated, coherence, community), the linguistic and discursive phenomena that relate to these issues (e.g. syntax, speech acts, turn-taking, and conflict management), and the specific methods and linguistic frameworks that can be used to study them (e.g. text analysis, pragmatics, conversation analysis, and interactional sociolinguistics). The final two categories, *participation* and *multimodal communication*, were added to Herring's later work (2013), and also indicate a shift away from the understanding of computer-mediated discourse as primarily text-based, and 'free from competing influences from other channels of communication and from physical context' (Herring, 2001: 612).

It is beyond the scope of this chapter to explain every single issue, phenomenon, and method in this table, but each of them is described by Herring and also in a large number of other textbooks, such as the accessible overviews in Culpeper et al. (2018), and some are mentioned in the examples below.

184   *Johann W. Unger*

Table 9.1 Reproduced from Page et al., 2014, drawing on Herring's (2013) 'Four levels of CMDA' and 'Multimodal communication as an additional level of CMDA'

	Issues	*Phenomena*	*Methods*
Structure	Orality, formality, complexity, efficiency, expressivity, genre characteristics, etc.	Typography, orthography, morphology, syntax, discourse schemata, formatting conventions, etc.	Structural/descriptive linguistics, text analysis, stylistics
Meaning	What is intended, what is communicated, what is accomplished	Meaning of words, utterances (speech acts), exchanges, etc.	Semantics, Pragmatics
Interaction	Interactivity, timing, coherence, repair, interaction as co-constructed, etc.	Turns, sequences, exchanges, threads, etc.	Conversation analysis, ethnomethodology
Social behaviour	Social dynamics, power, influence, identity, community, cultural differences, etc.	Linguistic expressions of status, conflict, negotiation, face- management, play; discourse styles/lects, etc.	Interactional sociolinguistics, critical discourse analysis, ethnography of communication
Participation	Affordances, norms of the community of practice	Participation patterns over time	Statistical analysis, ethnography
Multimodal communication	Mode effects, cross-mode coherence, reference and address management, generation and spread of graphical meaning units, media coactivity, etc.	Mode choice, text-in-image, image quotes, spatial and temporal positionality and deixis, animation, etc.	Social semiotics, visual content analysis

Discourse-centred online ethnography (DCOE)

While CMDA is a broad framework that allows for the analysis of different linguistic and discursive phenomena at different levels, DCOE is a particular methodological approach to research into digitally mediated texts and practices. Androutsopoulos (2008) draws on the tradition of ethnographic research, which involves researchers immersing themselves in a community or culture to attempt to gain a better understanding of the behaviours that they observe. Androutsopoulos (2008) proposes the following six guidelines for observation of digitally mediated practices and actors (people), reproduced here with some additional explanation and suggestions that adapt the framework for more contemporary digital media platforms in parentheses:

Digitally mediated discourse analysis 185

1) Examine relationships and processes rather than isolated artefacts (in other words, researchers should not just treat digitally mediated texts as static, but think about them in terms of part of a set of practices that change over time)
2) Move from the core to the periphery of a field (try to identify the most important sites, sections, pages, etc. of a digitally mediated context, and look at those first, then consider more marginal ones)
3) Repeat observation (observe the same people/groups on multiple occasions and different people/groups in comparable contexts)
4) Maintain openness (avoid approaching the data with a fixed mindset, and don't assume that what is observed the first time will always be true)
5) Use all available technology (consider how different people use a particular platform, with all its features and affordances, also how they might engage with digital media with different devices, operating systems, etc., and how actors involved might make use of different technologies as part of a set of practices, e.g. sharing images across multiple platforms)
6) Use observation insights as guidance for further sampling (let what is learnt about the sites/platforms/actors, such as what kinds of texts are written, or who the main actors are, inform further research, and be prepared to change plans if it seems appropriate as more information is uncovered)

These are followed by a further six guidelines for contact with the actors responsible for or involved in the texts and practices that have been observed:

1) Contacts should be limited, non-random, and include various participation formats (this means researchers should be focussed in their choice of contacts, based on observations of practices, and should have a clear goal in mind in their information-gathering. Participation formats here means the position/role of the participant, e.g. professional, amateur, moderator, frequent user, newbie, etc.)
2) Pay attention to the initial contact (first impressions count! It can be difficult for researchers to motivate participants outside their own friendship networks, so give yourself the best chance to engage participants in your research)
3) Formulate and customise interview guidelines (it is not necessary, or even desirable, to have a rigid script for interviews and ask everyone the same questions: interview questions should be based at least in part on the observed data and prior knowledge about the participant).
4) Confront participants with (their own) material (this allows for a greater understanding of texts and practices – by asking participants how and why they use digital media, researchers can gain valuable insights)

186   Johann W. Unger

5) Seek repeated and prolonged contacts (for ethnographic research, long-term contact between the researcher and participants is extremely valuable and allows for exploration of whether and how practices change over time)
6) Make use of alternative techniques whenever possible (this could include questionnaires, surveys, or public chat sessions (where not ethically problematic)) as well as individual interviews.

While CMDA on its own allows researchers to take an *etic* (from an outside observer's) perspective, DCOE allows the addition of an *emic* (from within the community/culture being studied) perspective, which can strengthen analyses and provide a rich source of insights and analytical detail. Androutsopoulos is, of course, not the only researcher to conduct digitally mediated ethnographies. For instance, Hine (e.g. 2015) provides in-depth accounts and guidelines on how to conduct digital ethnographies.

Digitally mediated discourse studies (DMDS)

As other chapters in this book show, discourse studies is a varied and eclectic field with no single methodological or theoretical framework. KhosraviNik and Unger (2016) argue that many of the same linguistic and discursive phenomena can be analysed in digital media as in more traditional contexts of language use. What is particularly needed to account for digitally mediated communication, however, is an understanding of media dynamics, and how these shape and are shaped by the way language is used in digital contexts. For the specific case of social media platforms, Figure 9.1 shows the interactions between users, institutions (i.e. companies and public institutions), and contexts.

Other approaches to digital media often ignore the corporate institutional contexts in which digital media platforms are provided. When someone posts on Twitter, Instagram, or Snapchat, for instance, platforms that are free to end-users, this potentially generates data that linguists could, if appropriate ethical procedures are followed, analyse in various ways. However, the data that is generated is then provided, usually indirectly and via particular algorithms that factor in personal information such as age, sex, sexuality, and more, to advertisers, who can then in turn target users with specific adverts (whether for products, services or political parties), that are based on their identities and preferences. Critical analyses of social media (and other digital media) should take into account the role of these institutions, even if only by describing them as part of the context in which communication takes place. More nuanced analyses take account of the role of these institutions in promoting or suppressing particular instances or kinds of communication, such as, for example, activism, hate speech, or advertising. Fuchs (2014) provides an accessible introduction to the theoretical underpinnings of this idea.

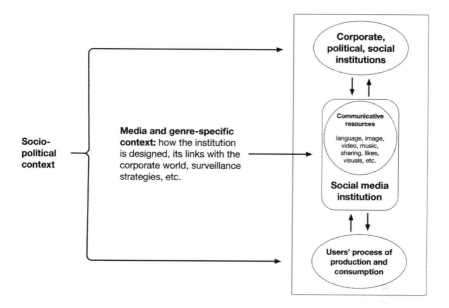

Figure 9.1 The dynamic of texts, society, and social media institutions (from KhosraviNik and Unger, 2016)

Identifying research questions

The most important consideration when choosing research questions is that they should be appropriate for the context and data (or vice versa – appropriate data and contexts should be chosen for specific research questions). Research questions in studies of digitally mediated discourse should ideally incorporate all of the following elements:

1) A question word or phrase (e.g. Why, how, what, do/does, to what extent)
2) A linguistic or discursive phenomenon
3) An issue
4) A particular social or institutional context in which digitally mediated communication occurs, or a group of people within such a context
5) A question mark

Examples of 2) and 3) are given in Table 9.1, above, though this should not be seen as a definitive list. Based on these guidelines, a typical question might therefore be:

> How[1] does face-work [2] contribute to community cohesion [3] in YouTube discussions around makeup vlogs [4]?[5]

188   *Johann W. Unger*

Several things are worth noting about this question: First, it contains a presupposition. Saying 'How does X contribute to Y' presupposes that X *does* contribute to Y. Another way of phrasing this question would therefore be 'Does face-work contribute to community cohesion in YouTube discussions around makeup vlogs and if so, how?' It is generally a good idea to avoid presuppositions in research questions, but sometimes they are unavoidable, or not problematic; for instance, research that is specifically concerned with hate speech, with data that has been selected because it is hate speech, does not need to ask whether hate speech occurs in the given context. The second notable feature is that everything before 'YouTube' could apply in numerous contexts, including those that do not directly involve digital communication. This is important because it reinforces what I have stated above: that many of the linguistic and discursive features, and by extension ways of analysing them, and the questions we might ask about them, are similar or the same in digital and non-digital contexts. Nevertheless, there will be interesting things to say about the digital context, and the way it interacts with the issues and phenomena under investigation. This can be left implicit, as in the question above, or could be turned into a separate question (perhaps for a different project!), such as:

> How do vloggers construct their identities in written YouTube discussions around their vlogs, and how does this differ from their identity construction in their videos?

This is potentially quite a broad question, which could incorporate a number of discursive phenomena, and may thus be a starting point for a more detailed investigation of specific phenomena once these have been identified as salient in an initial investigation. There could also be an ethnographic element. Following the guidelines outlined above as part of the DCOE approach, the observation of the vloggers' behaviour could be accompanied by interviews with vloggers in which they are asked about their identity construction practices).

It is worth noting that research questions, while they are often outlined near the beginning of an academic text, can evolve and change in the course of a project. The examples so far suggest that research into digitally mediated discourse focusses on the 'higher-level' issues and phenomena in the CMDA framework (see Table 9.1), such as social behaviours and multimodality. This is not necessarily the case, however – any of the phenomena and issues could be incorporated into a discourse studies project, e.g. investigating the use of specific orthographic conventions as an in-group identity marker on a social networking site, and how newcomers who are not familiar with the conventions are socially sanctioned or excluded.

It is also possible to pose a different sort of research question, which is concerned more with evaluating a particular theory or methodology in a digital context, e.g.

> Do the typical rules of turn-taking found in spontaneous spoken conversation between friends also apply in instant messaging?

This would allow the researcher to evaluate the conversation analysis framework, which was developed for non-digital interactions (see e.g. Ten Have, 2007), in digital contexts. Again, this is a rather broad question, so it may be advisable to narrow it down by including additional issues or phenomena. For instance:

> Do the typical rules of turn-taking, *in particular the turn allocation component*, found in spontaneous spoken conversation between friends also apply in instant messaging?

Or

> Do typical *gendered turn-taking strategies* found in spontaneous spoken conversation between friends also apply in instant messaging?

It is, of course, important to remember that there is now a substantial body of research into digitally mediated discourse from many different perspectives and research traditions. As such, any study that includes a more methodological or theoretical question should include a thorough literature search for recent journal articles and other scholarly publications that use data from digitally mediated contexts. This also allows for an *abductive research process*, i.e. applying the questions and concerns posed in existing scholarly literature to new data and contexts, and then, in light of your study, developing new insights about and explanations of both the theories you are applying and the contexts you are investigating. This is in contrast to more *inductive* forms of research, which would involve drawing conclusions from specific hypotheses about the data that can be tested in experiments or through systematic observation (abduction is discussed further in KhosraviNik and Unger, 2016).

Data collection and ethics

Ethical considerations

The different elements of the three frameworks described above provide the beginnings of a methodological framework for digital communication. I have only briefly mentioned ethical considerations so far, which should however be at the forefront of researchers' minds when undertaking any project involving human participants or their data. And, due to the

190   *Johann W. Unger*

participatory nature of many digitally mediated texts, and in particular social media texts, there is a huge amount of human-generated data that can be difficult to categorise as 'public' or 'private'. Page et al. (2014: 58) summarise the overarching ethical principle as 'avoid harm to yourself and others'. While this is a good start, it can be difficult to work out what might cause actual or potential harm. While ideally all human-generated data would only be collected and analysed after informed consent has been granted by the participants, this would make it almost impossible to study most publicly available social media data, because researchers are unlikely to get a high number of responses when they contact the people whose data they want to use. There is a useful overview in Page et al. (2014: Chapter 4), and a set of overarching guidelines published by the Association of Internet Researchers (Markham and Buchanan, 2012). However, I will here outline several key concerns that researchers should consider before embarking on a digitally mediated discourse studies project:

- *Public versus private*: The first judgement to make is whether participants had any expectation of privacy when they posted their data online. Clearly, a private WhatsApp group set up for friends to communicate with one another would be inappropriate for a researcher to use without getting consent from everyone involved. In fact, even asking for consent after being part of a context like this can create harm; participants may feel they were being surveilled without their knowledge by someone who was acting under false pretences. At the other extreme, a publicly available tweet by a well-known public figure or company is unlikely to have been posted with any expectation of privacy.
- *Anonymity and verbatim data*: There is little point in anonymising participants when publicly available data is quoted verbatim. Searching the internet for the quoted text will often turn up the original source very quickly. But unlike researchers in other disciplines and fields, discourse analysts cannot necessarily just aggregate data or change words around to make data more difficult to find, because we need to evidence our analyses with empirical data. So researchers have to make a choice around whether the topics in the data, the contents of data, or the participants' identities are sensitive, which means that they should not be exposed. For example, when researching a potentially sensitive topic like eating disorders, a researcher may not choose to include individual disclosures and descriptions of people's experiences, even if they are found in a public online discussion forum, because this may expose them further and potentially removes their ability to delete data about themselves. Digital media articles by journalists may be considered less problematic, by contrast. Where there is a potential risk to the people involved in digitally mediated data, texts should not be included verbatim (and perhaps not used at all, if too sensitive). However, it is also

possible that they can be used with little risk of harm to the participants that would supersede any possible risks from the original posting
(in which case they can be used without anonymisation, if institutional
ethics rules allow for this). This would apply, for instance, if someone's social media posts had been widely reported in the media. There
are two additional ways of resolving or mitigating this problem: first,
raw data can be withheld except from anyone involved in supervising
or assessing work, or from other researchers, and can be made available only on request. Second, when working with translated data, it is
often much harder for readers to trace the text back to an original
source.

- *Informed consent*: Some university ethics committees are considerably
  behind the times; for instance, they may require official names and sig-
  natures on paper forms for all participants, which may be completely
  impractical with digitally mediated research where participant and
  researcher are not physically co-present. Furthermore, by asking for
  official names, a layer of anonymity made possible by participants
  choosing their own screen names is removed. Fortunately, this practice
  seems to be changing, and ethics committees are becoming more flex-
  ible in this regard. If researchers do endeavour to seek informed consent (where appropriate), this should be done using the same means of
  communication as they are using to collect data, e.g. if recruiting participants on Facebook, via a direct Facebook message.
- *Access to data*: Although it is trivially easy to access huge volumes of
  data, this does not mean that it is all 'fair game', even if public. In particular, data that relates to sensitive or contentious subjects (e.g. political beliefs, eating disorders, and criminal activity) should be treated
  with great care. This is rarely a problem with academic texts that are
  only read by markers or dissertation supervisors, but can become
  a problem if the work is then made available online, or is seen by
  peers, friends or family. The relative anonymity of digital identities
  means that researchers may not know if someone whose data they are
  collecting is vulnerable (e.g. a child).
- *Unintended effects*: Following on from the previous point, there may be
  numerous unintended consequences of collecting and using participant
  data, for instance, data may still be available even if it has been deleted
  from the original social media platform; participants may gain more
  visibility than they would have had posting in some obscure forum
  known only to a small community of users.

As a rule of thumb, any data that can only be accessed by someone with
a personal username and password (e.g. Facebook) or that is between
individuals or within a small group (e.g. WhatsApp) should never be used
without gaining the participants' informed consent. Any data that is
publicly available should be assessed carefully in terms of how sensitive it

192 *Johann W. Unger*

is, and how much risk there is to participants (and the researcher themselves) before being used.

Collecting data

Before deciding what data to collect, it is first necessary to consider how much data is required to answer a particular research question and to be able to make claims with an appropriate degree of certainty. For instance, collecting only one tweet from a political leader will allow very little to be said about anything other than that specific tweet, which could however still have highly interesting features or be particularly important. Collecting all that politician's tweets, on the other hand, allows stronger claims to be made, but could be difficult to analyse within the scope of a time-limited research project. Ideally, to gain an insight into digitally mediated communication practices, a variety of texts should be collected, from different actors, over a specific time period, and from different genres. In Unger et al., (2016), we suggested that after reviewing existing theoretical knowledge (and after completing any required ethics processes), researchers should systematically collect available data and find out more about the context. This will give an overview of the research context, as well as indicating which types of data are available and what kinds of insights might be gained from them. This initial data collection could also include participant interviews (following the DCOE approach) alongside observations of participants' practices. Once this initial dataset has been collected, a subset can then be selected for specific analysis – for instance, choosing a smaller sample of social media texts that will help answer the research questions, based on transparent criteria. As an example, a study of racist ideologies on Wikipedia might start with a large number of contentious articles, and then gradually narrow this down to just one or a few for closer analysis. Measures used to downsize the sample could include text-external features (e.g. specific date ranges, presence on a list of widely-read articles) or text-internal features (e.g. presence of certain keywords, articles of a specific length, articles linked from a particular page, etc.).

Digitally mediated contexts lend themselves to the collection of large bodies of texts, though this can be difficult to reconcile with ethical requirements (see above). There are various sophisticated tools available (e.g. FireAnt for Twitter, WebCorp for general web corpora, and NodeXL for various platforms). These involve some time investment to learn to use effectively. Page et al. (2014: Chapter 8) outline a number of techniques for the collection and selection of social media texts. However, simpler tools, such as using the advanced search functionality of search engines can also be a useful way of collecting a variety of data, providing certain precautions are taken to avoid the 'filter bubble' effect caused by search engine algorithms tailoring content to specific users. Using a private browser window should ensure this effect is limited, and should also prevent researchers from accidentally collecting content that is only available to users who are logged in to a platform with a specific account. For critical discursive analyses of digitally mediated communication, often simple tools such as copying and pasting content from a platform into a word processor or spreadsheet, taking screenshots on mobile devices, or saving pages as PDFs can be sufficient. Where possible, data should be saved with its full set of multimodal features (including visuals, sound etc.), and then transcribed where necessary (e.g. written transcripts of videos) to be presented in an accessible format that conforms to ethical guidelines in academic texts.

Choosing data for a study of young successful female politicians

In most of the remainder of this chapter, I will illustrate some key points about analysis of digitally mediated communication using a specific example. In this case, I am interested in the political phenomenon of young, female politicians who have quickly risen to fame, and seem to have a strong traditional and social media presence. I would like to know more about how they achieve this success, how they discursively construct their and others' identities, and how they respond to media and social media attention. Although hate speech, misogyny, and trolling directed against these politicians (or other female public figures) would be a worthwhile topic to study, this is something that is already the subject of considerable scholarly attention (e.g. Hardaker & McGlashan, 2016), and I would prefer to focus more on their own strategies of positive self-representation, and how they position themselves to interact with their social media followers. As suggested above, any digitally mediated communication project should begin with an overview of theoretical frameworks and concepts, followed by systematic collection of a range data and as much information about the topic and context as possible. In this case, we will assume that I have read up on US politics, progressive populism, gender and politics, gender and social media, and other relevant areas, and have tried to establish what the latest relevant theoretical frameworks relating to discourse in social media contexts are (e.g. Fuchs, 2014; KhosraviNik and Unger, 2016). A number of politicians immediately spring to mind; for instance, Mhairi Black, the Scottish National Party Member of the UK Parliament (MP) who, at age 20, became the youngest MP in almost two centuries, and Jacinda Ardern, the Prime Minister of New Zealand, who at age 37 is the youngest female leader of a government in the world. However, I settle on Alexandra Ocasio-Cortez (AOC), a Congresswoman for New York who was elected in the US midterm elections in 2018 after beating a long-term incumbent for the seat in the Democratic primaries, and then took office in early 2019. While each of

194 *Johann W. Unger*

these three politicians is interesting in her own right, and could be the subject of a comparative analysis, I choose just AOC because her success is recent, making her the most topical choice, and because she is a highly active (and interactive) social media user. Any claims I make are therefore limited just to AOC, and not to the other two politicians, which limits the claims I can make about the topic in general (young successful female politicians). My initial data search tells me there is a huge amount of media coverage of her successes, from the primary win onwards (e.g. Embury-Dennis, 2018), and also that she is an active social media user herself. I start looking through her social media profile and narrow my search down to Twitter, on the grounds that the data here are easily accessible (her tweets are public) and that the risk of my conducting research on her tweets is very low, because she has a much more visible public profile than any research I do is likely to achieve, and is a public figure. For the purposes of this analysis, I will focus on two tweets which illustrate many of the features I find in her other posts. However, I note that were I completing a full-scale project, I would analyse her data systematically and make more transparent choices. To do this, I could use corpus techniques (see Chapter 7, this volume) to identify particular aspects of content or form that make her tweets characteristic compared to other Twitter users, such as her use of particular words, emoticons or syntactic constructions, and then choose specific examples that are 'typical' or 'atypical' of her style. Or, even without using corpus tools, I could select a larger number of random tweets and manually note down their features, to get a sense of all the different ways in which AOC uses Twitter, and then try to find tweets that illustrate these differences, to give a rich description of her social media practices. Alternatively, I could also focus on all the tweets within a specific date/time window, based on external events such as a policy announcement or an attack on her in the media. This could allow me to show how she uses her Twitter account in relation to specific political or media events. All of these approaches should be possible within the scope of a student project, bearing in mind the principle that the more data that is analysed, the less detailed the analysis can be: this is why the process of data selection (i.e. down-sampling) following a transparent process is so important.

Analysing and interpreting data

Having collected the data, I am now ready to begin a preliminary analysis. Figures 9.2 and 9.3, below show the two tweets by AOC. They are both examples of quoted tweets – a feature introduced by Twitter in 2015, whereby an existing tweet is shown in an inset box with the user's comment/response above it. Both tweets share a number of features: the standard layout of Twitter includes the profile photo, name and @username, a number of buttons for replying, retweeting, etc. AOC's

Digitally mediated discourse analysis 195

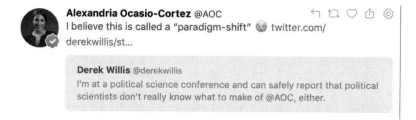

Figure 9.2 Political science conference tweet by Alexandria Ocasio-Cortez

Figure 9.3 Campaign contribution tweet by Alexandria Ocasio-Cortez

profile picture is partially overlapped by a tick in a blue rosette, which indicates she is a verified user (a public figure). The photo looks professional, and she is smiling directly at the camera, which Kress and van Leeuwen (2006) would describe as placing a *demand* on the viewer to engage with the image. Her very short username (only three characters), which she acquired in late 2018, suggests that she is serious about her social media identity – such short usernames are not easy to come by, and it seems likely she or her campaign bought it for a not inconsiderable sum of money. Without inside knowledge of her campaign, there is no way of knowing to what extent she personally controls her social media account, though it is not uncommon for politicians to manage at least some of their social media accounts at present.

In the first tweet (Figure 9.2), AOC replies to @derekwillis's comment about a political science conference. AOC here is doing some nuanced positioning work: on the one hand, her use of 'I believe' could indicate uncertainty, and the use of quotation marks around 'paradigm-shift' and indeed the hyphen in the term, might indicate she is distancing herself from the term as if not fully familiar with it. On the other hand, her use of a winking emoji suggest she is making a joke or being satirical. The term 'paradigm-shift' was coined by the philosopher Thomas Kuhn (1962) and has been widely used to describe shifts of thinking in academic fields such as economics, including for the radical departure from orthodox economics of John Maynard Keynes, whom AOC is presumably familiar with as a reported proponent of modern monetary theory. In other words, AOC is poking fun at the political scientists by playfully appropriating 'their' language, while also presenting herself as someone who wishes to bring about a marked change in US politics.

In the second tweet (Figure 9.3), AOC quotes a tweet about a press release from a (supposedly non-partisan) think-tank. The press release is about her approach to campaign funding, which eschews large donations and instead relies on grassroots members. Rather than just retweet this arguably rather positive article about her, AOC first tells a 'small story' (see Page, 2013). Numbers, and particularly large amounts of money, seem often to be used in political communications as a way of being persuasive (compare, for instance, Donald Trump's frequent tweets about how much money he has). Here, instead AOC is describing a very small amount ($1/month) because her aim appears to be to show that small donations can make a difference. She personalises the description of her campaign in the quoted tweet by describing a 'dishwasher in New Jersey' – this is a well-established technique in political speeches (compare for instance US Presidential candidate's John McCain's invocation of 'Joe the Plumber' in his 2008 campaign against Barack Obama). AOC's tweet uses empty lines to separate the story into three parts: the personal opening, then a more general philosophical point which follows from the dishwasher's selfless act, and finally a conclusion, followed by a link to her campaign donations page. Despite the white space, each subsequent part is linked to the opening through cohesive links: 'That gesture ...' and 'Because of him', and finally the story is linked with the present 'I can do more now' and a colon finally makes the connection with the donations page.

Overall, these two tweets appear to follow the pattern pioneered by Barack Obama and other Democratic US politicians: she engages with individual users, sends positive messages about herself and her campaign, uses a mix of light-hearted humour, appeals to pathos (emotion) and tries to differentiate herself from 'politics as usual' in various ways. Although there is not enough space to describe them in full here, it is worth briefly considering the next steps in a study of this kind. For example, this could involve observing reactions (in the form of replies, retweets, and media reactions) to AOC's tweets. Or an ethnographic element could be added, involving interviews with some of AOC's followers (supporters or detractors) along the lines suggested by Androutsopoulos (2008). Finally, although even looking at just two tweets can yield some interesting findings and interpretations, clearly a greater number of AOC's social media posts is needed, including examining her presence on different platforms, to present a fuller picture of her digitally mediated practices and their relation with the overall political context. This might also allow some reflection on the media dynamics at play here – popular and/or contentious politicians like AOC generate a huge amount of attention, which translates into revenue for private social media companies and their shareholders, not just political donations.

Presenting findings and results

Similarly to the other approaches detailed in this book, it is essential that findings from a study relate to the research questions, and that any claims that the writer makes are supported by evidence from the data, or are appropriately mitigated using hedges such as 'This may suggest that ...' where the evidence is open to interpretation. If researchers take a more qualitative approach to data analysis, as I have in the brief analysis of AOC's tweets above, there will inevitably be an element of interpretation in how the data is categorised and understood. These interpretations should however be made as transparent as possible by clearly setting out the framework for analysis and analytical categories (e.g. the discursive strategies described in Unger et al., 2016, or the elements of social media narratives outlined by Page, 2013).

As suggested above under the heading 'Ethical considerations', above, it is important to consider issues around anonymity and risk in presenting data For instance, including verbatim data in your work, even if you do not include usernames, may mean it is easy to find out the identity of the people whose data you are using. Furthermore, using data from particular groups may expose the researcher themselves to harassment or threats. However, generally speaking, it is necessary to quote verbatim data to provide evidence for analysis work, or at least to illustrate any claims being made. If work is being assessed but also shared publicly, it may be possible to put verbatim data in an appendix which is only available to the markers or can be provided to readers on request.

Where ethical considerations permit, it is good practice to provide screen-captured images of at least some of the data. Readers accessing the same digital platforms on different devices, or even a relatively short time period after the analysis was carried out, may see the data displayed in visually quite different ways due to differences between operating systems or changes in platform design over time. This also allows readers to see any non-verbal aspects of the data, where these are salient to the analysis.

198   *Johann W. Unger*

Issues and limitations

There are a number of limitations and issues in approaching digitally mediated communication as a researcher, some of which have already been outlined earlier in the chapter. First, there are considerable ethical barriers, which must be carefully negotiated to keep both participants and researchers safe. Second, there are some inherent features of digital media platforms that make researching them interesting, but sometimes challenging. One major challenge is the dynamic nature of many digital media texts. In many digital media contexts, including platforms like Facebook, Wikipedia, and online news sites, texts do not necessarily stay the same longer term or sometimes even for more than a few minutes. Researchers thus need to decide whether they take a snapshot and analyse the text as 'static at a particular time', or whether they attempt to capture this dynamism in their analysis for instance by documenting and discussing changes. However, not all platforms are as transparent as Wikipedia, which keeps accessible to users all changes that have been made, and it may be difficult for researchers to keep coming back to check for changes. A further issue, perhaps a limitation of existing research rather than a difficulty, is that it is very tempting for researchers to chase after new platforms, rather than focus on users' discursive practices within and across a range of platforms. Each new popular platform such Facebook, Twitter, Snapchat, has generated a raft of excited articles by academics documenting the 'next big thing', while the actual practices of users may not actually change all that much over time (Herring, 2004 warns of this danger). Finally, a problem for researchers is that they may wish to research a context that is relatively unfamiliar to them. This means not only that their lack of familiarity with conventions may be a barrier to gaining acceptance, but also that specific meanings may be obscure to them, due to the use of in-jokes, irony, particular registers and specialised lexis, or unfamiliar orthographies, to mention just a few problems. Nevertheless, through careful application of observations within a discursive framework, and the use of participant interviews where possible/desirable, these problems are surmountable.

Further reading

Page et al. (2014) provide an accessible introduction to language and social media. With specialised chapters focussing on ethics, qualitative and quantitative approaches and ethnography, this is a good place to start for researchers new to researching in digitally mediated contexts. Unger et al., (2016) is a chapter in a qualitative methods handbook which shows in more detail how the discourse-historical approach to critical discourse studies can be applied to social media data. Fuchs (2014) is an excellent introduction to social media from a critical, sociological perspective. It is not a linguistics textbook, but rather examines some of the broader societal and philosophical issues related to social media. Barton and Lee (2013) provides a highly accessible introduction to digitally mediated language, primarily from an ethnographic perspective.

References

Androutsopoulos, J. (2008). Potentials and limitations of discourse-centred online ethnography. *Language@Internet*, 5, article 8.

Barton, D. and Lee, C. (2013). *Language online: Investigating digital texts and practices*. London: Routledge.

Culpeper, J., Kerswill, P., Wodak, R., McEnery, A. and Katamba, F. (Eds.) (2018). *English language: Description, variation and context*. Basingstoke: Palgrave.

Embury-Dennis, T. (June 27, 2018). Everything you need to know about Alexandria Ocasio-Cortez, the 28-year-old socialist hailed as the 'future of the Democratic Party'. *The Independent*. London: Independent Print.

Fuchs, C. (2014). *Social media: A critical introduction*. London: Sage.

Gibson, J. (1977). The theory of affordances. In R. Shaw and J. Bransford (Eds.), *Perceiving, acting, and knowing: Toward an ecological psychology*. (pp. 67–82). Hillsdale, NJ: Lawrence Erlbaum.

Gillen, J. (2013). Writing Edwardian postcards. *Journal of Sociolinguistics*, 17, 488–521.

Hardaker, C. and McGlashan, M. (2016). 'Real men don't hate women': Twitter rape threats and group identity. *Journal of Pragmatics*, 91, 80–93.

Herring, S.C. (2001). Computer-mediated discourse. In D. Schiffrin, D. Tannen and H. Hamilton (Eds.), *The handbook of discourse analysis*. (pp. 612–634). Oxford: Blackwell.

Herring, S.C. (2004). Computer-mediated discourse analysis: An approach to researching online behavior. In S.A. Barab, R. Kling and J.H. Gray (Eds.), *Designing for virtual communities in the service of learning*. (pp. 338–376). New York: Cambridge University Press.

Herring, S.C. (2007). A faceted classification scheme for computer-mediated discourse. *Language@Internet*, 4, article 1.

Herring, S.C. (2013). Discourse in web 2.0: Familiar, reconfigured, and emergent. In D. Tannen and A.M. Trester (Eds.), *Discourse 2.0: Language and new media*. (pp. 1–25). Washington, DC: Georgetown University Press.

Hine, C. (2015). *Ethnography for the internet: Embedded, embodied and everyday*. London: Bloomsbury.

KhosraviNik, M. (2017). Social media critical discourse studies (SM-CDS). In J. Flowerdew and J.E. Richardson (Eds.), *Handbook of critical discourse analysis*. (pp. 582–596). London: Routledge.

KhosraviNik, M. and Unger, J.W. (2016). Critical discourse studies and social media: Power, resistance and critique in changing media ecologies. In R. Wodak and M. Meyer (Eds.), *Methods of critical discourse studies*. (pp. 205–233). London: Sage.

Kress, G. and van Leeuwen, T. (2006). *Reading images: The grammar of visual sesign*. London: Routledge.

Kuhn, T. (1962). *The structure of scientific revolutions*. Chicago: University of Chicago Press.

Markham, A. and Buchanan, E. (2012). Ethical decision-making and internet research v 2. Available: http://aoir.org/reports/ethics2.pdf.

Page, R. (2013). *Stories and social media: Identities and interaction.* London: Routledge.

Page, R., Barton, D., Unger, J.W. and Zappavigna, M. (2014). *Researching language and social media.* London: Routledge.

Ten Have, P. (2007). *Doing conversation analysis.* (2nd ed.). London: Sage.

Unger, J., Wodak, R. and KhosraviNik, M. (2016). Critical discourse studies and social media data. In D. Silverman (Ed.), *Qualitative Research.* (4th ed., pp. 277–293). London: Sage.

10 Experimental methods in discourse analysis

Christopher Hart

Introduction

This chapter introduces a quantitative approach to critical discourse analysis that is less concerned with the distribution of textual features, as in the previous chapter, and more concerned with the effects that particular features have on audience cognition. One way of empirically investigating the cognitive effects of textual choices is to use experimental methods. In this chapter, I introduce the rationale for using methods normally associated with psycholinguistics in critical discourse analysis (CDA). I introduce a number of key concepts fundamental to any experimental research and illustrate how these might be applied in designing, administering and reporting an experimental project in CDA.

Outline of approach

Experimental methods are not common in critical discourse analysis (CDA). Indeed, traditionally, researchers in CDA have explicitly rejected positivism. Instead, CDA has emphasised the social and historical situatedness of texts and argued that the meaning of a text is not reducible to something that can be studied and measured in a laboratory setting. The meaning of a text is always a function of the social and historical conditions in which it is produced and consumed and only analysts sensitive to these complex contextual factors, which laboratory methods fail to capture, can account for the meanings a text conveys. Nevertheless, many forms of CDA make claims, either explicitly or implicitly, about the effects of textual choices on readers' cognition. Indeed, CDA as a field is fundamentally Whorfian. Analyses in CDA involve attributing to different textual features contrasting effects on audience attitudes, emotions, beliefs, values, judgements, perceptions, decisions, and, ultimately, actions. And these are things that can, in principle, be investigated empirically in the lab. Some researchers who have been critical of CDA have in fact explicitly called for such a move. Widdowson (2004: 171), for example, states that 'whatever textual feature is identified as significant, be it lexical or

202 Christopher Hart

grammatical, or even typographical, can be systematically altered and the effects of the alteration empirically investigated'.

In the absence of any empirical evidence, however, CDA has been accused of presenting only subjective, politically rather than theoretically motivated, readings of texts which risk over-interpreting the impact that specific textual features have on the beliefs, values, judgements, decisions, etc. of audiences (Widdowson, 1995; Stubbs, 1997). In the context of such criticism, and as part of a more general commitment to 'triangulation' (Baker and Levon, 2015), approaches to CDA have developed which do more to address audience reception of texts. For example, using corpus linguistic methods in CDA (see Chapter 7, this volume) researchers are able to observe the general collocational behaviour of a target word and use this as a more reliable basis on which to draw conclusions about its evaluative function on a specific occasion of use (Coffin and O'Halloran, 2006; O'Halloran, 2007). The use of Cognitive Linguistics in CDA (see Chapter 6, this volume) also takes the reader into account, albeit an 'ideal reader' rather than actual readers on specific occasions, and, based on a psychologically motivated model of language, theorises the impact that language choices have on audiences (Hart, 2013a, 2013b, 2015). Both corpus linguistics and cognitive linguistics, then, move us closer to a form of reception studies in CDA. However, they do not get us all of the way. As Subtirelu and Gopavaram (2016: 39) note:

> Such work has made important contributions to CDA by providing plausible accounts of how texts might be taken up by 'typical' readers especially those only reading for basic comprehension (i.e., 'to get the gist'). Nonetheless, even when critical discourse analysts have attended specifically to cognitive theory and have used it to ground their explanations of the effects of discourse, they have rarely attempted to study listeners' or readers' uptake of texts ... This means that even CDA research grounded in Cognitive Linguistics usually lacks more direct evidence of audiences' uptake of texts.

There is now a small but growing body of work in (critical) discourse analysis which aims to provide precisely this kind of empirical evidence, attesting to the impact of textual choices on audience cognition, by exploiting experimental methods (Hart, 2018a, 2018b, 2019; Fuoli and Hart, 2018; Fuoli, van de Weijer and Paradis, 2017; Subtirelu and Gopavaram, 2016). There are also a number of studies in other fields of linguistics, and even other disciplines like media studies or political science, that are relevant to students of discourse keen to pursue experimental methods (e.g. Arpan et al., 2006; Fausey and Matlock, 2011; Landau, Sullivan, and Greenberg, 2009; Lau and Schlesinger, 2005; Robins and Mayer, 2000; Thibodeau and Boroditsky, 2011; Utych, 2017).

Fundamentals of experimental research

In experimental studies, researchers test a particular *hypothesis* by deliberately manipulating an *independent variable* and then measuring, in a scientific way, the effects of this manipulation on a *dependent variable*, while at the same time controlling for potential *extraneous variables*. Manipulations of the independent variable are described as different *levels* and are presented in the experiment in different *treatments* or *conditions*.

In CDA, independent variables are the textual features hypothesised to serve some ideological or persuasive function. This might include, for example, particular lexical choices, metaphors, or grammatical structures. Dependent variables are the things that these textual features are predicted to affect – the things you are measuring. In CDA, dependent variables would include audience attitudes, emotions, beliefs, values, judgements, perceptions, decisions, and, potentially, actions. So, for example, you might want to investigate the effects of animal metaphors for immigrants (condition 1) compared to literal descriptions (condition 2) on audience perceptions of immigrants and/or attitudes toward immigration policies. Extraneous variables are any variables besides your independent variable that could also have an effect on your dependent variable and thus may provide an alternative explanation for your results, in which case you are said to have a potential *confound*. In CDA, one particularly important extraneous variable, which should always be controlled for, is political orientation.

Experiments in linguistics make use of both *off-line* and *on-line paradigms*. This distinction has nothing to do with whether the experiment is conducted over the internet. Rather, on-line methods are those that investigate, directly or indirectly, real-time aspects of language processing. On-line measures include reaction-times, eye-tracking, and neuro-imaging. Off-line methods investigate the results of language processing and involve some conscious reflection on the part of the subject. Off-line measures include the kind of judgement tasks found in surveys and questionnaires. To date, experiments in CDA have made use only of off-line methods. However, it is perfectly conceivable that on-line methods could also be used to investigate the cognitive (including affective) impact of ideological language choices.

There are many different kinds of *experimental design*, which involve different numbers of groups and different numbers of variables. For example, one way of classifying an experiment's design is according to whether it is *between-subjects* or *within-subjects* (also known as *repeated measures*). In a between-subjects design, different groups of people are exposed to each condition and the responses of each group are compared. In a within-subjects design, the same group of people are exposed to all conditions and their responses in one condition are compared with their responses in the other. There are advantages and disadvantages to both

204 *Christopher Hart*

designs. For example, a major advantage of a within-subjects design is that it reduces the potential for *extraneous variability* arising from *individual differences*. In a between-subjects design, there is a risk that subjects in one group will differ from subjects in the other group with respect to some factor other than the independent variable, such as age, gender, literacy level, educational background, test-anxiety, or other personality trait, not all of which can be controlled for. In a within-subjects design, there is only one group, with the same subjects tested in each condition, effectively acting as their own control. Any effect found therefore cannot be attributed to such extraneous variables. Another advantage of a within-subjects design is that they have greater statistical power meaning that fewer participants are required in order to find a statistically significant effect. However, a major disadvantage of a within-subjects design compared to a between-subjects design is the risk of *carry-over effects*, whereby subjects' behaviour in one condition is influenced by their exposure to and behaviour in the other condition. Carry-over effects include subjects becoming more adept at the task and performing 'better' as they progress through the experiment (practice effects). Conversely, subjects can become tired or bored and perform 'worse' as the experiment unfolds (fatigue effects). Responses in one condition may also be made relative to responses in another condition, rather than representing 'true' judgements or behaviours (contrast effects). Another serious risk in a within-subjects design is that, since subjects are exposed to each condition, they will recognise the manipulation you have made, figure out your hypothesis, and modify their responses as a result.

In each design, there are ways to mitigate against these problems. For example, a between-subjects design can mitigate against errors arising from individual differences by assigning subjects to groups *randomly*. This is, in fact, an 'essential characteristic of experimental studies' (Abhul, Gass, and Mackey, 2013: 119). *Random assignment* minimises the likelihood that subjects who have some factor other than the independent variable in common will end up in the same group. The alternative to random assignment is a *block design* whereby subjects are matched according to some factor that the researcher suspects could influence the dependent variable and are then deliberately split between groups. Another way that a between-subjects design can address the issue of error variance is by collecting demographic information relating to potential extraneous variables at the end of the experiment and factoring this into subsequent analyses. A within-subjects design can mitigate against carry-over effects through *counter-balancing*, whereby randomly assigned subjects complete the different conditions in different orders. So, if you are testing the effects of animal metaphors for immigrants then half of your participants would be exposed to the animal metaphor text first while the other half would be exposed to the literal text first. A within-subjects design can try to prevent subjects from working out what is being tested by including at least as many *filler* stimuli as *target* stimuli. Filler stimuli are those included in the experiment as a decoy but discarded in the analysis later on. However, it should be noted that introducing filler stimuli will increase the length of the experiment and therefore enhance the risk of fatigue effects.

Another way of classifying an experiment's design is according to the number of independent and dependent variables. The simplest design consists of one independent variable and one dependent variable. This is known as a *single-factor, univariate* design. However, it is possible to have more than one of each type of variable. When you have more than one independent variable this is known as a *multi-factor* (or factorial) design. When you have more than one dependent variable this is known as a *multivariate* design. An example of a single-factor, multivariate design is Hart's (2018a) study of event-perception in media discourses of political protests. In this experiment, subjects were presented with a news article reporting violence at a fictitious political protest. Each subject was randomly assigned to one of four conditions, which reported the violence using different grammatical constructions. There was thus one independent variable with four levels. After reading the news report, subjects had to indicate (i) where they placed the blame for the violence that occurred and (ii) how aggressive they perceived the actors involved to be. There were thus two dependent variables: blame assignment and perception of aggression. An example of a multi-factor, univariate design is Hart's (2018b) study of fire metaphors in media reports of political protests. Here, subjects were presented with a news article also reporting violence at a fictitious political protest. This time, one manipulation concerned metaphor with the report either using fire metaphors or literal equivalents to describe the violence. In addition, however, the stimulus texts also included images of protest which either contained or did not contain fire. There were thus two independent variables, each with two levels. Once subjects had read the article, they were asked to make a judgement on the acceptability of police using water cannon to control the protests. There was thus only one dependent variable.

Factorial designs are common in psycholinguistics. The crucial advantage they have is that they allow the researcher to investigate the effects of more than one independent variable separately (known as *main effects*) while also establishing whether the effect of one independent variable is contingent upon another (known as *interaction effects*). The simplest multi-factor design is the between-subjects 2x2 factorial design. In this design, there are two independent variables, each with two levels. This gives rise to four treatment combinations to which subjects are then (randomly) assigned. An example of this design is found in Landau, Sullivan, and Greenberg's (2009) study of body-politic metaphors and attitudes to immigration. They gave subjects a popular science article about airborne bacteria that was described either as harmful or harmless. They then gave subjects a short essay addressing a range of

206   *Christopher Hart*

domestic policy issues (other than immigration). One version of this essay made use of body-politic metaphors (e.g. After the Civil War, the United States experienced an unprecedented *growth spurt*, and is *scurrying* to create new laws that will give it a chance to *digest* the millions of innovations) while the other did not. Subjects' attitudes toward immigration were then measured. The researchers found no main effect. That is, neither the manipulation in the bacteria text (harmful versus harmless) nor the manipulation in the policy text (metaphor vs. literal) had any effect on their own. However, they did find an interaction effect such that among subjects exposed to the body-politic metaphor, those who had previously been primed with the harmful bacteria text showed significantly more negative attitudes toward immigration than subjects in the harmless bacteria condition. By contrast, the bacteria manipulation made no difference to subjects who read the literal policy text and the body-politic metaphor made no difference to subjects who had read the harmless bacteria text. In other words, the metaphor framing effect in this study is shown only to arise under specific circumstances, here dependent on a heightened sensitivity to threat from contamination.

Of course, it is also possible to a have a multi-factor, multivariate design as in Fuoli and Hart's (2018) study of trust-building strategies in corporate discourse. In the end, which experimental design is adopted will depend on a number of things including your research questions and the resources (including participants) available to you. Which design is adopted will also have consequences for the type of statistical analysis you perform later. One thing we can say, however, is that experimental studies in or relevant to CDA have tended to favour between-subjects designs.

Identifying research questions

Research questions are inextricably linked to hypotheses. Indeed, a hypothesis can be viewed as an answer to a particular research question. In experimental research, a hypothesis is a statement that makes a prediction about the relationship between at least two variables. A hypothesis always has two sides to it. The *null hypothesis* states that there is no relationship between the variables under investigation. The null hypothesis is important for statistical analysis – it is in fact the one that gets tested. However, in experiment reports, it is often left implicit in the statement of hypotheses. The *alternative hypothesis* is the positive counterpart and the one explicitly formulated in response to your research question. The alternative hypothesis predicts an effect, a difference or a correlation between variables. So, for example, in Hart's (2018b) study of fire metaphors in media discourses of civil disorder, the research question and hypotheses were set out as follows:

RQ: Do fire metaphors in media discourses of disorder contribute to a perceived legitimacy of using water cannon in police response to civil unrest?

H1: The presence of fire in images of protest will facilitate support for police use of water cannon.

H2: The presence of fire in metaphors of protest will similarly facilitate support for police use of water cannon.

In CDA, research questions and experimental hypotheses should be driven by attested textual data and previous qualitative analyses. Research questions should centre around a linguistic or other semiotic feature that is part of real discourse produced and consumed in a specific social context, rather than representing a hypothetical, non-attested discursive practice. This may be a textual practice you yourself have noticed or one that has been identified as characteristic of a particular discourse in a previous study. Likewise, hypotheses concerning the functions of a given linguistic or other semiotic feature should represent predictions that emerge from prior analyses rooted in a particular theoretical framework. In that sense, hypotheses are often generated by previous research conducted within other approaches to CDA. So, for example, Hart's (2018b) study of metaphor was motivated by previous studies that had found fire metaphors to be a recurrent feature of discourses of disorder with predictions about the consequences of fire metaphors in this context emerging from analyses based in cognitive linguistic theories of metaphor (Charteris-Black, 2017; Hart, 2014; Hawkins, 2014).

A further constraint on research questions and hypotheses is, of course, that they must be capable of being addressed in an experimental setting. Researchers must think realistically about what can and cannot be achieved in an experiment. For example, although CDA theorises the social action effects of texts, no causal connection between texts and social action can ever be directly observed. By contrast, the cognitive effects of texts, which intercede any social action effects, are within empirical reach.

Data collection and ethics

Once research questions and hypotheses have been identified and the basic design has been decided, it is time to start thinking about data. Data in experimental CDA is not textual data that is the subject of close critical analysis but numeric data, obtained in an experimental setting, and subjected to statistical analysis. In getting ready to collect data, we need to think about three further elements of any experiment: measures, materials, and participants.

Measures

Recall, dependent variables are the things we are measuring in order to ascertain the extent to which they are affected by an independent variable.

The question that then arises is how do we actually measure our dependent variable? In experimental CDA, off-line methods are normally employed in a questionnaire-embedded experiment. Off-line methods are most appropriate for measuring the attitudes, opinions, judgements, etc. that may be influenced by discourse. Several types of measure are available, including free-response, yes-no, forced-choice, and rating scale. An example of a *free-response* task is found in Fausey and Matlock (2011). Fausey and Matlock investigated the effects of grammatical aspect in descriptions of political candidates' past actions on judgements about electability. Subjects in this experiment first read a short text about a fictitious senator that was up for re-election. The text described past actions that were either positive or negative using either the perfective or imperfective aspect: *collected donations/was collecting donations* (positive) versus *took hush money/was taking hush money* (negative). Subjects were randomly assigned to one of the four conditions. Having read the description, one of the questions subjects had to answer was '*Please estimate the total amount of donation money (in dollars)*' (positive valence condition) or '*Please estimate the total amount of hush money (in dollars)*' (negative valence condition). This is a free-response task because there are no constraints on the values that subjects can give; they can estimate any amount of money. Results of the experiment showed that grammatical aspect affected the judgements that people made in relation to negative actions. Estimates were significantly higher when the senator *was taking* hush money (imperfective) compared to when they *took* hush money (perfective). Judgements about positive actions were unaffected by grammatical aspect.

Fausey and Matlock's study also contained an example of a *yes–no* task. As well as giving a dollar estimate, subjects were asked '*Will this candidate be re-elected? (circle Yes or No)*'. They were also asked to express a confidence value in relation to their decision. Unsurprisingly, results showed that subjects in the positive action condition were significantly more likely to respond 'yes' compared to subjects in the negative action condition. More interesting is the influence of grammatical aspect. While aspect did not affect confidence in 'yes' decisions following positive actions, subjects were significantly more confident about their 'no' decisions when the senator *was doing* the negative action compared to when they *did* the negative action.

The yes–no task is a particular type of *forced-choice* task. A forced-choice task is one in which the subject is asked to select from a fixed number of pre-defined alternative responses. This can be *binary* as in the yes–no task or involve more than two options. Another kind of binary forced-choice task is found in Hart (2019). Hart (2019) investigated the effects of point of view and relative spatial values in pictures (as well as linguistic descriptions) of political protests. Specifically, in one of the experiments reported, he was interested in the influence of perspective on perceptions of aggression. In a within-subjects design, he gave participants six pairs of pictures showing a protester and a policeman engaged in a violent encounter. The only difference between the two images in each pair was that in one the protester was on the left while in the other the protester was on the right (this was counter-balanced across the six trials). For each pair of images, the subject had to say in which one was the protester the most *aggressive/unfriendly/intimidating/frightening/threatening/hostile*. The choice was thus between spatial values left and right. Results showed that subjects were significantly more likely to associate the left spatial position with higher levels of aggression. Hart repeated the study for spatial values front and back and found an even stronger effect with the back (and ego-opposed) position being associated with higher levels of aggression.

There are advantages and disadvantages to different types of measure. A major disadvantage of the free-response task is that its open-endedness can lead to an enormous amount of variability in the data, which can be unwieldy and cannot always easily be attributed to manipulations of the independent variable. For example, in Fausey and Matlock's (2011) study, subjects might have started with wildly different conceptions of what constitutes a large amount of money and this, rather than grammatical aspect, may account for the range of dollar estimates. An advantage of forced-choice tasks is that they are relatively easy to administer while having increased statistical power (Schütze and Sprouse, 2013: 32).[1] Forced-choice tasks compare two or more conditions directly (rather than indirectly as in scalar response tasks). However, in contrast to a free-response task, forced-choice tasks are highly restrictive and can produce effects that are exaggerated, arising as a function of the task itself rather than the targeted factor. For example, in Hart's (2019) study, there was no option for 'neither left nor right' or 'neither front nor back'. The task, as its name suggests, forces a response and this may not necessarily reflect the subject's true position. It is therefore a good idea to include a 'neutral' or 'don't know' option. Another limitation of a forced-choice task is that it does not directly tell us about the size of any difference between conditions. For example, Hart's (2019) study does not tell us how much more aggressive actors are perceived as being when they appear in the left position compared to the right. A forced-choice task, then, may be optimal for ascertaining a qualitative difference between conditions. Very often, however, there is reason to be interested in quantitative differences, in which case a numerical task is likely to be more appropriate.

The most common type of measure, which is especially well-suited to measuring attitudes and opinions, is a *rating scale*. Rating scales come in several different forms. However, two of the most widely used are *Likert scales* and *semantic differential* scales. In a Likert scale, subjects are given a statement and asked to rate their level of agreement with it on a 5- or 7-point scale with endpoints 'strongly agree' and 'strongly disagree'. It is important that the scale consists of an odd number of points because this provides a mid-point representing a neutral 'neither agree nor disagree' position. An example of a Likert scale is found in Utych's (2017) study of dehumanising metaphors in immigration discourse. Utych was interested in the potential for such metaphors to increase feelings of disgust toward immigrants. Utych took perceived threat from contamination as a proxy for disgust and asked subjects to rate their agreement, on a 7-point scale, with the statement: 'Illegal immigrants make Americans more prone to infectious diseases'. In a semantic differential scale, subjects are presented with a question rather than a statement and asked to indicate their response to it on a scale whose endpoints represent polar opposite values. Scales typically consist of 5 or 7 points but can consist of 9, 11, or even more points. Semantic differential scales capture the broadly positive or negative traits associated with a given object, entity, action, or event. Endpoints of this scale are therefore typically labelled using antonymic adjectives or other ways of expressing opposite connotative associations. An example of a semantic differential scale is found in Hart (2018a). In Hart (2018a) subjects were given news reports of violence at a fictitious political protest that contained either transitive or reciprocal verbs (as well as differences in voice and information sequence within these verb-types). They were then asked 'How aggressive do you think the protesters were?' and 'How aggressive do you think the police were?' Responses were given on a 7-point scale with endpoints labelled 'not aggressive at all' and 'extremely aggressive'. The same semantic differential scale was used in Hart's (2019) study of point of view and perceptions of aggression in pictures of political protest.

Scales are more convincing and more powerful when they are made up of more than one item addressing the dependent variable. *Multi-item scales* are more comprehensive in their capture of the dependent variable and therefore less prone to random measurement error (increased *validity*). They also allow for greater degrees of discrimination (increased *sensitivity*). For example, Hart (2018b), in his study of metaphor in media discourses of disorder, used a two-item semantic differential scale to capture different dimensions of legitimacy: 'How logical was the police decision to use water canon?' and 'How justifiable was the police decision to use water canon?' In Landau, Sullivan, and Greenberg's (2009) study of dehumanising metaphors and their effects on attitudes toward immigration, they used a six-item Likert scale that included statements such as 'It's important to increase restrictions on who can enter into the United States' and 'An open immigration policy would have a negative impact on the nation'. With multi-item scales, subjects' responses across items can either be aggregated or averaged to create a single composite data point.

Any scale also needs to be *reliable*. There are different types of reliability. One form of reliability concerns the extent to which a scale will elicit similar responses when deployed on different occasions. A form of reliability that relates specifically to multi-item scales concerns the internal consistency of the scale. A scale is described as reliable, in this sense, to the extent that subjects respond to items, intended to target the same underlying factor, in a similar way. A formula commonly used to measure this type of reliability is known as *Cronbach's alpha coefficient*. It is beyond the scope of this chapter to describe how this measure is calculated (see Kaplan, 2004). But since some studies will report this measure, it is worth noting that a value exceeding 0.80 is usually taken as indicating high levels of reliability (DeVellis, 2012: 109). For example, for their six-item Likert scale measuring attitudes toward immigration, Landau, Sullivan and Greenberg reported a Cronbach's alpha value of $\alpha = 0.87$. When designing a new study, then, it is not always necessary to develop new scales. If your dependent variable is one that has been investigated elsewhere, it is a good idea to use or adapt scales that have been used previously and which have proven to be reliable. In their study investigating trust-building functions of stance-taking acts in corporate discourse, for example, Fuoli and Hart (2018) made use of several pre-existing multi-item scales measuring different dimensions of trustworthiness.

Besides your dependent variable, you need to measure other, potentially confounding, factors like age, gender, and political orientation. This is normally done at the end of the experiment before a final debriefing message. Age and gender are relatively straightforward variables to measure. However, note that at the very least gender categories should include 'male', 'female', and 'non-binary'. Political orientation is more difficult to measure. In CDA, it is sometimes treated as a nominal variable with subjects asked to indicate their political orientation based on political parties (e.g. Hart, 2018a, 2013b). Other times, it is treated as an ordinal variable with subjects indicating their orientation on a scale ranging from 'liberal' to 'conservative' (e.g. Fuoli and Hart, 2018).

Materials

Once you have identified your research questions and decided on the most appropriate measures for your dependent variable it's time to start putting together the materials that make up your experiment. This consists of the experiment itself but also an information sheet for your subjects, a consent form, instructions, and a final debriefing message. The information sheet is important because it tells subjects roughly what the researcher is investigating (without giving too much away so as to influence the outcome of the experiment), what is expected of subjects completing the experiment, what will happen to the data, and whom to contact for further information or in case of any concern. The experiment itself is made up of stimuli representing your independent variable(s) and measures of your main dependent variable(s). It is also a good idea to collect demographic information such as subjects' age, gender, political orientation, or educational background. This data can be used later on with factors included as independent or control variables in your analyses. It should be collected at the end of the experiment.

Stimuli contain the manipulations of your independent variable(s). In CDA, it is important that stimuli texts are authentic, representing as closely as possible the content, style, and format etc. of real texts produced in the target genre. In other words, researchers should strive for maximal *ecological validity*. This is important in order that experimental findings can be generalised to real-world contexts, thus preserving their relevance for CDA researchers. For example, in their study of trust-building strategies in corporate discourse, Fuoli and Hart (2018) created an About Us webpage for a fictitious pharmaceutical company that was based on the About Us page of the real pharmaceutical company GlaxoSmithKlein (see Figure 10.1). In some studies, such as Fuoli and Hart (2018), a *pilot study* is conducted prior to the main experiment (using different and smaller numbers of subjects) to determine the authenticity of stimulus materials, as well as the validity and reliability of measurement scales.

In addition to stimuli materials and measures, some experiments also contain manipulation or attention checks. The purpose of these checks is to ensure high-quality data. An *attention check* ensures that subjects have properly engaged with the task and read the stimulus texts carefully. For example, in Hart (2018b) subjects were asked to list three words they remembered from the stimulus news text before being presented with the dependent measures. A *manipulation check* goes a step further and checks not only that subjects have read the stimulus text carefully but also that the manipulations of the independent variable have been effective. Such checks are not without problems, however. For example, if they feature after the presentation of stimuli and before measures of the dependent variable, it is possible that their inclusion will affect experimental outcomes (see Hauser, Ellsworth, and Gonzalez, 2018 for discussion). Manipulation checks in particular risk making hypotheses known to subjects who may respond to dependent measures differently as a result. Alternatively, if they feature at the end of the experiment, then they may not be so effective. The decision on whether or not to include an attention or manipulation check, and if so where, is a matter of design that involves weighing up risks and rewards.

One context in which it seems most appropriate to include an attention or manipulation check is when experiments are administered over the internet. Running experiments on-line is now commonplace in linguistics and psychology. It affords a number of obvious advantages. These include the ability to access more diverse population samples, which compared to most student populations may be more representative of society in general, and the ability to collect large quantities of data quickly and efficiently. There are some questions, however, over the quality of data obtained on-line compared to data collected via more traditional means (e.g. pen and

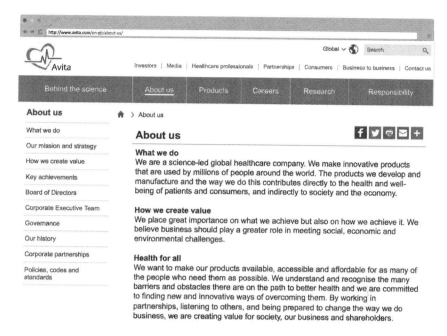

Figure 10.1 About Us page from Fuoli and Hart (2018)

paper). It is, for example, more difficult to monitor subjects' engagement with the task. Given appropriate checks are in place, though, and sufficient quantities of data are collected so as to compensate for any 'noise', several studies now point to the reliability of on-line survey-based experiments (Behrend et al., 2011; Buhrmester, Kwang, and Gosling, 2011; Paolacci, Chandler, and Ipeirotis, 2010). Several platforms are available for conducting experiments on-line. The one with the most functionality and favoured by most professional researchers is Qualtrics (www.qualtrics.com). Most UK universities will hold a licence for Qualtrics that allows student use of the software. However, simple survey-based experiments can also be conducted via open platforms like Survey Monkey (www.surveymonkey.com) and Google Forms (https://google.co.uk/forms/about).

Participants

Now you have designed your experiment, all you need is participants. The number of participants you need depends on your expected effect size. As a rough guide, for medium to large effect sizes, 30 participants per condition should be sufficient to provide the level of statistical power normally considered acceptable (Cohen, 1988).

Most studies in CDA and applied linguistics more generally use *convenience sampling methods* to obtain participants. Convenience sampling is a non-probabilistic sampling paradigm in which subjects are selected on the basis that they are easily accessible and willing to participate. This is in contrast to random (probabilistic) sampling and more targeted forms of non-probabilistic sampling (sometimes called purposive sampling), which require participants to meet highly specific criteria, such as having lived with a particular illness or through a particular time period. This is not to say that convenience methods have no sampling constraints at all. For example, you may want to sample native speakers of English only.[2] You may also want to use 'quotas' to ensure that your sample is either balanced or representative. For example, you may want an even number of men and women in your study. Alternatively, you may want the gender profile of your sample to reflect the gender profile of the general population. A potential issue with convenience methods, then, is the *representativeness* of the sample. Convenience samples often show a *selection bias*. The classic example of this is university lecturers using undergraduate students as participants in their research. A sample made up exclusively of university students is clearly not representative of the population at large. This affects the generalisability and thus real-world relevance of your results. Arguably, the ability to recruit participants over the internet has made it easier to access more diverse populations and thus, potentially, to obtain more representative samples (Buhrmester, Kwang, and Gosling, 2011). Many studies in or relevant to CDA have recruited participants this way using various kinds of crowdsourcing platform. For example, Hart (2018a) recruited participants through *r/SampleSize* (www.reddit.com/r/SampleSize) while several studies have recruited participants via *Amazon's Mechanical Turk* (www.mturk.com/) (e.g. Fuoli and Hart, 2018; Hart, 2018b; Subtirelu and Gopavaram, 2016; Thibodeau and Boroditsky 2011).[3] Convenience samples are also gathered through social media sites like Facebook and Twitter.

Any study involving human participants will require formal ethics approval from your university. Eckert (2013) provides a useful overview of various ethical dimensions that must be properly taken into account before embarking on any linguistic research. Here, I highlight a few of the most important things to consider. However, it is absolutely essential that you do not begin any form of participant data collection until you have spoken with an academic supervisor about the specific ethics requirements and procedures in your institution.

- *Data storage and identity protection* – Will your data be anonymised? Will it be stored securely? How long will it be stored for? How will it be used? Who else will have access to it?
- *Incentive and consent* – Will your subjects be rewarded for their participation? Is this fair remuneration? Could subjects feel obliged or coerced into

participating? How will subjects give their consent? How will you ensure that subjects are properly informed of what they are consenting to and that they have the capacity to consent?

- *Impact of study on participants* – What level of inconvenience does participation entail? Is participation likely to result in any short- or long-term physical or psychological discomfort (e.g. by being exposed to offensive language or distressing images)?
- *Deception* – Does your study involve misleading subjects or not disclosing details about the experiment? How will this be redressed (e.g. in a debriefing message)?
- *Risks to researcher* – Does your study place you, as the researcher, in any danger or at any risk of physical or psychological discomfort?

It must be stressed that although institutional approval is required and your university's ethics committee will provide some guidelines, there are not always official, agreed-upon standards to follow. It is often up to the researcher to be guided by their own personal ethics. An example of this is remuneration for participants recruited via Amazon's Mechanical Turk. There is no minimum level of payment dictated. However, in good conscience, you might want to pay a pro-rata rate that at least meets the living wage in the country where your subjects are resident.

Analysing and interpreting data

Once you have run your experiment you will have your data in its raw form. The first thing you need to do is get that data into a format that makes it easy to process. In most cases, this means something like an Excel spreadsheet. Organise your data so that subjects are represented in rows and variables are represented in columns. This makes it easier to transport data to environments for statistical analysis. So, for example, if you are investigating the effects of metaphor in a given context and testing for these effects using a 7-point semantic differential scale comprised of two items, whose average you will take as your dependent measure, you would want to organise your data along the lines shown in Figure 10.2, which also takes into account potential extraneous variables.

The next thing you need to do is to 'clean' your data. Data gathered in an experiment is often messy and incomplete. It is at that stage, known as *pre-processing*, that you may take decisions to exclude subjects from subsequent statistical analysis. It is important that any decisions to exclude subjects are fully justified, taken systematically and made transparent in your write-up. For example, you will most likely want to exclude subjects who failed an attention check or who did not complete the whole experiment. These are easy decisions to justify. Slightly more difficult to justify but commonly practised is exclusion based on time taken to complete the experiment (software packages like Qualtrics give you this

216   Christopher Hart

	A	B	C	D	E	F	G	H	I
					Averaged				
			Scale	Scale	Scale	Political			Time
1	Subject	Condition	Item 1	Item 2	Response	Orientation	Gender	Age	Taken
2	1 Metaphor		6	5	5.5	Liberal	Male	20	
3	2 Literal		3	3	3	Liberal	Female	35	
4	3 Literal		3	4	3.5	Conservative	Male	26	
5	4 Metaphor		7	5	6	Liberal	Other	42	
6	5 Metaphor		4	5	4.5	Conservative	Female	33	
7	.....		.....	.....	....	....	....	......	....

Figure 10.2 Organising your data

data). For example, a markedly long or short time may indicate that the subject was either distracted or that they did not respond to items honestly. The question then, though, is what counts as a markedly long or short time? Unfortunately, there is no definitive answer to this. However, as a general rule of thumb, it is usually considered acceptable to exclude data from subjects where the time taken to complete the experiment falls three standard deviations above or below the mean. In some cases, there are reasons to exclude subjects on the basis of their responses. For example, if their responses are inconsistent or erratic. However, excluding subjects based on their responses is extremely difficult to justify and requires applying very complex criteria (see Hart and Fuoli, forthcoming for an example). It is obviously not acceptable to exclude subjects because their responses do not support your hypothesis.

Once any pre-processing is done, you can move on to analysing your newly cleaned data. This is the point at which you get to see the results of your study. Analysis at this stage means statistical analysis, which comes in two forms: *descriptive statistics* and *inferential statistics*. Descriptive statistics are the first step in quantitative analysis. They give us information relating to the overall shape of the data. Descriptive statistics include, for example, *mean, median,* and *standard deviation* values for data that is continuous (see below) and *mode* and *per cent* values for data that is categorical (also see below). Descriptive statistics also enable us to compare within our data to gain some insight into *potential* patterns. So, for example, we could compare the mean response of subjects in one condition with the mean response of subjects in another condition or the proportion of subjects who respond a certain way in one condition with the proportion of subjects who respond the same way in a different condition. However, we cannot know whether any differences found at this stage are large enough to be considered meaningful. In other words, we do not yet know whether the results of our experiment are *statistically significant*. This is where inferential statistics come into play.

Inferential statistics use the data you have collected to put your hypothesis to the test. In actual fact, it is your null hypothesis that is tested with inferential statistics. In other words, inferential statistics tell us whether or not there is no relationship between our dependent and independent variables. If it is found not to be the case that there is no relationship, then this leaves open the possibility at least that our experimental hypothesis is true. What inferential statistics give us, then, is a measure of how likely it is that the null hypothesis is true. This probabilistic measure is known as a *p value*. In applied linguistics and psychology, a *p* value of less than 0.05 (written as '$p < 0.05$') is usually taken as indicating significance. What this expresses is that, given the data, there is less than a 5% chance of the null hypothesis being true and we therefore reject it in favour of the alternative experimental hypothesis, which we assume to be the most likely explanation for the data. Put another way, a *p* value of 0.05 is an indication that were the same experiment to be run repeatedly, only one in 20 times could we expect the same results if the null hypothesis were true.

A *p* value, then, is the output of a statistical test. Unfortunately, there is no single statistical test that gets applied. There are a great many statistical tests out there and choosing the most appropriate one is not always easy. Which test you should use depends on several things, including the distribution of the data, the type and number of variables involved, how many levels each variable has, and whether the design of the experiment is between-subjects or within-subjects (repeated measures). It is beyond the scope of this chapter to describe all the different statistical tests available and the motivations for selecting one over another (see van Peer, Hakemulder, and Zyngier, 2007 for a good overview). However, I try to provide some basic principles. It is also worth noting that statistics is a fast-moving area with new methods and models emerging and new trends evolving all of the time.

The most fundamental distinction is between *parametric* and *non-parametric* tests. Parametric tests include *t*-test and ANOVA and assume your data is *normally distributed*. When plotted on a graph, data that is normally distributed will take the form of a bell-shaped curve. Mathematically, in normally distributed data, 95% of data points fall within 1.96 standard deviations above or below the mean (see Johnson, 2013 for further discussion). Non-parametric tests, by contrast, make no assumptions about data distribution and are therefore used when the data does not follow a normal distribution or when it does not make sense to ask if the data is normally distributed. Non-parametric tests include chi-square and Mann–Whitney U. Parametric tests are the more powerful while non-parametric tests are more conservative.

Which particular parametric or non-parametric test you use is determined by the type and number of variables that you have (both independent and dependent) and the number of levels to each variable. There are two basic types of variable: *continuous* and *categorical*. Since in

CDA, independent variables are most likely to be categorical (e.g. literal versus metaphorical treatment), we will discuss principles that apply only to cases where the independent variable is categorical and the appropriate statistical test then rests on the dependent variable type (see Figure 10.3). I will also limit the discussion to cases involving just one independent and one dependent variable.

A variable is continuous if it takes a numerical measurement which, theoretically, can be of any value. An example of a continuous dependent variable is found in Fausey and Matlock (2011), where subjects were asked to estimate the amount of money a politician had obtained as either charitable donations or hush money. Continuous variables often follow a pattern of normal distribution and are therefore typically analysed using parametric tests. When the dependent variable is continuous, you use a *t*-test if your independent variable has two levels (i.e. there are two treatment conditions) and an ANOVA if it has more than two levels (i.e. there are more than two treatment conditions).[4] There are also versions of these tests for within-subjects designs: paired-samples *t*-test and repeated measures ANOVA respectively.

A variable is categorical if its values fall into two or more discrete categories. Categorical variables, in turn, are classed as either *nominal* or *ordinal*. Nominal variables are those whose values do not have any natural

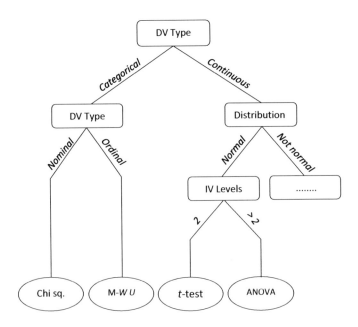

Figure 10.3 Basic decision tree for statistic tests

Experimental methods in discourse analysis   219

order to them. In Fausey and Matlock (2011) study, the yes–no question concerning whether or not the politician would be re-elected measures a nominal variable. By contrast, ordinal variables are those whose values have some intrinsic order to them. Variables measured by Likert scales or semantic differential scales are ordinal variables. Since means and standard deviations cannot be calculated for categorical variables, the issue of distribution does not apply. Categorical variables are therefore analysed using non-parametric tests. If your dependent variable is nominal, then the relevant statistical test is chi-square while in the case of an ordinal dependent variable the relevant test is Mann–Whitney U. Equivalents of these tests for within-subjects designs are Wilcoxen's and McNemar's tests respectively.

It is not always easy to tell the difference between types of variable and social scientists disagree on what type of variable certain measures are associated with. For example, the distinction between continuous and ordinal variables is not necessarily immediately clear. And indeed, variables measured using ordinal scales such as Likert or semantic differential scales are often treated as continuous.[5] When or even if this is acceptable, however, is the subject of much debate. Composite scores derived from multi-item scales are more similar to continuous data since the range of values they can take is almost unlimited.

Researchers sometimes also *recode* data both within and between variable types. For example, you might want to collapse the categories of a nominal variable to create a smaller number of broader categories. This was the approach Hart (2018a) took in his study of blame assignment in discourses of disorder. Subjects were asked to indicate where they placed the blame for the violence reported between police and protesters at a recent political demonstration. For purposes of analysis, Hart merged the categories 'police mainly to blame' and 'police fully to blame' into a single category 'police to blame'. The same was done for protesters to create the category 'protesters to blame'. In Fausey and Matlock (2011), a continuous variable in the form of dollar estimates was recoded as a nominal variable. They achieved this by creating two categories – 'low' and 'high' – defined by the overall median ('low' = below the median, 'high' = above the median). This enabled them to compare the proportion of subjects giving high and low estimates in their two treatment conditions (perfective vs. imperfective aspect) and to test for significant differences using chi-square.

The advantage of recoding data this way is that it generally makes the data easier to handle and allows for clear presentation of results. However, there are problems with this practice. For example, collapsing two or more categories into one ignores any differences between the original categories. As a result, statistical power is reduced and an effect that is there may not be found (known as a *type II error*). Conversely, recoding a continuous variable as nominal exaggerates the distance between values close to the cutpoint and as a result runs the risk of finding an effect that isn't really

220   *Christopher Hart*

there (known as a *type I error*). Although recoding is a standard procedure in many of the social sciences, then, it should be recognised that in wider academic circles there is much controversy surrounding this practice.

Underpinning every statistical test is a complex mathematical formula. Fortunately for us, data can be fed into a statistical software environment where these tests can be run automatically. Such software packages include IBM SPSS (www.ibm.com/uk-en/analytics/spss-statistics-software) and R (www.r-project.org).[6] It is beyond the scope of this chapter to provide introductory tutorials for these programmes but see Field (2013) and Field, Miles, and Field (2012) respectively. There are also several very handy websites with free and easy to use on-line calculators capable of performing a variety of statistical tests. My favourite is www.social statistics.com. What you do need to know, of course, is what data to actually give a statistical calculator. For continuous variables, you enter, on a separate line, the response of each subject. You do the same for ordinal variables. Note that if you have multiple items in your measure, the value you enter will be the composite score derived by averaging or aggregating responses across items for each subject. Where an ordinal variable is not measured using numeric values, as can be the case for Likert scales, numeric values need to be assigned to each interval. So, for example, you might assign numbers as follows: 1 = strongly disagree, 2 = somewhat disagree, 3 = neutral, 4 = somewhat agree, 5 = strongly agree. For nominal variables, you enter the total number of responses that fall into each category, by condition. Figure 10.4 shows a typical chi-square contingency table.

When doing experimental research relating to political discourse, it is important to recognise that political orientation will also have an effect on the dependent variable you are measuring and that this may interact with your independent variable in a number of different ways. For example, political orientation could overlap with your independent variable so that all of your subjects in one experimental condition happened to identify as conservative while all your subjects in the second experimental condition happened to identify as liberal. In this case, you would have a confound and could not know whether any effect found is due to the manipulation made in the stimulus texts or due to prior political disposition. It is

	Category 1	Category 2
Condition 1		
Condition 2		

Figure 10.4 Typical chi-square contingency table

Experimental methods in discourse analysis 221

therefore important to account for political orientation in your analyses. You can rule out a confound by reporting the political make-up of each group. Hopefully, having randomly assigned conditions, political orientations will be distributed more or less evenly across groups. It could also be that the effect of the textual manipulation is greater for one political orientation than another, in which case you have an interaction effect. For example, in Hart's (2018b) study of fire metaphors in media discourses of civil disorder and their role in legitimating police use of water cannon it was found that subjects reporting a liberal orientation were more likely to be influenced by the metaphor manipulation than subjects reporting a conservative orientation. A simple way of testing for this is to run separate analyses for subjects with different political orientations and compare the results. You can do the same for other variables like age or gender.

There are more sophisticated and reliable ways to factor variables like political orientation into your analysis, either as control variables or as second independent variables, using more advanced forms of statistical modelling (e.g. analysis of covariance (ANCOVA), two-way ANOVA, structural equation modelling, or different types of logistic or linear regression depending on the types of variables you have). These procedures, however, are too complex to cover in this chapter.

Presenting findings and results

Now the results are in, you need to think about communicating them to your audience. There are standard formats for reporting experimental studies that vary slightly depending on discipline. Generally, however, an experiment report adheres to some version of the following structure:

Abstract
1. Introduction
2. Background
3. Hypotheses
4. Method

    4.1 Participants
    4.2 Materials and Design
    4.3 Measures

5. Results
6. Discussion and Conclusion
References
Appendices

Here, we focus on presenting the results of your experiment. The results section is dedicated to reporting descriptive and inferential statistics in relation to your hypotheses. At this point, then, you are confirming whether or not your hypotheses are borne out by your data. Comments on the implications of your study and explanations as to why some hypotheses might have been confirmed while others were not should be saved for the discussion section.

A key to communicating results effectively is *data visualisation*. As well as reporting descriptive statistics verbally, it is often helpful to present them visually in the form of tables and figures. Graphs are especially useful for illustrating a dramatic difference between conditions or for showing an interaction effect in a factorial design. The most commonly used types of figure, in scientific research, are *line graphs* and *bar graphs*. Pie charts usually are best avoided. Bar graphs are normally preferred when the dependent variable is categorical or in single-factor designs involving a continuous dependent variable. Line graphs are preferred for multi-factor designs where the dependent variable is continuous.

Typically, in any graph, the X-axis represents treatment conditions and the Y-axis a measure of the dependent variable, such as mean response or proportion of sample falling into a given category. When you have a categorical dependent variable, categories of the variable are shown through the shading of bars in a bar graph. Categories can be represented by separate bars or, as illustrated in Figure 10.5, within a single bar. In either case, the contrasts in shading should be stark enough to stand out in black and white print. It is also important to label your axes and provide a legend where necessary. The most important advice that can be given for creating graphs is to make them simple and effective. You should therefore avoid the overly fancy designs that many word processing packages now offer.

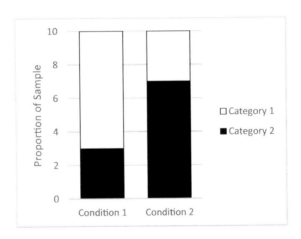

Figure 10.5 Example of bar graph for categorical variable

Experimental methods in discourse analysis   223

When it comes to reporting inferential statistics, there are certain conventions to follow. Remember, results can only be described as 'significant' if they are *statistically significant*. In applied linguistics and psychology, the cut-off point for statistical significance is a p value of 0.05 or less. For all statistical tests, then, you need to report the p value. If the p value is less than 0.05, it is reported as 'p < 0.05'. However, if it is less than 0.01, then it gets reported as 'p < 0.01' and if less than 0.001 as 'p < 0.001'. In addition to the p value, you also need to report the test-specific values using the appropriate designation. So, for example, a chi-square value of 6.4 is reported as '$\chi^2 = 6.4$'. Other tests get reported the same except that in a t-test you report a t-value, in a Mann–Whitney-U test you report a U-value, and in an ANOVA you report an F-value. For chi-square, t-tests and ANOVAs, you should also report the number of *degrees of freedom* (*df*).[7] All this information is given inside brackets. So, for a dependent variable that is nominal, you might report something like the following:

- The metaphor manipulation had a significant effect. In the literal condition, 45% of subjects said they would support the policy while in the metaphor condition 60% of subjects said they would support the policy ($\chi^2 = 4.51$, df = 1, $p < 0.05$);

while, for a dependent variable that is continuous, you might report something like:

- The manipulation of grammatical aspect had a significant effect. Subjects in the perfective condition gave lower estimates (M = 3.8; SD = 1.9) than subjects in the imperfective condition (M = 4.9; SD = 1.7) ($t = -2.96$, *df* = 58, $p < 0.001$).

Issues and limitations

Running an experiment can be a daunting task. For students whose training to date has been at the qualitative end of research in linguistics, there are a lot of new concepts, skills, and terminologies to confront. Reading experimental research and conducting and reporting your own experimental project often require new academic literacies. Knowing where to start in designing your own experimental project can be especially difficult given the vast array of different designs open to you. The best advice here is to try to keep things simple and take inspiration from previous studies inside or outside of CDA. Practical issues include access to participants and access to platforms for collecting and analysing data.

The use of experimental methods in CDA is very much a new thing. Disciplinary norms have yet to be established and the methods used are evolving quickly. More complex designs and more advanced forms of

224 *Christopher Hart*

statistical analysis are being used all of the time. Students coming to experimental CDA for this first time may therefore find it hard to keep up with current practice.

Epistemologically, experimental methods do not sit well with all CDA researchers. For many, the link between discourse and social action is not something that can be studied quantitatively in a laboratory setting. Experimental studies are necessarily decontextualised to a certain extent. However, as van Dijk (2014: 134), has argued, the link between discourse and social action necessarily presupposes a link between discourse and cognition:

> There are no direct links between social structures and discourse structures, because all discourse production, comprehension and uses are mediated by the mental representations of the participants. Thus, if in critical studies a link is established between discourse and social power, such an account should be seen as a shortcut, as incomplete or as tacitly presupposing mental structures of members and processes that remain unaccounted for in the analysis.

Thus, if we can empirically demonstrate the influence of textual choices on audience cognition, in political contexts, then we have at least not broken the first link in the discourse-cognition-society triangle and are halfway to validating our analyses.

Further Reading

There are, as yet, relatively few studies in the nascent area of experimental discourse analysis. Hart (2018a) and (Hart, 2018b) both describe relatively simple experiments involving single-item scales or two-item scales respectively with results analysed using non-parametric statistical tests. Fuoli and Hart (2018) present a more complex factorial design, involving several multi-item scales, with results analysed using a more advanced statistical technique known as structural equation modelling.

Notes

1 Statistical power refers to the probability of detecting a significant effect and is relative to sample size (Schütze and Sprouse, 2013)
2 This is common in psycholinguistics but from a CDA perspective is problematic because it would result in a sample that does not reflect wider society.
3 r/SampleSize is aimed at audiences who enjoy answering surveys and has the advantage of being free. Amazon's Mechanical Turk requires you to pay 'workers' who complete the task but presents a much larger participant pool and the platform has much greater functionality.
4 Note that if you have two independent variables that are categorical and are interested in whether they have an interaction effect on a continuous dependent variable, as in a classic 2x2 factorial design, then the statistical test required is a two-way ANOVA.

5 The distinction has to do with the intervals between values. With continuous variables, intervals are consistent. So, in the case of money, we can say that the difference between $10 and $20 is the same as between $30 and $40. We can also say that $40 is twice as much as $20. By contrast, the same consistency between intervals is not present in ordinal variables. So we cannot say, for example, that the difference between 'disagree' and 'strongly disagree' is the same as the difference between 'agree' and 'strongly agree' or that a response of 4 on a semantic differential scale is twice as positive as a response of 2.

6 SPSS requires a paid subscription. Many universities will hold an institutional licence that extends to students. R is an open software environment.

7 It is not possible to explain the concept of degrees of freedom here. All we can do is note that whether or not a test-specific value reaches the threshold for significance depends on the number of degrees of freedom there are. As an example, for Chi square, degrees of freedom is calculated by taking the number of rows in a contingency table (conditions) minus one and multiplying it by the number of columns (categories) minus one. So, in a basic contingency table such as shown in Figure 10.4, degrees of freedom equals one. For t-tests of independent samples that are the same size, degrees of freedom equates to total number of subjects minus two.

References

Abhul, R., Gass, S. and Mackey, S. (2013). Experimental research design. In R.J. Podesva and D. Sharma (Eds.), *Research methods in linguistics*. (pp. 116–134). Cambridge: Cambridge University Press.

Arpan, L.M., Baker, K., Youngwon, L., Taejin, J., Lorusso, L. and Smith, J. (2006). News coverage of social protests and the effects of photographs on prior attitudes. *Mass Communication & Society*, 9(1), 1–20.

Baker, P. and Levon, E. (2015). Picking the right cherries? A comparison of corpus- based and qualitative analyses of news articles about masculinity. *Discourse & Communication*, 9(2), 221–236.

Behrend, T.S., Sharek, D.J., Meade, A.W. and Weibe, E.N. (2011). The viability of crowdsourcing for survey research. *Behaviour Research Methods*, 43, 800–813.

Buhrmester, M., Kwang, T. and Gosling, S.D. (2011). Amazon's Mechanical Turk: A new source of inexpensive, yet high-quality, data? *Perspectives on Psychological Science*, 6, 3–5.

Charteris-Black, J. (2017). *Fire metaphors: Discourses of awe and authority*. London: Bloomsbury.

Coffin, C. and O'Halloran, K. (2006). The role of APPRAISAL and corpora in detecting covert evaluation. *Functions of Language*, 13(1), 77–110.

Cohen, J. (1988). *Statistical power analysis for the behavioral sciences*. (2nd ed.). Hillsdale, NJ: Erlbaum.

DeVellis, R.F. (2012). *Scale development: Theory and applications*. (3rd ed.). Thousand Oaks, CA: Sage publications.

Eckert, P. (2013). Ethics in linguistic research. In R.J. Podesva and D. Sharma (Eds.), *Research methods in linguistics*. (pp. 11–26). Cambridge: Cambridge University Press.

Fausey, C.M. and Matlock, T. (2011). Can grammar win elections?. *Political Psychology*, 32(4), 563–574.

Field, A.P. (2013). *Discovering statistics using IBM SPSS Statistics*. (4th ed.). London: Sage.

Field, A.P., Miles, J.V.N. and Field, Z.C. (2012). *Discovering statistics using R: And sex and drugs and rock 'n' roll.* London: Sage.

Fuoli, M. and Hart, C. (2018). Trust-building strategies in corporate discourse: An experimental study. *Discourse & Society, 29*(5), 514–552.

Fuoli, M., van de Weijer, J. and Paradis, C. (2017). Denial outperforms apology in repairing organizational trust despite strong evidence of guilt. *Public Relations Review, 43,* 645–660.

Hart, C. (2013a). Event-construal in press reports of violence in political protests: A Cognitive Linguistic Approach to CDA. *Journal of Language and Politics, 12*(3), 400–423.

Hart, C. (2013b). Constructing contexts through grammar: Cognitive models and conceptualisation in British Newspaper reports of political protests. In J. Flowerdew (Ed.), *Discourse and contexts.* (pp. 159–184). London: Continuum.

Hart, C. (2014). *Discourse, grammar and ideology: Functional and cognitive perspectives.* London: Bloomsbury.

Hart, C. (2015). Viewpoint in linguistic discourse: Space and evaluation in news reports of political protests. *Critical Discourse Studies, 12*(3), 238–260.

Hart, C. (2018a). Event-frames affect blame assignment and perception of aggression: An experimental case study in CDA. *Applied Linguistics, 39*(3), 400–421.

Hart, C. (2018b). 'Riots Engulfed the City': An experimental study investigating the legitimating effects of fire metaphors in discourses of disorder. *Discourse & Society, 29*(3), 279–298.

Hart, C. (2019). Spatial properties of action verb semantics: Experimental evidence for image schema orientation in transitive vs. reciprocal verbs and its implications for ideology. In C. Hart (Ed.), *Cognitive linguistic approaches to text and discourse: From poetics to politics.* (pp. 181–204). Edinburgh: Edinburgh University Press.

Hart, C. and Fuoli, M. (forthcoming). Subjectification outperforms objectification in military interventionist discourse. *Journal of Pragmatics.*

Hauser, D.J., Ellsworth, P.C. and Gonzalez, R. (2018). Are manipulation checks necessary? *Frontiers in Psychology* 9: 998.

Hawkins, S. (2014). Teargas, flags and Harlem shake: Images of and for revolution in Tunisia and the dialectics of the local in the global. In P. Werbner, M. Webb and K. Spellman-Poots (Eds.), *Global protest: The Arab Spring and beyond.* (pp. 31–52). Edinburgh: Edinburgh University Press.

Johnson, D.E. (2013). Descriptive statistics. In R.J. Podesva and D. Sharma (Eds.), *Research methods in linguistics.* (pp. 288–315). Cambridge: Cambridge University Press.

Kaplan, D. (2004). *The Sage handbook of quantitative methodology for the social sciences.* London: Sage.

Landau, M.J., Sullivan, D. and Greenberg, J. (2009). Evidence that self-relevant motives and metaphoric framing interact to influence political and social attitudes. *Psychological Science, 20*(11), 1421–1426.

Lau, R.R., and Schlesinger, M. (2005). Policy frames, metaphorical reasoning, and support for public policies. *Political Psychology, 26*(1), 77–113.

O'Halloran, K. (2007). Critical discourse analysis and the corpus-informed interpretation of metaphor at the register level. *Applied Linguistics, 28*(1), 1–24.

Paolacci, G., Chandler, J. and Ipeirotis, P. G. (2010). Running experiments on Amazon Mechanical Turk. *Judgement and Decision Making, 5,* 411–419.

Robins, S. and Mayer, R.E. (2000). The metaphor framing effect: Metaphorical reasoning about text-based dilemmas. *Discourse Processes*, *30*(1), 57–86.

Schütze, C.T. and Sprouse, J. (2013). Judgement data. In R.J. Podesva and D. Sharma (Eds.), *Research methods in linguistics*. (pp. 27–50). Cambridge: Cambridge University Press.

Stubbs, M. (1997). Whorf's children: Critical comments on critical discourse analysis (CDA). In A. Ryan and A. Wray (Eds.), *Evolving models of language*. (pp. 110–116). Clevedon: England.

Subtirelu, N.C. and Gopavaram, S.R. (2016). Crowdsourcing critical discourse analysis: Using Amazon's Mechanical Turk to explore readers' uptake of comments about Language on RateMyProfessors.com. *CADAAD*, *8*(1), 38–57.

Thibodeau, P.H. and Boroditsky, L. (2011). Metaphors we thing with: The role of metaphor in reasoning. *PLoS ONE*, *6*(2), e16782.

Utych, S.M. (2017). How dehumanization influences attitudes toward immigrants. *Political Research Quarterly*, *17*(2), 440–452.

van Dijk, T.A. (2014). Discourse-cognition-society: Current state and prospects of the socio-cognitive approach to discourse. In C. Hart and P. Cap (Eds.), *Contemporary critical discourse studies*. (pp. 121–146). London: Bloomsbury.

van Peer, W., Hakemulder, J. and Zyngier, S. (2007). *Muses and measures: Empirical research methods for the humanities*. Newcastle: Cambridge Scholars Publishing.

Widdowson, H.G. (1995). Discourse analysis: A critical view. *Language and Literature*, *4*(3), 157–172.

Widdowson, H.G. (2004). *Text, context, pretext: Critical issues in discourse analysis*. Oxford: Blackwell.

Index

abductive 189
adjacency pairs 27–29, 31
affordances 146, 180–182
agency 65, 72–73, 83, 159
agentless passive 62, 65, 83, 159
Amazon Mechanical Turk 214
angle *see* point of view
annotation 47–48, 88, 93, 106, 118, 119, 128–129, 154; annotation tools 106, 119, 154–155
anonymisation of data 39, 86, 128, 190–191, 197, 214
AntConc 129–130, 131, 135
appraisal 56, 57, 58, 154, 161
archives *see* databases
aspect 115–116, 208, 209, 219
ATLAS.ti 47, 106, 154–155
attention, windowing of 100–101, 111, 113–114
attention check 212–213, 215

body movement 23, 33, 151, 145
body posture 38, 145, 151, 161

categorisation of data 48, 75, 88, 131–134, 153–154, 197
cherry-picking 125
clause-type 56–58
cleaning data *see* pre-processing
coding *see* annotation
cognitive grammar 105, 106
cognitive linguistics 14, 97–120, 168, 202; *see also* conceptual metaphor theory
cognitive psychology 98, 119
coherence 15, 56, 147, 164–165
cohesion 56, 58, 67, 148, 164–165, 166; intersemiotic cohesion 166–168, 170, 196

collocation 124, 125, 126, 129, 130, 131, 133–134, 136, 139, 140, 148, 166, 202
comparative analysis 66, 102–103, 126, 151, 194
computer-mediated communication 182
computer-mediated discourse analysis 183–184
conceptual blending theory 79
conceptual metaphor theory 78–81, 105, 145, 149, 174; invariance hypothesis 79
conceptualisation 98–101, 102–116; *see also* conceptual metaphor theory
concordance 88–89, 130, 132, 133, 134, 135–138, 139
confirmatory research 151–152
confound 203, 211, 220–221
connotation 147, 154, 161–164
consent 11, 23, 46, 67, 86, 128, 153, 190, 191, 211, 214–215
construal *see* conceptualisation
context: definitions of 41
conversation analysis 19–34, 36, 48, 145, 183, 189
copyright 11, 128, 152, 153
corpora: building of 13–14, 50, 87, 105, 127–128, 130, 152; definitions of 124; existing 23, 126–127, 136; reference 130, 136
corpus linguistics 12, 86–92, 103, 104, 124–140, 202
corpus tools 127, 129–130, 139, 192
co-text 68, 92, 135, 147, 154
critical stance 2, 10, 16, 106, 108, 145, 147, 154
critical discourse analysis 2, 10, 16, 33, 41–42, 54–55, 97–120, 126, 127, 140, 143, 145, 149, 154, 174, 183, 186, 201–207, 212, 214, 218, 223–224

critical metaphor analysis 81–84, 93, 100
crowdsourcing 214

data storage 214
databases 87, 104, 127, 128
deductive 153
deixis 101, 103, 115
denotation 147
description 65, 66, 74–75, 86–87, 105
diagrams: use of 74, 92, 117, 119
dialectic 16
dialogic 10, 86, 103
digitally mediated communication
  180–199
digitally mediated discourse studies
  186–187
digital social media 67, 128, 132, 139,
  153, 181, 182–183, 186–187, 190,
  191, 192
discourse: definitions of 6–8
discourse-historical approach 42
distance *see* point of view

ecological validity 212
embodiment 32, 81, 98–99, 145, 149
emic 37–39, 49, 50
emotion 71, 78, 81, 88, 119, 147, 196,
  201, 203
ethnography 12, 36–51, 66, 103, 188,
  197; discourse-centred online
  ethnography 180, 183, 184–186
ethnomethodology 19–20
exclusion of social actors 62, 100, 159
exclusion of subjects 215–216
experimental design 203–206
exploratory research 43, 46, 149

Facebook 9, 182, 191, 198, 214; *see also*
  digital social media
facial expression 145, 161
fieldnotes 9, 36–37, 38, 44–45
fieldwork 41, 43, 44, 50
focus groups 13, 14
force 68, 81
frame semantics
framing 100, 109–110, 170; *see also* metaphor framing effect
frequency lists 129

gaze 23, 31, 38, 145, 156, 161
genre 9, 191
gesture 8, 23, 31, 33, 38, 143, 145,
  147, 161

grounded theory 47
grounding: temporal 115–116

Hansard 87
hypothesis 203, 206–207, 217

ideology 15, 41, 54, 60, 62, 80–85, 91,
  93, 97, 99, 101–103, 105–119, 138,
  144, 147, 149, 150, 156, 170, 174,
  192, 203
image act 154, 161–162, 167, 195
image schema 84, 99, 106, 107–112
inductive 153–154, 189
information value 56, 58, 164, 165–166,
  167, 174
interactional sociolinguistics 33, 41, 42,
  48, 145, 183
interactional sociology 20, 48, 145
interdiscursivity 151, 170–171
interpretation 10, 44, 65, 66, 74–75,
  86–87, 97, 105, 106, 117, 125, 126,
  139, 140, 154, 171, 172; over-
  interpretation 92, 202
intersemiotic relations 148–149,
  151–152, 166–168, 170
intertextuality 12, 41, 170
interviews 9, 14, 32, 43, 44, 48, 183, 185,
  188, 192, 197, 198
intuition 92, 106

keywords 130–132

legitimation 99, 102, 103, 105, 106, 148,
  149, 156, 207, 210, 221
log-likelihood 130, 131, 133, 140

manipulation check 212–213
meaning-potential 146–147
measures 207–211; off-line vs online 203
mediated action 15
meta-data 87, 152
metafunction 55–58, 147, 150, 166;
  ideational 56–57, 155–159, 166–167;
  interpersonal 57, 159–164, 167; textual
  58, 164–166
metaphor 48, 68–69, 99, 100, 101,
  102–103, 104, 106, 108, 109–110,
  111, 117; entailments 80, 92–93;
  extraction 87–88; framing effect
  203, 205–206, 207, 210, 215, 221;
  identification procedure 89; over-
  interpretation of 92; primary 81, 82;

230   *Index*

scenarios 83–84, 91; *see also*
  conceptual metaphor theory
metonymy 62, 65
modality 57, 161
monologic 10, 12, 13, 86, 103
mood 57, 161
motion 106, 107–116; default motion
  event 107–108; manner of 108–110;
  rate and iteration of 111–112; self vs
  caused 114
multimodal 8, 33, 38, 48, 69, 183, 193;
  discourse analysis 143–176; ensemble
  145; interaction analysis 145, 152, 153;
  metaphor 86, 149, 151, 154, 168–171

Nexis 104, 105, 127
nominalisation 62, 65, 68, 164
normalisation of data 92, 118, 139, 171

participant observation 37, 39, 44
participant recruitment 191, 213–215
participant roles 60–61, 156–159
pilot study 212
plexity 110–111, 112
point of view 101, 115, 145, 151, 159,
  161–164, 170,174–175, 208–209
political orientation 203, 211, 220–221
polysemy 146, 148
positivism 201
preferred response 29–31
pre-processing of data 215–216
process types *see* transitivity
production 111–113
prosody 125, 133, 136
proximisation 103, 115, 116
public vs private 153, 190

qualitative 10, 47, 74, 102, 104, 117, 125,
  130, 131, 132, 139, 140, 150, 151, 152,
  154, 171, 172, 197, 207, 223
Qualtrics 213, 215
quantitative 10, 54, 69, 74, 92, 102 104,
  117–118, 119, 151, 152, 154, 171–172,
  216, 224

reception 13–14, 191, 146, 174–175, 202
recoding 219–220
reflexivity 38, 39, 46, 50
reliability 210–211

repair 29
representativeness 125, 152, 212, 214

sampling 152, 185, 214; down-sampling
  192, 194
saturation 152
scales 209–211, 219, 220
small story 196
social actor representation 60–65, 71–73,
  153, 154, 156, 159
social constructionism 81
social media *see* digital social media
speech act 57
standardisation *see* normalisation of data
statistics: descriptive 216, 222; errors
  219–220; inferential 118, 216–217;
  p-values 217, 223; power 204, 209,
  213, 219; significance 118, 131, 204,
  216, 217, 223; tests 118, 130, 139, 140,
  217–219, 221, 223; tools 220
stimuli 204–205, 211–213
subjectivity 106, 174, 202
systemic functional linguistics 48, 54–75,
  106, 145–149, 154

tagging *see* annotation
telicity 115–116
tense 115–116
thematic structure 58, 165–166
transcription 9, 23–26, 32, 67, 193
transitivity 57, 58–65, 68, 74, 148, 153,
  154, 155–159, 166–167
triangulation 44, 202
turn-taking 20, 26–27, 32, 189
Twitter 128, 181, 182, 186, 192, 194,
  198, 214; *see also* digital social media

usage-based 98

variable: categorical vs continuous
  218–219; dependent vs independent
  203–206, 207; extraneous 203, 204
vectors 155–156
viewpoint *see* point of view
visual message elements 167–168
visualisation of data 92, 118, 139, 222

Wmatrix 88, 129